# Mission after Christendom

# Mission after Christendom

*Emergent Themes*
*in Contemporary Mission*

EDITED BY

Obgu U. Kalu
Peter Vethanayagamony
Edmund Kee-Fook Chia

WESTMINSTER
JOHN KNOX PRESS
LOUISVILLE · KENTUCKY

*First edition*
Published by Westminster John Knox Press
Louisville, Kentucky

10 11 12 13 14 15 16 17 18 19—10 9 8 7 6 5 4 3 2 1

*Book design by Sharon Adams*
*Cover design by Lisa Buckley*
*Cover art: Spiral staircase at Convento de Cristo; courtesy Corbis*

**Library of Congress Cataloging-in-Publication Data**

Mission after christendom : emergent themes in contemporary mission / edited by Ogbu U. Kalu, Peter Vethanayagamony, Edmund Kee-Fook Chia.
  p. cm.
  "All the essays in this volume were presented in some forum of the CCGM, with most from the 2008 World Mission Institute, celebrating the centenary of the World Missionary Conference held at Edinburgh in 1910"—Pref.
  Includes bibliographical references.
  ISBN 978-0-664-23465-2 (alk. paper)
  1. Missions—Theory. I. Kalu, Ogbu. II. Vethanayagamony, Peter. III. Chia, Edmund. IV. Chicago Center for Global Ministries.
  BV2063.M5553   2010
  266.001—dc22

2009028358

*In Memory*
*of*
*Obgu U. Kalu*
*(1942–2009)*

# Contents

# Preface

Christian global mission has been a central concern of three seminaries located on the south side of Chicago: Catholic Theological Union, the Lutheran School of Theology at Chicago, and McCormick Theological Seminary. These three schools represent Roman Catholic, Lutheran, and Reformed theological traditions of the church. Their commitment to global mission brought them into close ecumenical collaboration for several decades, sharing resources in equipping the saints for ministry in the global church. Among several collaborative academic projects and programs, the Chicago Center for Global Ministries (CCGM) stands as a unique witness to what can be achieved when Christians, committed to mission, come together. Besides bringing the mission professors of the three seminaries together through seminars, public lectures, and symposia, the CCGM organizes an annual World Mission Institute, gathering missiologists from around the globe. All the essays in this volume were presented in some forum of the CCGM, with most from the 2008 World Mission Institute, celebrating the centenary of the World Missionary Conference held at Edinburgh in 1910.

The CCGM set in motion the centenary celebration of Edinburgh with the annual Scherer Lecture of February 2008 and especially the World Mission Institute, held in April 2008 at the Lutheran School of Theology at Chicago. All this was during the visionary leadership of Ogbu Kalu, who was the CCGM director at the time and until his sudden death on January 7, 2009. Thus CCGM wishes to record its deepest appreciation for Professor Kalu's seven "Chicago Years," the culmination of a long and distinguished career in theological education. We dedicate these pages in loving memory of him.

We thank many persons for making this publication possible. First and foremost are the authors of these essays, who represent both the Global South and the Global North. The book likewise owes much to the services of David Dobson, editor of Westminster John Knox Press, who enthusiastically supported this project from its inception. The editors also acknowledge the services rendered by Dean David Esterline and President Cynthia M. Campbell, both of McCormick Theological Seminary, for negotiations with the WJK Press.

A special word of thanks to faculty members of the three schools who served on CCGM's Council and others who have always been a support: Stephen Bevans, Anna Case-Winters, James Chukwuma Okoye, Luis Rivera, José David Rodriguez, Kenneth Sawyer, Robert Schreiter, Roger Schroeder, Michael Shelley, Mark N. Swanson, and Mark W. Thomsen. Two persons served us very dedicatedly and incredibly well as executive secretary of the CCGM office: Sr. Joan Delaney and Ms. Gwendolyn Sampson. Then we have our deans and presidents, without whom the CCGM would not have been: Kathleen Billman, Cynthia Campbell, James Kenneth Echols, David Esterline, Gary Riebe-Estrella, and Donald Senior. Our gratitude and thanks go out to them.

Peter Vethanayagamony
Edmund Chia
June 2009

# Acknowledgments

After the sudden death of Dr. Ogbu Kalu in 2009, the Chicago Center for Global Ministries asked Associate Director of the Center, Dr. Peter Vethanayagamony, to take over completion of this project and final preparation of the edited volume for publication. The Presidents and Deans of the Lutheran School of Theology at Chicago and McCormick Theological Seminary are deeply grateful to Dr. Vethanayagamony for the care, dedication, and editorial skill he brought to this work. Indeed, the volume would not have reached completion without his scholarly competence and commitment, and for that we, and all the contributors to this project, are deeply grateful.

Cynthia M. Campbell
President, McCormick Theological Seminary

# Contributors

**Nancy Bedford** has been the Georgia Harkness Professor of Applied Theology at Garrett-Evangelical Theological Seminary in Evanston since 2003; she is also Profesora Extraordinaria No Residente (Nonresident Professor) at the Instituto Universitario ISEDET in Buenos Aires, Argentina, where she taught systematic theology from 1995 to 2002. She was born in Argentina and obtained her doctorate in theology at the University of Tübingen in Germany. Dr. Bedford has published over fifty articles and book chapters, as well as five books as author or editor. Her latest book is *La porfía de la resurrección: Ensayos desde el feminismo teológico latinoamericano* (2009).

**Stephen Bevans** is a priest of the Society of the Divine Word and is currently Louis J. Luzbetak, SVD, Professor of Mission and Culture at Catholic Theological Union, Chicago. He is past president of the American Society of Missiology (2006) and former board member of the Catholic Theological Society of America (2007–2009). Among his publications are *Models of Contextual Theology* (2002), *Constants in Context: A Theology of Mission for Today* (with Roger P. Schroeder, 2004), and *An Introduction to Theology in Global Perspective* (2009).

**Edmund Kee-Fook Chia** is originally from Malaysia, where he began his career as a secondary schoolteacher and youth minister. He obtained a BA in Psychology, an MA in Human Development, and an MA in Religion from universities in the United States. He was then based in Thailand, where he served as executive secretary of Ecumenical and Interreligious Affairs for the Asian Bishops' Conferences. After completing his PhD in Intercultural Theology from the University of Nijmegen in the Netherlands, he joined the faculty of the Catholic Theological Union in Chicago. He is editor of *A Longing for Peace: The Challenge of a Multicultural, Multireligious World* (2006) and *Dialogue: Resource Manual for Catholics in Asia* (2001).

**Gemma Tulud Cruz** is originally from the Philippines, where she completed a BSc in Education and an MA in Religious Studies. She taught for more than ten years before obtaining a PhD in Intercultural Theology from Radboud Universiteit Nijmegen in the Netherlands. Migration theology is her ongoing research interest, and she has published much on it as well as presented papers on the theme in Asia, Europe, and the United States. She was Assistant Professor of Theology at St. Ambrose University in Iowa before moving to Chicago, where she currently serves as Visiting Assistant Professor of Catholic Studies at DePaul University.

**Ogbu U. Kalu** was the Henry Winters Luce Professor of World Christianity and Mission at McCormick Theological Seminary, Chicago (2001–2009). He served as the Associate Director (2002–2005) and Director of the Chicago Center for Global Ministries (2005–2009). Kalu also served as the Secretary of West African Association of Theological Institutions, Chairman of Conference of African Theological Institutions, and one of the three Directors of the Commission on the History of the Church in the Third World, an arm of the Ecumenical Association of Third World Theologians. Kalu taught as a full professor at the University of Nigeria, Nsukka (southeastern Nigeria). His notable publications include *Power, Poverty and Prayer: The Challenges of Poverty and Pluralism in African Christianity, 1960–1996* (2000); *Clio in a Sacred Garb: Essays on Christian Presence and African Responses, 1900–2000* (2004, 2008); as editor, *African Christianity: An African Story* (2005, 2007); and *African Pentecostalism: An Introduction* (2008).

**Dawn M. Nothwehr** is Associate Professor of Ethics at Catholic Theological Union in Chicago. The ethics of power and racial justice in our globalized, terrorized, ecologically threatened world are the foci of Dr. Nothwehr's current research. Her latest book is *That They May Be One: Catholic Social Teaching on Racism, Tribalism, and Xenophobia* (2008). Of equal interest to her are global climate change, environmental ethics, and ecotheology. Her ongoing attention to mutuality as a formal norm, the feminist ethics of power, and the relationship of ethics and spirituality informs her study. Additional involvements include empowerment of the poor and vulnerable, human/environmental relations, and relations in moral disagreement. Her research has also involved the moral "Other" and how Franciscan theology shapes eco-theology and ecological ethics.

**Robert J. Priest** is Professor of Mission and Intercultural Studies and Director of the PhD Program in Intercultural Studies at Trinity Evangelical Divinity School. He holds the PhD in anthropology from the University of California at Berkeley. Among his more recent publications are *This Side of Heaven: Race Ethnicity and Christian Faith* (coedited with Alvaro Nieves, Oxford, 2007) and *Effective Engagement in Short-Term Missions: Doing It Right* (Oxford, William Carey Library, 2008).

**David M. Rhoads** is Professor of New Testament at the Lutheran School of Theology at Chicago. He is the author of *Reading Mark, Engaging the Gospel* (2004); *Mark as Story: An Introduction to the Narrative of a Gospel* (rev. ed. with Joanna Dewey and Donald Michie, 1999); *The Challenge of Diversity: The Witness of Paul and the Gospels* (1996); and *Israel in Revolution 6–74 C.E.: A Political History of Israel Based on the Writings of Josephus* (1976). He is the editor of *Earth and Word: Classic Sermons on Saving the Planet* (2007) and *From Every People and Nation: The Book of Revelation in Intercultural Perspective* (2005). Rhoads supervises the Web of Creation (www.webofcreation.org) and the Green Congregation Program. He is the author of *The Green Congregation Training Manual* (rev. ed., 2005).

**Barbara R. Rossing** is Professor of New Testament at the Lutheran School of Theology at Chicago. She serves on the executive committee and council of the Lutheran World Federation, where she also chairs the Lutheran World Federation's Theology and Studies Committee. Her publications include *The Rapture Exposed: The Message of Hope in the Book of Revelation* (2004); *The Choice between Two Cities: Whore, Bride, and Empire in the Apocalypse* (1999); two volumes of the New Proclamation Commentary, for preachers (2000 and 2004); "Prophets, Prophetic Movements, and the Voices of Women," in *A People's History of Christianity* (2005); and articles and book chapters on the apocalypse and ecology. She is an avid hiker and environmentalist.

**Robert Schreiter** is Vatican Council II Professor of Theology at Catholic Theological Union in Chicago. He is a past president of the American Society of Missiology and the Catholic Theological Society of America. He is editor of the Faith and Culture Series for Orbis Books, and coeditor of the journal *Studies in Interreligious Dialogue*. Among his publications are *Constructing Local*

*Theologies* (1985), *The New Catholicity: Theology between the Global and the Local* (1997), and *Mission in the Third Millennium* (2001).

**Peter Vethanayagamony** is Associate Professor of Church History at the Lutheran School of Theology at Chicago and has been serving as Associate Director of Chicago Center for Global Ministries since 2007. Before his current position at LSTC, he taught church history (1980–98) and held several academic administrative positions, including the office of the Dean (1993–98) at Hindustan Bible Institute and College, Chennai, India. He was raised in India. His graduate education includes degrees in theology, history, and philosophy from universities in India and seminary in the United States. He currently serves as the Director of the DMin program at LSTC.

**Amos Yong** is J. Rodman Williams Professor of Theology at Regent University School of Divinity in Virginia Beach, Virginia. His graduate education includes degrees in theology, history, and religious studies from Western Evangelical Seminary, Portland [Oregon] State University, and Boston [Massachusetts] University. He has published six books—on theology of religions, theological method, pneumatological theology, Pentecostal theology, and theology and disability—and is presently completing two manuscripts on Pentecostalism and political theology. He and his wife, Alma, currently reside with their three teenage children—Aizaiah, Alyssa, and Annalisa—in Chesapeake, Virginia. For his publications, see http://www.regent.edu/acad/schdiv/faculty_staff/faculty/yong.cfm.

# Introduction

PETER VETHANAYAGAMONY
AND EDMUND KEE-FOOK CHIA

Christianity is a world religion in every sense of the term. We are not referring here to how it dominates the world, as it tried to do in the last half a millennium or so. Instead, we are referring to how the face of Christianity is so diverse today that to associate it with any particular culture or continent would not only be naive but also a gross injustice. Thus, while in the past one might have regarded Christianity as a Western or European religion, today it is no longer the case, as shown by the shift of its epicenter from the Global North to the Global South. Although its former heartland, Europe, has by and large become post-Christian, Christianity in turn is by and large becoming post-Western. Indeed, if Christendom was a reality of the past in global history, its empire has all but crumbled with the fall of the European colonial empires.

As a consequence, what we have today is a polycentric Christian world, and the church's mission is also taking on a distinctively polyvalent flavor. Though previously mission was unidirectional, moving from the Western hemisphere to what were called mission territories, today mission seems to be from everywhere to everywhere. Obviously, this has resulted in not only a variety of understandings of Christian mission, but also a variety of its expression. If anything, today mission is no longer understood solely as coming from the "saved" Christians to the "lost" heathens. It is also no longer exercised solely from the center to the periphery or from a position of strength to beneficiaries who are powerless. Today, mission is, if we can use the negative, everything that Christendom did not stand for.

In this context, we have entitled this volume *Mission after Christendom*. And we reflect in concert with many other Christians throughout the world who are also exploring what and how mission should and would look like in this new millennium. Specifically, the centenary celebration of the World Missionary Conference held at Edinburgh in 1910 has provided the occasion for this reflection in our generation. The Edinburgh 1910 Conference is arguably the most significant event in the twentieth-century history of Christianity. It is rightly cited as the birthplace of the modern ecumenical movement in that it brought together Christians from very diverse denominations and missionary societies under one single umbrella. This eventually led to the founding of a number of ecumenical movements and unity agencies, including the World Council of Churches in 1948.

As a distant grandchild of this ecumenical movement, the Chicago Center for Global Ministries (CCGM), a collaborative venture between three seminaries—Catholic Theological Union, Lutheran School of Theology at Chicago, and McCormick Theological Seminary—representing major Christian traditions of the church, joined with the worldwide ecumenical community in a series of mission reflections, in view of contributing to the centenary celebration of Edinburgh 1910, which will be held again in Edinburgh in the year 2010. Sharing in the spirit of the Edinburgh 2010 process, the CCGM's own study process has ensured the ecumenical nature of its membership, as evidenced in the authors of this volume coming from a spectrum of the Christian tradition (Roman Catholics, Lutherans, Presbyterians, Anabaptists, Pentecostals), as well as from across the globe and representing diverse ethnic and national communities (Africans, Asians, and Americans).

In reflecting on *Mission after Christendom*, the authors of these essays begin with the premise that the contemporary terrain for doing mission is much different from what it was a century ago. Thus, if Edinburgh 1910 was primarily devoted to discerning strategies and more effective means for "carrying the Gospel to all the non-Christian world," Edinburgh 2010 will discuss the theme of "witnessing to Christ today" by beginning with an acknowledgment that the concept of witness will carry different meanings and the praxis of mission will take different forms. Significantly, the present mission terrain is foreshadowed by the third phase of globalization. This, in particular, is characterized by a complex combination of vast economic repatterning, communication technology, cultural exchanges, and social networking. These forces, in turn, purvey a secularist value system that challenges the church's voice in proclaiming and living out the *shalom* of God. Already, the sustainability of the environment is challenged by the process of industrialization, population growth, and various forms of human activities. The debate over ecological ethics and global warming captures much of the urgency and danger. New socioeconomic transformations create new gender relationships, class divisions, racial problems, and value systems in the church as well as in society. Moreover, globalization also adversely impacts local economies and state structures and catalyzes massive migration, disruption, dislocation, and disempowerment. To complete the picture, the twenty-first century has been characterized by various forms of oppression and occupation, violence and terrorism, ethnic strivings and civil wars, interstate conflicts and mineral wars. Much of the violence is allegedly connected to religion, though recent researches have shown that religion is only used to justify the violence, which is more often rooted in and caused by other factors, such as economics, politics, and so on.

Within the church, meanwhile, we have witnessed a seeming loss of missionary passion. But it might be that Christians are actually engaging in a critique of the old mission paradigms in view of enabling the emergence of new forms for doing mission. As the population of Christians explodes in the Southern hemisphere, as there is a retreat in the Northern hemisphere, missionary structures have changed. Evangelicals now dominate in the missionary enterprise; more agencies are engaged in short-term missions built around social services rather than proclamation; missionaries work with greater cultural sensitivity and attention to other religions; and missionaries cooperate with secular NGOs and international agencies in the task of serving God's kingdom. Then there is the phenomenon of reverse flow, indicating both the increased participation of Southern Christianity in global mission and its special entry into the Western world. Immigrant religion, to be sure, is revitalizing many Western religious strongholds, which have been seeing a decline in their traditional membership, as well as reshaping the religious landscapes of some cities in the North Atlantic. Quite notable is the rise of charismatic spirituality with its passion for evangelism, the resurgence of contemplative spirituality, and a vibrant social activism by progressive Pentecostals. In the final analysis, the crisis in mission is actually loaded with great opportunities. On top of that, the resurgence of religion in the public sphere has also disproved the prognostication of secularists. Religion is more alive today than it was a century ago. Its influence cannot be underestimated, and churches will continue to play significant roles, especially in sending out missionaries for the missions. In light of all these new circumstances and contextual realities, we believe Edinburgh 2010 to be an exciting event and momentous occasion of God's grace. It will certainly see numerous creative and groundbreaking theological insights; in such a spirit, the authors of these essays have set out to offer their own reflections.

The first chapter, by Stephen Bevans, provides an overview of the mission concerns today, as measured against what they were a century ago. Appropriately titled "From Edinburgh to Edinburgh," the essay is a compare-and-contrast analysis of how the 1910 Conference was run and how the forthcoming one is taking shape. Bevans, who serves on one of the 2010 conference's committees, looks at missiology's new opportunity, new context, new attitude, new means, and new content. He sums up the hundred-year journey by insisting that while missiology must be rooted in theology, theology must also be influenced by missiological themes. Missiological themes such as contextualization, justice and ecological commitment, peacemaking, dialogue among religions, and cultural awareness and sensitivity—these have to be considered by every theology. Hence, we see the preparatory commission of Edinburgh 2010 identifying nine "basic" themes and seven "transversal" themes (which run through all the basic themes) as constituting the content of today's thinking on mission. The other ten essays in this volume address some of these themes; the first six can fall under the rubric of "basic" themes, and the next four are "transversal" themes. These constitute the *Emergent Themes in Contemporary Mission*, the subtitle of the present volume.

Chapter 2, by Robert Schreiter, looks at some of these emergent themes. Postulating mission "from the ground up" as an approach to a theology of mission, Schreiter insists that the missioner must pay attention to the seeds of the Word and the signs of the times. This approach is rooted in the belief that ours is a missional God: the essential task of the missionary is to discern how God is already at work in a given situation and to learn to cooperate with that work. Schreiter then sketches four areas where he sees mission from the ground up as calling us today: (1) mission must take into account that in the past two decades there has been a religious resurgence in many parts of the world and across many religious traditions; (2) mission must respond to the challenges posed by the poorest billion people in the world, currently concentrated in fifty-eight countries, mainly in Africa and Central Asia; (3) mission must include inter-religious dialogue; (4) mission must deal with the challenges posed by globalization. Schreiter suggests that in the face of a globalized world where people struggle in their quest for meaning and purpose, the great ideas embedded in the various religious traditions offer the best hope for survival.

The globalization theme is taken up in Ogbu Kalu's essay, chapter 3 of the present volume. He argues that in a shrunken world, which is depriving cultures and people groups of isolation, the challenge confronting us is the maintenance of particularity in the face of universalizing tendencies. Ironically, globalization forces actually helped democratize religion and provided fuel for its explosion, resulting in the many new and diverse forms Christianity has taken, most clearly seen in the South. In this connection, especially the charismatic forms of Christianity have taken on a global face, employing media technology to the hilt and reaching out to all and sundry and to every nook and corner of the globe. Herein lies another irony, in that it was the Christian missionary from the North who first nurtured the seeds of globalization, only to be on the receiving end today on account of reverse missions. Moreover, the contemporary growth of Christianity and the emergence of new cultural trends influenced by global processes have scrambled the modes of Christian expressions, ministerial formation, theological education, and missionary structures and strategies.

Chapter 4, by Amos Yong, looks at the growth of the Pentecostal church. While Pentecostalism has been around for a while, only in recent decades have we witnessed its growth and expansion, especially in the Global South. Yong begins by surveying the twentieth-century Pentecostal paradigms of mission as it had developed in North America, exploring the missiological strategies employed, as well as the postcolonial forms it later embraced, especially in the Pentecostal missions emanating from the Global South. Of importance is his assertion that while Pentecostal missiologies have been intertwined with colonialism, they have also been developed independent of it. He then sketches a post-Christendom, postcolonial, and Pentecostal theology of mission by arguing that the many tongues of Pentecost open up to many different Spirit-empowered missionary practices. His primary thesis is that the many tongues and many practices can also be viewed as protest and resistance movements and that a post-Christendom theology of mission must also be postcolonial: it should proceed from the margins and the underside of history and society, rather than from the power and centers of empire.

From another perspective chapter 5, by Peter Vethanayagamony, looks at the consequences of globalization by focusing on Christianity's demographic changes and the concomitant implications for contemporary mission. Although a century ago 80 percent of Christians lived in the Global North, today the majority of Christians live in the Global South. Former mission-sending churches also continue to play significant roles in mission, but as recipients of mission, partly on account of the reverse migration from the rest of the world to the West, and also because of the sharp decline of Christianity in the West. Christians who migrate to the West not only bring with them their own forms of vibrant Christianity but also reach out to people of the secularized West and those who have abandoned the traditional forms of Western Christianity. Moreover, the theology of Southern Christians may be misread as identical with the conservative theologies of the North, missing the dynamics of the social-justice paradigm in contemporary mission and reinscribing the personal individual-salvation model of mission. This new era of mission suggests a mission theology and praxis, and ethics will not be dictated by the affluent Global North but by the blending of the salvation and social-justice needs of the Global South.

An example of developing a mission theology from the margins and the South is in the context of the phenomenon of migration. Gemma Cruz addresses this issue in chapter 6. She begins with startling statistics that disprove the prevailing myths about migration, such as the West being the destination of migrants when Asia actually receives more migrants than North America. Her starting point is that the great surge in migration in the postcolonial era is largely born from and bred by global economic injustice. She argues, therefore, that mission in the context of contemporary migration must be contextually liberative. Today migrants are their country's primary "exports" and have become globalization's flexible, expendable, and disposable capital; hence, Christian mission needs to proclaim that God is meaningful even in contexts where people face isolation, alienation, and discrimination. It must be both empowering as well as transforming, especially of forces that prey on the vulnerability of the poor migrants. At the same time Christian mission must also equip migrants to witness to and celebrate their faith amid different cultures and religions, while creatively drawing from the richness that comes from this migration-induced cultural and religious pluralism.

The change in world order and flux resulting from the globalization phenomenon has also given birth to what has now been referred to as short-term missions. Robert Priest's essay, chapter 7, explores noncareer missionaries who go on mission for anywhere from several years to as brief as a week. In certain cases these short-term missions have actually come to replace the youth camps, which were once popular in the United States. Though the majority of short-term mission teams head to the Global South, this does not mean that the missioners are equipped to engage the Christians there, many of whom are more devout and dynamic. This new paradigm of mission is often more for the benefit of the missioners and their home church than for those on the receiving end. On the other hand, the benefits reaped by the host communities are in no way insignificant. Priest points to a case study in Peru, where the rich North Americans, through the linking of social capital, were able to financially help the Peruvian Christians both directly and indirectly, opening doors to evangelism and education, enhancing the local church's credibility, and providing strategic leverage for social change.

After looking at some of the basic themes that contemporary mission has to address in the twenty-first century, we now turn to what Edinburgh 2010 considers "transversal" themes. These themes cut across all subjects of interest and have to be dealt with in all mission theology. The first of these is the gender issue, addressed in Nancy Bedford's essay, chapter 8 in the present volume. She points out that even if it was a group of women who were the first to receive the common mission to share the good news from the risen Jesus, the church, even from the very beginning, has been hesitant in believing that Jesus' commission bestows sufficient authority on women. Bedford argues for a theological feminism to move the church forward toward gender equality and women empowerment, since only a healthy, liberating, antiracist, decolonial, joyful, and pneumatic theological feminism can and must help the church to be more faithful to the good news of Jesus. Citing examples from all over the globe, Bedford shows how women, even in quite difficult situations, seem to be able to find ways to fulfill the commission of the risen Jesus to women. Taking seriously the commission to women means that missiology must (1) take a pneumatological approach so as to provide more space for the opening up of new possibilities for ministry; (2) revisit its theological anthropology so as to check androcentrism; (3) look at ecclesiology realistically and acknowledge the important role that women play in the development of churches. It is unfortunate that even until today, it seems to be mostly women who are taking seriously Jesus' commission to women.

Another transversal theme that needs to be examined is that of racism, discussed in chapter 9, by Dawn Nothwehr. Recounting how V. S. Azariah, an Indian delegate, unmasked the issue of racism at Edinburgh 1910, Nothwehr admonishes that unless we sharpen our moral sensitivity to the dynamics of power, we are doomed to let history repeat itself and to enable racism to rear its ugly head. She identifies three forms of racism that require our particular attention today: color-coded racism (where one group targets another on account of phenotype), tribalism or ethnocentricity (where a group harbors strong feelings of loyalty to the exclusion of others), and xenophobia (fear of strangers). Pointing to the mixed record of the church with regard to these concerns, she implores that its ministers be engaged in experiential learning so as to prevent racism's sinful violence. Nothwehr then sheds light on some official documents of the Roman Catholic Church that teach against racism. Although these documents certainly rob racism of any ethical legitimacy, much more can and should be done. Most important is that the antiracism agenda should truly be "transversal" and be integral to the mission and ministry of all Christians everywhere and for all time.

Chapter 10, on ecology, by David Rhoads and Barbara Rossing, addresses yet another theme that must feature in all missiology and theology. Examining the crisis presently confronting the earth, the authors warn that mission conceived from an anthropocentric perspective risks focusing exclusively on humans, to the detriment of mother earth. Nothing short of a thoroughgoing reformation is needed for churches to transform their teaching and practice so as to make caring for all creation foundational to every mission. Five key mandates are offered to guide such a transformation: (1) We need to take the trouble to learn about the degradation of God's creation. (2) Our Christian ethic must emphasize the interrelationship between ecological conditions and issues of human justice. (3) We must highlight the biblical tradition, which presents care for creation as fundamental to our human vocation and mission. (4) Our mission to all creation leads us to theologize in new ways. (5) Earth care is integral to the mission of all Christian ministries and communities. Rhoads and Rossing conclude by stating that ours is the mission to restore God's creation and to form a sustainable life for God's beloved earth community.

In the final essay, chapter 11, Edmund Chia discusses the transversal theme of dialogue. Focusing specifically on the church in Asia, Chia, who also serves on one of Edinburgh 2010's study commissions, advocates for a mission theology that takes seriously the imperative of dialogue. Instead of confronting or conquering other religions, Christianity should be engaging and learning from them in respectful dialogue and collaboration. This dialogue begins with immediate concerns such as the contextual realities of poverty and suffering, as well as of religious and cultural pluralism. It is what the Federation of Asian Bishops' Conferences calls the "triple dialogue," of the church with the poor, with the cultures, and with the religions of Asia. In this dialogue the Christian missionaries immerse themselves as friends and copilgrims into the lives of the people of Asia. They work together in partnership with these people, even and especially those of other religions and cultures, in alleviating the suffering of the oppressed and poor of the continent. Through such humble acts of service and association, from a position of powerlessness and vulnerability, the church acquires its missionary credentials and establishes its ministerial authority.

It is also in this spirit of dialogue that we here in Chicago have engaged in this mission-reflection project, which culminates in the present volume. The dialogue first began at meetings of the Chicago Center for Global Ministries among mission professors of the three schools represented. This dialogue was then continued in official platforms such as the annual Scherer Lectures, the World Mission Institutes, and the Student-Faculty Forums organized at various junctures throughout the year. We are presenting the fruits of our dialogue here with the hope that others, especially the delegates of Edinburgh 2010 and mission leaders all over the world, will join with us in reflecting on where the churches ought to be headed in terms of their missionary movement for the twenty-first century.

At the point of writing, the Chicago Center for Global Ministries is undergoing its own transformation in view of the current economic crisis. Whatever happens, the agenda and vision of the CCGM will remain a firm commitment of our three schools and their faculty. Even if it is no longer under the purview of a center or commission, global mission will continue to be integrated into the life of our schools. With or without a center for global ministries, the Catholic Theological Union, the Lutheran School of Theology at Chicago, and the McCormick Theological Seminary will continue to be engaged in mission studies, especially in places where the Spirit can encourage dialogue and continuing reflection on the meaning of mission in the twenty-first century.

Perhaps that might also be where the 2010 Edinburgh Missionary Conference is headed. With or without an official forum or a future conference such as Edinburgh 2010, we trust that the churches in the North and in the South, in the East and in the West, will continue to maintain Christianity's missionary thrust and vocation (chap. 1). With or without Edinburgh 2010, we trust that mission will always be from the ground up (chap. 2). With or without Edinburgh 2010, we trust that mission will take heed of the challenges posed by globalization (chap. 3). With or without Edinburgh 2010, we trust that mission will acknowledge that many tongues make for many practices (chap. 4). With or without Edinburgh 2010, we trust that mission will be sensitive to the changing landscapes of mission (chap. 5). With or without Edinburgh 2010, we trust that mission will expand its boundaries and attend to the challenges posed by migration (chap. 6). With or without Edinburgh 2010, we trust that mission will explore ever new and evolving paradigms of mission (chap. 7). With or without Edinburgh 2010, we trust that mission will take seriously the commission that the risen Jesus gave to women (chap. 8). With or without Edinburgh 2010, we trust that mission will be decidedly antiracist (chap. 9). With or without Edinburgh 2010, we trust that mission will embrace care for the earth and all of God's creation (chap. 10). And finally, with or without Edinburgh 2010, we trust that mission will be dialogical in spirit (chap. 11). Happy reading!

# 1

# From Edinburgh to Edinburgh

## *Toward a Missiology for a World Church*

STEPHEN BEVANS

## INTRODUCTION

I would like to draw the outlines of a theology of mission—or a missiology—that is both relevant and challenging for the Christian church in today's world, as we head into the twenty-first century and consciously experience ourselves for the first time in history as a world church. How I'd like to do this is to take the 1910 Edinburgh World Missionary Conference as an icon of

This essay was originally delivered as the 2008 Scherer Lecture at Lutheran School of Theology at Chicago on February 19, 2008. This endowed lecture was funded by the Scherer family in honor of their parents, Eleanor and Arnold Scherer. The author is honored to be part of a legacy of missiological reflection that includes Kosuke Koyama, his colleague Tony Gittins, Andrew Walls, and the late Paul Hiebert. He also wishes to record his gratefulness to Dr. Brian Stanley of the Henry Martyn Institute in Cambridge, England, perhaps the foremost scholar today of the 1910 Edinburgh Conference, for making available to him several unpublished lectures that he delivered in 2006 at Princeton Theological Seminary. Brian Stanley later published these lectures as *The World Missionary Conference, Edinburgh 1910* (Grand Rapids: Wm. B. Eerdmans Publishing Co., 2009). The author is particularly indebted to Dr. Stanley's work in this book as well. He is particularly honored and grateful, however, to be the 2008 Scherer Lecturer, since it gives him an opportunity to pay homage in some way to Professor Jim Scherer, who has been his colleague, collaborator, and most important, his friend for almost the whole twenty-two years he has been on the faculty of Catholic Theological Union. To Jim and his wife, Frances, this essay is humbly dedicated.

missiological understanding at a time that proved to be the high point of the Age of Progress and the Age of Colonialism. In contrast to this icon, I want to indicate how different today's church and world is, and how very different our understanding of the church's missionary task must be.

I do this not to deny the importance or historical significance of the great Christian assembly that Edinburgh was, but only to highlight the missiology that we must develop today in a world of quite new sensibilities and circumstances. I am rather sure that not much of what I say will be startling or new, but I hope it will bring together a number of things that we, as faculty members of the Chicago Center for Global Ministries, have been reflecting on, discussing, and maybe even arguing over for the last several years.

## FROM EDINBURGH TO EDINBURGH: MISSIOLOGY'S NEW OPPORTUNITY

The Boston *Missionary Herald* may have exaggerated when it spoke of the 1910 World Missionary Conference as "the most important ecclesiastical assembly since Nicaea,"[1] and the conference's charismatic chair, John R. Mott, perhaps indulged in a bit of rhetorical flourish when he wrote that "never has there been such a gathering in the history of the Kingdom of God on earth."[2] Nevertheless, even though there had been large missionary conferences going back as far as 1854,[3] James Scherer tells us that the 1910 meeting in Edinburgh "was unprecedented in terms of scope, preparation, and consequences."[4] Even though the 1910 Edinburgh Conference was no Nicaea, or Trent or Diet of Augsburg, I do think we can rightly claim that it was *one* of the most important gatherings of Christians in history—certainly in modern history.

From June 14 to 23, 1910, for 10 days, 1,215 delegates—overwhelmingly white and male but working as missionaries in virtually all parts of the world— listened to some 300 hundred speeches of 7 minutes each during the day and 24 speeches in the evening that lasted up to 40 minutes.[5] The wide-ranging topics were based on 9 voluminous reports that had been meticulously prepared before the conference began. They included volumes of several hundred pages each on carrying the gospel to the non-Christian world, the local church in situations of mission, education, non-Christian religions, missionary training, church-state relations, and Christian unity. Every delegate had received a set of these volumes.[6]

Many of the major figures of nineteenth- and twentieth-century Christianity were present as delegates: Temple Gairdner, John R. Mott, A. G. Hogg, Pandita Ramabai, V. S. Azariah, Charles Gore, and Charles Henry Brent. The president of the United States, Theodore Roosevelt, was registered as a delegate, although "to his own deep regret,"[7] says Temple Gairdner, he was unable to be present. The famous politician and future Scopes Trial lawyer, William Jennings Bryan, was present as a delegate and addressed the conference as well. Due to illness, the great pioneer of mission studies, Gustav Warnek, was not able to attend the conference (he died later that year) but wrote a message that was read in the assembly. Significant as well was the fact that many young men who served as stewards and ushers at the conference would become major church leaders in years to come. Among these were the future theologian John Baillie, the biblical scholars Otto Dibelius and T. W. Manson, and the future archbishop of Canterbury and ecumenical leader William Temple.[8]

The mood was electric. As the editor of the *Christian Century*, Charles Clayton Morrison, wrote in the July 7, 1910, issue of the magazine: "Everyone feels the presence in the conference of a power not ourselves, deeper than our own devices, which is making for a triumphant advance of Christianity abroad. And not less are the delegates thrilled by the sense that the conference foreshadows a new era for the church at home."[9] It was a time, says Andrew Walls, "of dreams and visions." All were convinced that, indeed, the world *could* be evangelized in *this* generation, as Mott had famously proclaimed.[10] And while Brian Stanley warns of oversimplification, Walls notes that "not for nothing are the origins of the modern ecumenical movement conventionally dated from this meeting."[11] Out of the strengths and weaknesses of the 1910 Conference arose the International Missionary Council and the two groups of Faith and Order and Life and Work; out of the latter two groups emerged the World Council of Churches, inaugurated in Amsterdam in 1948, which by 1961 included the IMC.[12]

Edinburgh 1910 is an event worth remembering, and this is what a number of events planned for 2010 and into 2011 aim to do. James Scherer points out that the Lausanne Committee for World Evangelization, the Boston Theological Institute, and the Pentecostal Partners in Mission all have plans to mark the centenary; there will be "a common celebration jointly sponsored by many groups," to take place in Edinburgh on June 12–15, 2010. In addition, the WCC's Conference on World Mission and Evangelism has proposed a commemoration late in 2011.[13] And on a much smaller scale, CCGM's annual World Mission Institute for 2008 took the Edinburgh World Mission Conference 1910 for its theme, as this volume attests.

So 1910 produced an amazing event, one clearly worth commemorating. A century's distance, however, can not only point out a lot of the rather naive and even arrogant presuppositions of the time, presuppositions that have given the missionary movement such a bad name in our time. It can also show us, by contrast, how we might think about and engage in mission today. There are a number of important contrasts between Edinburgh and "Edinburgh," if you will, and these can help us glimpse a missiology more suited to today's world church.

## FROM EUROCENTRIC TO WORLD CHURCH:
## MISSIOLOGY'S NEW CONTEXT

Of the 1,215 delegates to the conference, the overwhelming majority were
*men* from Britain and the United States. Although accounts of numbers vary,
Brian Stanley writes that 509 of the delegates were British, and 491 were
North American. In addition, there were 169 delegates who originated from
the European continent, and 27 came from white South Africa, Australia,
and New Zealand.[14] There were only 19 representatives from what the conference (mistakenly!) called the "younger churches," and all of them were
from Asia—4 from India, 4 Japanese, 3 from China, and 1 each from Korea,
Burma, and Turkey. There was only 1 "indigenous black African Christian"
in attendance: Mark C. Hayford from Ghana. Hayford's name, however, does
not appear in the lists of the official delegates, with the result that scholars had
concluded that there was no indigenous African in attendance.[15] The 5 (pos-
sibly 7) male and 1 female African American delegates were often mistaken by
participants and the press as Africans.[16] But, with the only exception of Hayford, "the voice of African Christianity was not heard at Edinburgh."[17] There
was no representation from the Pacific Islands or from the Caribbean.[18]

Latin American representation was ambiguous. One of the conditions for
Anglican participation in the conference was that it should exclude places
where Catholics, Orthodox, or even other Protestants were the targets of missionary activity. "Such endeavors could be included only when, as in parts
of Latin America, they were directed toward statistically identifiable groups
of aborigines or recent immigrants—islands of heathenism with the boundaries of Christendom."[19] Nevertheless there were no Orthodox or Roman
Catholic representatives present, although American delegate Silas McBee
read a lengthy letter of greeting from Bishop Geremia Bonomelli, bishop
of Cremona, Italy, addressing the issue of Christian unity. What is intrigu-
ing for history is that Bonomelli had befriended a young priest by the name
of Angelo Roncalli, the future Pope John XXIII, who convoked the Second
Vatican Council almost a half century later, a council whose chief aim was the
promotion of Christian unity. Who knows the influence that this pioneer of
Catholic ecumenism had on his friend, the future pope?[20] Noting the absence
of the Roman Catholic and Orthodox delegates, Temple Gairdner reflects
prophetically: "Who, on this ridge of memories and of hopes, can say what
the future may bring forth?"[21] Charles Henry Brent, the Episcopal bishop of
the Philippines, wrote that Bonomelli's letter was "the little cloud not larger
than a man's hand to-day, destined tomorrow to cover the Roman heavens."[22]

What was clear from the small numbers of representatives from what
we call today the two-thirds world is that the organizers of the conference

conceived or imagined the world as relatively sharply divided into two parts. There was a "Christian" world, the duty of which was to be a *sending* church, and there was a "non-Christian" world, which was to be evangelized, or at best be a "receiving church." As Andrew Walls puts it with his usual eloquence:

> The best analysts and thinkers of 1910 could take for granted that there was a reasonably homogenous fully evangelized world, and a world beyond it that was unevangelized or only partly evangelized. From the fully evangelied world of Europe and North America the Home Church must send forth its choicest to carry the Gospel to the non-Christian world, where the Native Church, a tender young plant, stands as earnest of the future.[23]

If there is anything that has changed in mission today, it is this situation of a neatly divided world, of a section of the world that could call itself Christendom, of a basically Eurocentric church. Walls himself, along with Lamin Sanneh and, more popularly, Philip Jenkins, have all pointed to the seismic shift in Christianity in our day from North to South, from Europe, North America, and Australasia to Latin America, Africa, and significant parts of Asia.[24] At the turn of the twentieth century, the largest Catholic country in the world was France; now it is Brazil, followed by Mexico, the Philippines, and the United States (due in part to our influx of Latino/a migrants). And while now Christianity is actually shrinking in what Edinburgh 1910 regarded as the Christian world over against that of the heathen, it is in the latter where Christianity is now flourishing. Missionary activity is not only going on "in six continents,"[25] as a famous World Council of Churches meeting expressed it in 1963; it is becoming increasingly a two-thirds world movement to the West and the North, and every congregation has as its task that of becoming a "missional church."[26] Representatives of the missionary movement today, therefore, as we move from Edinburgh to Edinburgh, will have to come from the entire world, not just from one part of it, for the whole context of missionary work has changed dramatically and radically. And any missiology *for* a world church has to be a missiology *of* a world church.

The meetings mentioned above that will commemorate Edinburgh 1910 will be quite different in content and character from it. While Western theologians, missiologists, and missionaries will certainly be present, the vast majority of delegates will be from the thriving churches of Asia, Africa, and Latin America. Among these will be scholars who have contributed to recent works of missiology written out of a two-thirds world perspective: men and women like Jehu Hanciles, Philomena Njeri Mwaura, Chukwudi A. Njoku, Lalsangkima Pachuau, Jacob Kavunkal, Evangeline Anderson-Rajkumar, and Julie C. Ma.[27]

# FROM MODERNITY TO POSTMODERNITY:
## MISSIOLOGY'S NEW ATTITUDE

Edinburgh 1910 was held at the height of the missionary movement that had begun, by Protestants, at the beginning of the nineteenth century—the "Great Century," as Kenneth Scott Latourette called it[28]—and for Catholics, several years later. It was a heady time, one of optimism and belief in inevitable progress. John R. Mott saw a real confluence of the power of the gospel and the power of modern science, and it was this that convinced him of the possibility of the conversion of the world by the end of what others had called "the Christian Century." The church, Mott and many others believed, "stood at a *kairos* moment,"[29] and the doors that were open might not stay open indefinitely. Now was the time to seize the opportunity, in bold action for the sake of the gospel.

Who could have guessed in 1910, however, how soon those doors would indeed be closed. Just four years later, as the "guns of August"[30] lined up against each other, the hopes of the nineteenth century would come crashing down, and there would begin the long, painful, yet inevitable process of decolonialization and—despite the untold amount of good that missionary work had done—the unmasking of the evil that Christian mission had condoned or brought about itself. Today we still have the wonders of science, which fueled the visions of the nineteenth-century West. Scientific progress has brought amazing things like jet travel and computers and instant communication to almost anywhere in the world. But scientific rationalism and arrogant belief in progress, we know, have also resulted in the proliferation of nuclear weapons, the poisoning of our planet, and the very ambiguous phenomenon of globalization.

Edinburgh 1910 was held at the height of Western modernity, but it was an age that was soon to collapse in on itself. A century later we find ourselves still in the aftermath of that collapse and can only speak of ourselves in terms of *post*modernity. A century ago the answers to life's questions seemed clear and inevitable; today there are more questions than answers. A century ago there was no doubt of the superiority of Christianity over the other world religions: the modern "master narrative" was in full force. This was evidenced at Chicago's 1893 World Parliament of Religions and at Edinburgh itself, where the demise of the other world religions was confidently predicted if Christians would take the initiative boldly and quickly. Yet today, Islam, Hinduism, Buddhism, and traditional religions throughout the world have experienced a renaissance, and theology recognizes in the famous words of Max Warren that "God has not left himself without a witness in any nation at any time. . . . God was here before our arrival."[31] The "great new fact of *our* time" is the validity of religious pluralism, while still acknowledging the uniqueness and absolute necessity of the revelation of God in Jesus of Nazareth.

Missiology today, however, is born not so much out of uncertainty as out of humility. We *must* continue to preach the gospel with our whole hearts: the church is missionary by its very nature. But our attitude has changed as we first of all repent of and ask pardon for the mistakes and even sins of those who have gone before us. While we can introduce and make use of the best of Western thinking and science—in medicine, in agriculture, in computers—we need also to respect and learn from local wisdom, from relationships with the people among whom we work, and from their often simple yet effective and more earth-friendly technology. While we must continue to share the riches of the God of Jesus Christ, with David Bosch we also have to acknowledge that while we do indeed *know*, we *do* know only in part.[32]

If we truly believe in the God of Jesus Christ as a God constituted of dialogue as such—this is the essence of Trinitarian faith—we will share in the mission of that God by ourselves being in dialogue and being changed by the Others in our lives. Moving from Edinburgh to Edinburgh will give us this new attitude—an attitude of "bold humility," as David Bosch characterized it, or of "prophetic dialogue," as my congregation, the Society of the Divine Word, has named it.[33]

## FROM POWER TO VULNERABILITY: MISSIOLOGY'S NEW MEANS

At the time of Edinburgh in 1910, mission was an exercise of power—the power of Christendom aimed at "heathendom," the power of the West to the "rest," the power of colonizing Europe and North America to colonized India, footholds in China and Japan, Africa, Native Americans and Maoris. The language at Edinburgh, Bosch points out, was military language: "Mission stood in the sign of world conquest. Missionaries were referred to as 'soldiers,' as Christian 'forces.' References were made to missionary strategies and tactical plans. Military metaphors such as 'army,' 'crusade,' 'council of war,' 'conquest,' 'advance,' 'resources,' and 'marching orders' abounded."[34] Brian Stanley speaks of how "Edinburgh 1910 was conceived as a great deliberative council of the Church Protestant that would prepare its missionary armies to launch a concerted and final onslaught on the dark forces of heathendom that still ruled supreme beyond the frontiers of western Christendom."[35] Stanley goes on to quote Bishop James Bashford, Methodist bishop of China, who spoke of mission at the time among youth and laity as "a crusade for world evangelization quite as striking [as] and far more providential than the crusade of Peter the Hermit for the recovery of the Holy Land."[36] Mission—for the most part, even though *many* missionaries were critical of it—had colonial might on its side, and missionaries were supported by thousands of affluent and middle-class men and women in the home countries. "The money power in the hands of believing Christians," rhapsodized Mott in his presentation at the Conference on June 15, "is enormous."[37]

Journeying from Edinburgh to Edinburgh, we have moved from a missiology of power to a missiology of relationship and vulnerability. "Mission," writes Nigerian Theresa Okure, "is not about conquest but reconciliation, proclamation of the good news of liberation to all nations. So no nation is to be conquered by another, even for Christ."[38] Kosuke Koyama wrote famously of the need for missionaries today to be converted from a "crusading mind" to a "crucified mind";[39] and in one of his last lectures, titled "The Vulnerability of Mission," David Bosch focused on Shusaku Endo's powerful novel *Silence*, in which the missionary's identity is not with the powerful Portuguese merchants and colonists but with imprisoned Japanese Christians and, ultimately, with the crucified Christ.[40] And as missionaries come increasingly from poorer countries such as those in Africa, Asia, and Latin America, mission work will be done increasingly, as the Latin American bishops have put it, "out of poverty."[41]

What this means in concrete is that being in mission is about sharing deeply in people's lives: building real relationships and friendships with those we serve, living not at a standard above the people we live among, but if necessary, sharing their poverty and their own vulnerability, undergoing the self-emptying of learning Others' languages and culture. Perhaps the most important and controversial address at the 1910 Conference was that of Bishop V. S. (Vedanayagam Samuel) Azariah from India, but it probably expresses best the way of doing mission without power that I am speaking of here. Although his words at the end were greeted with stunned silence and cries of disagreement, Azariah's talk unmasked the racism and superiority of many foreign missionaries in India. He spoke of "a certain aloofness, a lack of mutual understanding and openness, a great lack of frank intercourse and friendliness. . . . Too often you promise us thrones in heaven, but will not offer us chairs in your drawing rooms." His address reached a climax with the following words: "Through all the ages to come the Indian Church will rise up in gratitude to attest the heroism and self-denying labours of the missionary body. You have given your goods to feed the poor. You have given your bodies to be burned. We also ask for *love*. Give us FRIENDS."[42]

## MISSIOLOGY FOR MISSIONS OR FOR THE CHURCH? MISSIOLOGY'S NEW CONTENT

I have already emphasized the fact that the basic dynamic of the 1910 Edinburgh Conference was of the "evangelized," "Christian," "Western" world focusing on the "unevangelized," "heathen," "rest" of the world. The Christian West, in other words, thought missiologically not about itself—it was already converted, it was already "the church." Missiology was for the sake of the evangelization of the Others, the missions, so that they might one day be fully church. The titles of the eight reports that made up the conference's agenda reflect this focus and provide an outline of what made up missiological thinking at the time. First and foremost was mission's evangelical task, to bring the gospel to the world. There was concern about the status of the "churches in the mission field" that were still not quite mature. Education in relation to the Christianization of the various nations where missions existed was discussed. Commission IV proposed a rather open and challenging discussion of Christianity in relation to other religions; it was the report that received the most attention at the conference. The final three reports spoke of missionary preparation, the importance of the home, sending church, and— the topic that was to be what the conference would be best remembered by the wider church—cooperation and Christian unity.

To see how the content of missiological thinking has changed—and in some ways remained the same—it might be helpful to review the themes that an international committee developed in July 2006 in preparation for the 2010 commemoration events.[43] I had been on the committee that presented the first draft of this document in a meeting in June 2005. We had tried to keep the themes to eight, as an echo of the original eight reports for the 1910 Conference, but as you will see, this did not happen: there are actually nine "basic" themes and seven "transversal" themes, which run through all the basic themes. Time will not permit the development that each of these themes deserve, but simply naming them will give an idea of the content of today's thinking about mission as we journey from Edinburgh to Edinburgh.

The first theme is titled "Foundations for Mission" and firmly anchors mission within the very life and mission of the Trinitarian God. Second, the fourth theme of the original conference is taken up under the title "Christian Mission among Other Faiths." The third theme focuses on "Mission and Postmodernities" and will reflect on postcolonialism, economic structures, internationalism, and information technology. Fourth, preparation for Edinburgh 2010 will consider the complex relation between mission and power and "will assess the function of both power and weakness in our understanding

and practice of Christian mission." A fifth area of reflection is titled "Forms
of Missionary Engagement" and will sort out the various groups—churches,
organizations, parachurches—and ways of doing mission. Sixth, there will
be a focus on "Theological Education and Formation," and a seventh theme
will reflect on "Christian Communities in Contemporary Contexts," such as
urbanization, migration, poverty, and the world of the blog (Web log) and the
Internet. The eighth theme continues the eighth theme of Edinburgh 1910 as
it reflects on "Mission and Unity—Ecclesiology and Mission," and finally, a
ninth theme speaks about "Mission Spirituality and Authentic Discipleship."
The "transversal" themes are (1) women and mission; (2) youth and mission;
(3) reconciliation and healing; (4) Bible and mission, and mission in the Bible;
(5) contextualization; (6) subaltern voices; and (7) ecological perspectives.

This is quite an agenda, immensely broader than the themes studied a century ago for the original conference. But they are broader in another way
that goes beyond their content: they are themes that *every* theology needs
to consider if it can claim authenticity in today's world. To say this another
way, what missiology is claiming today is that there cannot be just a theology any more: all theology has to be missiological. In a world church, in
a postmodern world, in a world where the test of authentic personhood is
no more power and might and domination, but vulnerability and relationship—all theology needs to draw from the richness of the church's missionary
commitment. There cannot be, for example, a doctrine of God that does not
engage seriously in interreligious dialogue or contextualization; there cannot
be an ecclesiology that does not understand the church's essence in relation
to commitment to the preaching and witnessing of God's present and coming
reign. There cannot be a theology of grace that does not ponder God's mys-
terious presence outside explicit faith in Christ. There cannot be a theology
and spirituality of ministry that does not call church leadership to cultural
sensitivity. There cannot be a Christian life that is not committed to justice,
to peacemaking, to Christian unity, to ecological responsibility. A missiology
in a world church can only be a theology for a world church; a theology for
a world church can only be a missiology in a world church. This is what the
journey from Edinburgh to Edinburgh teaches us.

## CONCLUSION

A century is a long time, and the metaphorical journey from Edinburgh to
Edinburgh has been a long one. The opportunity, the context, the attitude, the
means, the content that have developed along the way may serve as a worthy
agenda for the church's theological and missiological reflection for the next

century and the next stage of the road. Yet there may be things that are left out, or topics that will prove to be dead ends. But one thing we know: the Lord is with us on the journey, with us on the road. He was with the disciples on the way to Emmaus (Luke 24:13–35), and as he assured the wavering disciples on the mountaintop, he will be with us till the end of the ages (Matt. 28:20).

# 2

# Mission from the Ground Up

*Emergent Themes in Contemporary Mission*

ROBERT SCHREITER

## INTRODUCTION

This essay presents a series of emergent themes in contemporary mission that will have to be addressed in the coming years. It is part of a larger endeavor that the Chicago Center for Global Ministries (CCGM) has undertaken in response to the call from the planners of Edinburgh 2010 to envision mission for the twenty-first century. At the outset it is important to situate the themes chosen here in light of the larger efforts of the CCGM in its reflections on the state of contemporary mission.

The 2008 World Mission Institute of the CCGM took another read of the current situation. Besides what appears in this essay, a major manifestation of Christian mission is the rapid growth of Pentecostal and charismatic forms of faith. Many observers would see this phenomenon as the single most salient feature of Christian mission today. Amos Yong addresses this in chapter 4 of this book. A host of other themes have also received attention, as indicated by the other chapters in this book: themes of globalization, migration, ecology, racism, gender, and short-term mission. Some of these themes are on the planning committee's list; others represent themes of special importance to the North American context (such as short-term mission).

What is presented here has to be seen within the context of these other reflections coming out of the efforts of the CCGM. I will present four of these emerging themes in this essay. These represent either relatively new themes for mission, or older themes viewed from a different angle. They should not be considered as the most pressing or urgent themes; ecological themes may hold that special position. Nor are they necessarily the largest; Pentecostal and charismatic forms of faith probably claim that category. But they do represent areas that have the potential to change the entire landscape of mission in the decades to come. To be sure, predicting the future is a hazardous and perhaps foolish action. Edinburgh did not foresee the imminent collapse of the context of contemporary mission at that time: Europe's imperial adventures around the world. Nor did it pick up on a phenomenon that was already beginning: Pentecostal faith. Our descendents will no doubt say the same about us. But it is nonetheless incumbent upon us to peer into the immediate future as best we can. It is part of our responsibility to be faithful to the God who is calling us in mission.

I will proceed in the following way. First, there is a short reflection on what "Mission from the Ground Up" is trying to say. It is about a method of mission. How we set out to do mission has important implications for what mission appears to be for us, and how we evaluate our relative effectiveness in missionary work. Thus, our way of conducting mission grows out of a particular theological understanding of what mission is intended to be. "Mission from the Ground Up" bespeaks one of those understandings. Then we will move on to four emergent themes of mission:

- Reimagining secularity
- Accompanying the "Bottom Billion"
- Revisiting the religious interface
- Tracking the unintended interfaces of globalization

## MISSION FROM THE GROUND UP

Over the course of the past two hundred years, mission has been approached in a variety of ways. Behind each of these approaches, one can discern a theology of mission as well as the outline of how mission was to be carried out. I suggest here that "mission from the ground up" might be considered one of those approaches to mission. Here I briefly sketch four of these approaches. These by no means exhaust the possibilities, nor do they completely chart all such approaches that have been used over the past two centuries. But together they help to set the conditions under which mission will be taken in these first decades of the twenty-first century.

The first is *mission theologically driven*. At the end of the eighteenth century, mission *ad gentes* (to the nations) began to be taken up with great focus and energy among the Protestant churches. Through the millennium and more before that time, Luke 14:23 ("compel people to come in") had dominated missiological thinking. In the 1580s the Lutheran theologian Justinian Welz focused on Matthew 28:19–20 as the biblical motivation for mission. Roman Catholic missionaries, who had been especially active in the first Portuguese and Spanish imperial ventures, had begun to act upon the so-called Great Commission.

While missiology began to develop as a formal academic discipline, concerns for its theological foundations and the consequent imperatives to be drawn from there began to take clearer shape. The importance of saving souls and of furthering the frontiers of the visible church became the most salient themes. They remain so for many missionaries today, especially of the more conservative mode. These two themes continue to shape missionary strategy as well: direct proclamation of the gospel, baptism, and church planting.

A second approach to mission might be called *sharing what we have*. Besides being engaged in direct proclamation of the gospel, a great many missionaries over the past two hundred years have been sharing what would be seen as the developments of Western civilization: education, health care, the codifying of languages in dictionaries and grammars, agricultural technology, and all those things that can be brought under the umbrella of "development." Many missionaries made such acts of "mission" their life's work.

Some of this was motivated by imperial ideologies of helping "primitive" people move toward "advanced" societies. But much of this found direct gospel inspiration in passages such as Matthew 25, the parable of the final judgment, or in Paul's injunction of Diaspora Christians to help the church in Jerusalem. Thus such means of building up or improving the lives of "mission churches" have provided the motivational and procedural framework for missionaries and mission societies.

A third kind affects those who stayed home more than those who were sent abroad into the "mission fields." This is *mission out of our surplus*, whereby networks of supporters of mission would provide the funds and other means of support for missionary work. This caritative (charitable) approach might seem to some to be external to mission, but it is hard to imagine how much of the mission from the Global North to the Global South would have been able to do so much without it. "Mission promotion" or "mission development" was to become an essential part of mission for any individual congregation or mission society as it allowed for all Christians to participate in the missionary activity of the churches in a special way.

Here the episodes we find in the New Testament of the early Christians holding their goods in common for the sake of the entire community have had special valence. It fostered awareness that the Christian church is more than a single, defined congregation; instead, it encompasses the entire of the Christian *oikoumenē*.

The fourth kind of mission understanding became particularly strong in the middle of the twentieth century and has enjoyed a certain new appeal at the turn of the twenty-first. Like the first one mentioned above, it is especially theologically motivated. This is the concept of the *missio Dei*. In this understanding, mission begins with the entry of the triune God into creation, especially in the incarnation of the Second Person, and the sending out into the world of the Third Person. These are not arbitrary acts, but instead represent God's purposes for the world, to redeem and heal the world, and to bring about total reconciliation of the world at the end of time. Such a sense of mission, therefore, is not in the first instance centered upon the church, but rather upon the very action of God. The church plays a central mediating role but is itself not the final destination of this work of God. There is a strong sense, at least in the current understanding of the *missio Dei*, that the work of God goes ahead of the church and its missionaries. A central task of the missionary is to discern how God is already at work in a given situation and to learn to cooperate with that work. To use a patristic designation, finding the *semina Verbi* (seeds of the Word) already at work in a culture, and a capacity to read the "signs of the times," a scriptural reference appropriated especially by the Roman Catholic church at the Second Vatican Council—these become distinctive missionary activities. They are significant not only in places where the gospel has never been heard, but also where the faithfulness of the baptized has grown slack.

It is this attending to the seeds of the Word, to the signs of the times, that I am calling here "mission from the ground up." This entails listening before speaking, contemplating before acting. Only by focusing our attention in such a way as to be able to see God's movements in the world can we hope to participate in God's reconciling the world. To be sure, our capacity to listen and discern is heavily conditioned by our own backgrounds and upbringings. But the very principle of the incarnation of Christ as Jesus of Nazareth demands particularity even as we seek some measure of universality. Christ did not take on human form in some general, nonspecific way. He was born in a certain time and place, with all the limitations and possibilities that such implies. But particularity here does not become a license for solipsism. The catholicity of our faith requires us also to be in communion with all those trying to follow Jesus, and all those people of goodwill beyond the confines of Christian faith. Only through such polyphonic witness can we hope to hear how God might be speaking to us. It takes the blend of many voices to achieve this one single word to us.

Mission from the ground up, therefore, grows out of this spiritual discipline of listening. The actions that follow from that listening must also be put to the test of the many forms of witness and action of Christians, both in our own time and in times past.

Having said all of this, we can now turn to four places where, I believe, mission from the ground up is calling us today. These are by no means the only four places. The four do not include the rapid spread of Pentecostal and charismatic faith, a topic being given close reading by Amos Yong in chapter 4 of this book. But these are four that are, in some fashion, just beginning to emerge. Whether all of these will eventually become new horizons of mission is, at this time, difficult to determine. But they deserve our attention as sites where we might be observing a new call to mission.

## REIMAGINING SECULARITY

In the past fifteen years, the standard narrative about secularization has been shifting. Heretofore it had followed a pattern laid out by sociologist Max Weber at the turn of the twentieth century: the modernization process of European society that began a half millennium ago has had a twofold effect on religion (meaning here, Christianity). First of all, the modernization process has gradually banished religion from the public sphere, making it a privatized phenomenon that people may or may not choose to follow. Second, in that marginalization and privatization, religious practice and belief will decline and eventually disappear altogether, leaving a secular worldview that is determined mainly by science. This secularization process began in Northern Europe, but it is spreading throughout the world as modernization takes hold. Thus religion will finally disappear as reason replaces faith and other forms of nonrational thinking.

Since the middle 1990s, this standard narrative of secularization has been challenged by events. What became startlingly evident in that time was a resurgence of religion in many parts of the world rather than a decline. This resurgence took on many forms, from revitalization of practices of religion to narrow fundamentalism. Because this resurgence of religion coincided with the sharp rise in armed violence after the fall of the Soviet Empire (1989–91), opponents of religion linked this religious resurgence to violence, asserting that religion was a major cause of this violence. There were connections, to be sure, but more recent analysis suggests that the connections between religion and violence are not principally causative ones; rather, religion is often enlisted to legitimate violence in order to cloak other motives, such as desire for dominance, greed for precious goods, or settling old scores.

The rise of religion has also coincided with the collapse of secular utopian thinking in that same time, especially of Marxist ideology with the collapse of the Soviet Union and its hegemony over Eastern Europe. Postmodern assertions notwithstanding, people can live only so long with fragments of an overarching narrative. Although there is widespread distrust of totalizing, utopian narratives as being in the final instance oppressive, master narratives are still sought. Amid the apparent failure to construct credible human utopias, people turn again to religious traditions.

Moreover, in some parts of the world the spread of modernization has not necessarily meant secularization, in the sense of the disappearance of religion. The most notable exception to this is the United States, where a vibrant religiosity persists amid advanced modernization. In parts of Asia, modernization has been successfully introduced by authoritarian governments (in Singapore, China, and Vietnam), thus calling into question whether the modernization process only happens in one way. Modernization has been introduced with no significant drop in religiosity in some countries, such as India, or has been accompanied by increase in religiosity, as in China. As a result, modernity is no longer seen as a single phenomenon; it may be better to speak of "modernities" than "modernity" in the singular.[1] Rather than looking to Europe as the vanguard of the disappearance of religion, it may represent rather a special case, a *Sonderweg*.[2]

As a result of the resurgence of religion, new narratives about secularization are emerging, especially in Europe and North America. The German philosopher Jürgen Habermas, an avowed unbeliever, startled the world in his October 2001 address upon being awarded the Peace Prize of the Frankfurt Book Fair; he stated that religion retains its intrinsic value even in a highly secularized society. European society cannot be understood in its current form without acknowledging the role of faith in its genealogy. Habermas has gone on to affirm this, notably in his 2004 public dialogue with then-Cardinal Joseph Ratzinger (now Pope Benedict XVI),[3] and in his address in 2005 upon receiving the Holberg Prize from the Norwegian Parliament.[4] We are living in what he calls a "postsecular society," by which he means that a crude kind of scientism cannot establish itself as the sole arbiter of what constitutes reality. Religion has its rightful place in the discourse of society, although it may carry the "asymmetrical burden" of having constantly to prove itself in the face of secular reason.

The Canadian philosopher Charles Taylor, a Roman Catholic, has also presented a new narrative of secularization in a long and carefully argued book, *A Secular Age*.[5] He asserts that one cannot tell the story of secularization and the decline of religion by means of "subtraction theory," wherein religion is subtracted from the sum of Western society. Rather, society has continued to be a "mixed" reality: religion has both rational and nonrational elements, but so too does secularity. An example of this is the place that human rights discourse holds in the Western imagination. Human rights theory posits the dignity and equality of all human beings, but it does not give a rational ground for believing that such is the case. In point of fact, Western human rights discourse, now seen as utterly secular, has its roots in religion. Human rights were founded theologically upon the assertion that all human beings were created in the image and likeness of God (Gen. 1:26–27). To be sure, this theologically founded idea rests upon a nonrational assertion, but so does the secular human rights discourse. For Taylor, religion and secularity exist side by side, with each trying to negotiate the questions that modernity raises.

To ground his position on this coexistence of religion and secularity, Taylor provides a more extensive rereading of history than does Habermas. He finds the roots of secularity in the various movements for reform that marked Western Christianity from the twelfth century onward. These reforms imagined a more orderly society, in which all are called to live according to certain high ideals. The desire for such order gradually shaped a political theory that imposed a discipline on the entirety of society and created a situation in which society itself became self-grounding. This led to a "providential Deism," which sidelined a God who is active and intervenes in history. Gradually, in the secular view of this matter, God became utterly extrinsic to creation. In its crudest forms, this secularity became antitheistic (Taylor associates this darker side of modernity with Romanticism and especially with the philosopher Friedrich Nietzsche), so that today we have a three-way approach to dealing with questions and values in society: a religious one, a relatively neutral secular one, and a more hostile antireligious option.

What does this rethinking of secularity mean for mission? The most widespread response has been built upon the "subtraction-theory" version of the secularization narrative: that religion has been privatized and marginalized in society. The general religiosity that remains in society is vague and undefined; these are remnants of "Christendom," of a time when Christianity was part of the warp and woof of society. The Christendom mentality needs to be expunged: Christianity will never again play a dominant role in society. Rather, what must be cultivated now are small, disciplined communities that have vigor to serve as leaven in the larger society. This is a strategy shared, at least in its general contours, by certain strands of the Reformed tradition, most notably, in the work of the late Lesslie Newbigin, in the Gospel and Our Culture Network, and the "little flock" approach of Pope Benedict XVI.

What the now-proposed narrative suggests is somewhat different. It recognizes the "asymmetrical burden" that religion carries in a secular society, but tries to meet it on three related fronts. First, this narrative seeks to have a public church, embodied in the central city churches in Europe, often of architectural and historical significance, that become centers for art, cultural activities, social outreach, and religious activities. Such an approach recognizes that religiosity reaches farther than the tightly disciplined community. It also exhibits the fact that religion, art, and culture have been deeply inter-twined in the West. The sharp identification of religion with a set of beliefs is a seventeenth-century configuration, growing out of the Thirty Years' War. Religion, for most of the world, is more a way of life than a view of life. This public-church approach calls for a more ample definition of religion rather than a narrower one.

Second, there is an important place for the intentional community. But how it is envisioned is a bit different from the post-Christendom approach: here it locates itself in the larger "quest for the whole" that marks postsecular society. It acknowledges that, to orient themselves, human beings cannot live long on fragments. It recognizes the harm that utopias of human construction dating from the nineteenth and twentieth centuries have wrought in recent history. Time-tested ways to achieve the whole are not without their dangers; but his-torical testing can highlight the pitfalls along the way. By embracing Christi-anity in such historic communities, these intentional communities can offer themselves as a place to belong, a place to be part of something larger than themselves, a place of spiritual quest—thus a place that does not devolve into sectarian thinking.

Third, there is a conscious alignment of religion with secularity, of the more objective or neutral sort, that works together for the betterment of human society. Religion and secularity share a common origin in the reform-ing movements of medieval Europe, and together they address the challenges that modernity is posing to both. They also stand together against the darker sides of both: religious fanaticism and cults of power and exclusivism that are trying to subdue secularity.

## ACCOMPANYING THE "BOTTOM BILLION"

Oxford economist Paul Collier has been a prominent voice in the global dis-cussion of alleviating the acute poverty that some 20 percent of the world suffers. His own work focuses especially on Africa. In 2007 he published *The Bottom Billion: Why the Poorest Countries Are Failing and What Can Be Done about It*.[6] Though acknowledging the considerable progress that the global-ization of trade has helped to create, Collier sees 20 percent of the world's population locked out of the potential benefits of globalization by larger structural factors that need to be addressed. This billion people at the bottom are concentrated in fifty-eight countries, most of them in Africa and Central Asia. The structural factors blocking the alleviation of poverty constitute four "traps" in which these countries are caught, and the poorest countries are caught typically in more than one of these traps at the same time. The four traps are (1) protracted warfare, (2) being landlocked with hostile neighbors, (3) dependence upon a single source of income (either extractive resources or an agricultural product), and (4) bad governance. Here I wish to explore only the first two of these and their implications for mission.

The first trap is protracted warfare, usually internal to a country, but often abetted and sustained by neighboring countries as well. Some 80 percent of the wars today happen in the world's twenty poorest countries. The chances of warfare reerupting in those countries within five years are 50 percent. One-sixth of the world's population experiences five-sixths of the wars being fought today. A number of countries have experienced this protracted warfare now for half a century. The impact on population, resources, and infrastructure is enormous. For a generation to grow up knowing nothing but war, or marginal existence in a camp for displaced persons, restricts the social imagination necessary for building a civil society.

It has become increasingly evident that our sense of mission must now include skills in peace building and reconciliation, alongside well-established skills in education, medicine, and agronomy. There is a growing awareness of this, as more and more mission agencies come to realize that warfare can quickly wipe out any advances made in development, health, and literacy. The skills in this area do not simply represent handy instruments in the missionary's toolbox, but also embody a profound gospel message of the good news itself: the *shalom* of God and the reconciliation that the triune God is bringing about in the world itself. The churches have begun to recognize this: the 2005 conference of the Committee on World Mission and Evangelism of the World Council of Churches made reconciliation a central theme of its reflection. The Special Synod for the Bishops of Africa, held in the Vatican in 2009, is devoted principally to peace building and reconciliation.

Another implication for "mission from the ground up" is what happens on the ground itself. In places of protracted warfare, outsiders such as the UN peacekeepers, foreign investment, and the NGOs tend to leave and then stay away. It is often only the missionaries who stay. Accompanying the bottom billion is part of the mandate "to bring good news to the poor" (Luke 4:18). There surely come situations when even that presence is no longer possible, but it must not be forgotten as something that missionaries try to live up to.

A second of Collier's traps is too much reliance on a single product for national income. This single product is often something that can be extracted (such as oil, timber, or gold) or a single agricultural product. To be sure, the latter had been encouraged by international institutions such as the World Bank, to spur economic growth. But it also causes countries to become dependent upon the vagaries of the world market. Here I focus on just one part of this trap as it manifests itself in the growing food crisis, to be followed by a water crisis in many parts of the world, also.

The food crisis lies at the intersection of a number of challenges. On the one hand, the majority of the world's population now lives in large cities, which means they have little opportunity to produce their own food. At the same time, subsistence farming may provide for a single family, but it does not produce the surplus needed to feed the rest of the world. For example, two-thirds of Mexico's farmers produce only 12 percent of the food that Mexico needs. On the other hand, moving toward large-scale farming as practiced in North America and parts of Brazil raises questions about environmental sustainability and the use of genetically manipulated seeds and animals.

The food crisis that became evident in 2008 represents the potential of this crisis. From March 2007 to April 2008, the world price of wheat, the world's second most consumed staple, rose 130 percent. In the first three months of 2008, the price of rice, the most consumed staple worldwide, rose an astonishing 100 percent. This steep rise in the cost of food staples is not an accidental or short-term thing. Many economists believe that this will be a long-term crisis, such as the world has not seen in thirty years. Moreover, it will likely take two decades to reverse this trend.

Four factors are contributing to the crisis. First, bad weather, especially drought, in parts of the world (such as Eastern Australia) upon which the world depends for large-scale production. Second, the rise in the cost of oil, especially for the transport of food to countries that do not produce enough to sustain their population—such as shipping rice to the Philippines and supplies for chemical fertilizers. Third, the production of biofuels in and for the wealthy world, which diverts basic foodstuffs into ethanol, ostensibly for environmental purposes, though the production of ethanol sometimes wipes out the carbon emissions differential. Fourth, increased meat and dairy consumption as people move out of poverty, as occurred in Asia.

The best projections available now suggest that the world's population will top out at about nine billion persons by the middle of the twenty-first century. This estimate is lower than previous figures, but still represents about 50 percent more people living on the earth than do today. The church stands at the intersection of these formidable challenges—adequate provision of food, sustainability of agricultural practice, the growth in population, the dignity of human beings—as we face mission on the ground today. Holistic evangelization, something supported across most of the spectrum of the churches, calls us to think theologically about these challenges and to embed that thinking in our missiological practice.

## REVISITING THE RELIGIOUS INTERFACE

Interreligious dialogue has now figured into the understanding of mission for many of the churches for half a century. Such dialogue has taken on many forms. The Roman Catholic Church, for example, distinguishes four kinds of dialogue: (1) the dialogue of life, wherein dialogue is constituted by simple witness of life; (2) the dialogue of social action, where people from different traditions engage in common project for development or for furthering justice; (3) the dialogue of theological ideas, where experts in two traditions discuss fundamental concepts and ideas of their respective traditions; and (4) the dialogue of mystical experiences, where adepts in the traditions compare their experiences of God and the transcendent realm.

Dialogue within missiological practice often focuses upon building trust between the parties, with assurances that dialogue is to be understood as a respectful exchange and not a covert strategy to engage in proselytism. To be sure, that building of trust is fundamental for any kind of dialogue whatsoever.

In recent years, a dialogue of social action has come to take a special precedence over the other forms. It is a dialogue in which religious leaders have a special role. This dialogue comes in two forms. The first is a dialogue in which two traditions engage in a common witness for the sake of the community in which they find themselves. A common site of this today can be found in Europe or North America, where traditions such as Islam or Hinduism are now present in what had been Christian majority settings. The fact that the religious leaders in a neighborhood or district are known to be in friendly contact with one another helps to set the scene for caring for the well-being of all inhabitants of that area. Respecting each tradition's holy days and customs, coming to the aid of those distressed or subjected to prejudice, engaging in a common project for the good of the entire community—these all constitute practices of dialogue that underscore mutual respect and honoring of communities. Moreover, engaging in common projects helps to build networks of association that help differentiate how people identify themselves: multiple, cross-thatched identifications reduce the hardening of identities into combative opposites, especially in times of stress in the community.

The second form is closely related to the first and involves the dialogues that build peace within and between communities, especially when lines of difference coincide with lines of religious affiliation. Local religious leaders are key to the peace-building process. They are, first of all, important in preventing violence. By stanching rumors about the misbehavior of the other group, by not allowing religious beliefs to inflame and legitimate acts of violence—in these ways they can keep tensions from escalating into outright physical conflict. Similarly, religious leaders can contribute to the healing after violence, by bringing the symbolic and ritual resources of their traditions to bear upon acts of healing and reconciliation. They can channel experiences of suffering into the narratives of their own tradition that make the suffering more redemptive than prone to vindictive or retaliatory behavior. They can use traditions of forgiveness to heal wounds in the community. And they can use the opportunities of having overcome violence to deepen the understanding in their respective traditions of the meaning of peace.

Because religious difference is so often wielded as a way of inflaming difference and legitimating violence, it is important to counter these strategies, emphasizing religious traditions as a path to peace. Despite all those instances where people can point to religion as a source of violence, one can also point to the manifold ways that religions work to build peace. As recognized above, peace and reconciliation are signs of the good news of Jesus Christ, signs that the reign of God is indeed drawing near.

## TRACKING THE UNINTENDED CONSEQUENCES OF GLOBALIZATION

The world finds itself well into the second decade of this round of globalization. The compression of time and space that is part of the experience of globalization means that events can come upon us quickly, and consequences arise that were not anticipated. Balances of power can shift quickly, and the ever unsurely balanced financial markets can quickly totter and wreak havoc around the world. Because of globalization, physical features of our environment, such as disease, spread more quickly through air travel. The threshold of trust, needed to maintain such ephemeral but essential aspects of our world, such as the value of paper money, is always precarious. And features such as climate change cannot be kept at bay by territorial boundaries. Globalization heightens the sense of risk.[7]

I point to just two aspects of the current experience of globalization that pose challenges for Christian mission today. The first has to do with the power of ideas, but the attendant weakening of ideologies. As already noted, the grand utopian schemes of the nineteenth and twentieth centuries have not proved to be patterns for the improvement of human well-being. Rather, communism and fascism in their various forms have proved to be ruinous. If the new narratives of secularity gain ground, we will find an ideology of a world without God being replaced by secularity and religion living alongside each other, grappling together with the common challenges about the future. Religion itself can surely be reduced to ideology, especially in times of uncertainty and fear, when the ramparts of identity are heightened and the paradoxes of belief are flattened out into simple certainties. Yet the best of religious traditions is generally not expressed in distilled dogmas, but by the narrative of how those traditions see God working in the world. As mentioned above, people cannot live long with fragments. Sooner rather than later they will craft idols out of them as tangible substitutes for much greater realities. The great ideas embedded in our religious traditions—embedded in persons, in events, in stories—constitute the best hope for living in a globalized world that offers no meaning and purpose of its own beyond production and consumption.

The second consequence to attend to in globalization is the increase in the number of young people—especially young men—who, on the juggernaut of globalization, find themselves displaced, disoriented, disappointed, and dispossessed.[8] Not the poorest of the poor, but those whose hopes have been dashed, become the pool of people who can be recruited to violence. Contemporary studies on the making of terrorists and suicide bombers point to this. Mission needs to be directed especially to this group in the population. Their energies need to be engaged for constructing a better world, not an angry riposte to a disingenuous one. Can we help them see the visions that the prophet Joel promises to the young (2:28)?

## CONCLUSION

In many ways, Edinburgh 1910 was a watershed moment for the Christian church. Its vision of the future may have proved to be inadequate in many ways, but the energies it gathered and released had immense consequences for mission and the entire church in the century that followed. Whether Edinburgh 2010 will be principally a retrospective commemoration or an impulse to something new and engaging remains to be seen. Using the best analysis of which we are capable, and a firm trust in the Holy Spirit, we can hope to make it a *kairos* for our time.

# 3

# Globalization and Mission in the Twenty-first Century

OGBU U. KALU

## ANATOMY OF THE GLOBALIZATION DISCOURSE

Globalization has become the buzzword of our contemporary world: lauded for all that is good, creative, and inspiring, but blamed for all that is bad. This immediately raises issues about explanation of causality and our sense of history because the concept of globalization has deep roots and has evolved through time. Different genres of the history of globalization include (1) the archaic globalization of the fifteenth century, symbolized by the Iberian voyages of discovery; (2) the protoglobalization that followed the intensified commercial rivalry and mercantalist theory of the eighteenth century; (3) the modern globalization of the nineteenth century, with its imperial instrumentalization of power; and (4) the postcolonial globalization after the World Wars.[1] By the decade of the 1960s, the concept of the *global village* provided a new way of conceptualizing the changing vistas of world order and global relationships, including religion and, specifically, Christianity. Since the literature has burgeoned, suffice it to summarize that globalization is a relational concept explaining how technological, economic, and cultural forces have fostered cultural contacts, which have reduced vast distances in space and time and, at the same time, brought civilizations and communities into closer degrees of interaction. Everybody may not be amused, but many find the process ineluctably absorbing.

In the 1960s when Marshall McLuhan talked about the "global village," he pointed to the impact of communication and technology on cultures:

Gutenberg's invention of the printing press and massive communication technology have gradually turned the world into multisites webbed together by electronic languages and symbols; thus whatever happens in one part of the globe is immediately known in another part.[2] Thomas L. Friedman put it more graphically in his book *The World Is Flat: A Brief History of the Twenty-first Century*.[3] Friedman's list of "flattening influences" includes such milestones as the advent of the Netscape Web browser, work-flow software, outsourcing, offshoring, and supply-chaining. He demonstrates that technology has become even more complex since McLuhan's ringtone, "The media is the message," enthused the public. The electronic media have knotted many cultures, societies, and civilizations together into unavoidable contact, depriving them of their isolation and threatening their particularity. All are caught in the complex embrace. We are concerned about the delicate balance between particularity, which could lead to isolation, and universality, which could lead to homogenization.

Technology has reshaped human economies, cultures, and lifestyles. Friedman uses China to illustrate the benevolent face of the process, showing how isolated societies and economies have grown through the power of globalization. When Marco Polo visited China in the thirteenth century, he found a rich land known for its invention of paper, printing, gunpowder, and the compass. China's per capita income exceeded that of European nations. Its ships dominated the Indian Ocean right up to the shores of East Africa. In the fifteenth century, however, China retreated into a splendid isolation and its inventive spirit faded; by the nineteenth century it lagged behind Europe and was forced to accept a humiliating colonial domination. Internal turmoil followed. China changed course under Deng Xiaoping's leadership in the late 1970s: fueled by a commitment to education, technological innovation, and global commerce, it regained its position as a world economic superpower. Lurking under the success story are ethical dimensions: the inequalities in wealth distribution, the divinity of the market, and a certain spirit that commodifies human relationships breed inordinate consumption habits and pollute the environment—a fate that China has been forced to confront for hosting the 2008 Olympic Games.

The galloping process of globalization not only affected the theory of knowledge but also had two other results. Beyond the fact that it has created a new landscape and human challenges for production, dissemination, and utilization of knowledge, it has generated a new global culture, likewise the intensification of cultural and value clashes. As cultures are pressed together, the problem of identity looms large. Religion is manipulated as a marker of identity and ultimacy, invested with the symbol of prideful heritage, deployed as a tool for boundary maintenance, and promoted as the mooring for scapegoating the Other. A combination of these factors engenders the wider politics of difference and compels devotees to do difference in avoidable ways.[4] The discomfort of enforced intimacy could be illustrated by the fact that globalization has been used to explain the phenomenon of intensified religious violence in the twenty-first century. Some scholars emphasize the psychosocial analysis of religious violence: individuals who engage in religious violence perceive themselves as engaged in a cosmic battle larger than the individual; violence is used as an antidote to perceived marginality and humiliation, as an attempt to establish equality with rivals, opponents, and oppressors in the new global space, which threatens everyone with a homogenized culture.

Theories on the connection of violence and religion point to the fact that the twenty-first century has been distinguished by "categorical violence," a violence directed against people on the basis of their belonging to a certain religious group. Categorical violence has three distinctive features: excessiveness, the discourse on purification, and a ritual. We recognize the fact that nonreligious ideologies could also produce violence. Categorical violence has been powered by a metaphysical meaning embodied in the notion of preserving the good and true against relativizing global forces. Destruction is thought of as divine' and restorative. Thus, the restoration of orthodoxy in the face of alleged corruption or desecration of the pure could be achieved through divine destruction.[5]

Sacrifice is an essential ingredient of scapegoating: the impetus to identify a contrast group onto which we can project the root problem and that provides an explanation of that problem. Scapegoating is like ritualization of violence, as used to maintain the power of the dominant group. The concept of fundamentalism as a label for the new passionate religions may no longer suffice because the manifestations in the political, economic, and theological realms yield contradictory conclusions. Two irreducible dimensions are the increased use of violence in religious matters and the spilling of such violence into political, social, and economic realms. Secularism, another icon of the globalization process, has failed to turn the public space into a neutral arena. Thus, the concept of globalization may harbor internal contradictions: at once multidirectional, complex, and inherently paradoxical; incorporating movement, flows, countermovements, and blockages.

Some, therefore, argue that the new global culture is not from any particular region; others believe that it is a product and an internal requirement of capitalism, that much of the global violence is connected to the competition for resources, a drama heightened by the character of the new economic order and aroused appetites. The allure to and capacity for consumption explain why many fear the American domination dubbed as "McDonaldization," underpropped by political and economic ideologies: liberal democracy and market economy.[6] When Francis Fukuyama declared "the end of history" in 1989 because of the fall of Communist Soviet Union, he actually surmised the end of virulent ideological contests and the victory of capitalism and liberal democracy. He intoned that the impact of 1989 was not just political; it also unleashed cultural, technological, and economic forces that reshaped the globe. Big business would pacify the clash of cultures; trust would emanate from shared cultural values and shared interests. He further argued that beyond theories, basic self-interest is the basis of modern economic interdependence; in a market-dominated world, the primary human interaction would be competition, not support and solidarity. He virtually prophesied that the new world order and its asymmetrical power relations would intensify the scourge of poverty among the weaker communities such as Africa. Stronger economies would create an osmotic pull, engendering massive emigration or brain drain.

Some may demur, alleging an incomplete social analysis. Indeed, Thomas L. Friedman's earlier book *The Lexus and Olive Tree: Understanding Globalization* explores the tension between globalization on the one side, and culture, geography, tradition, and economy on the other. He assesses both the benefits and problems of globalization. What is certain is that globalization has acquired many characteristics based on the lenses used to interpret how certain cultural forces and values (economic, cultural, social, and political) have woven the *oikoumenē* into a certain order, sharing identical values and bound by economic, cultural, and religious forces, which are so strong that some inherited values must be surrendered and development trajectories modified or abandoned. This is an emergent global culture, utilizing technology, commerce, and monetary power to weld disparate peoples and cultures. Sometimes the cord is so strong that a sneeze at one end causes flu at the other end. Sometimes the bind is so ineluctable that even losers cannot extricate themselves.

The caveat is that matters have shifted from the global village concept to a rather bewildering disintegration and flux. First, questions arise about the pace and direction of the change. Global cultural flow is not unidirectional. In *The Travels of a T-Shirt in the Global Economy*, Pietra Rivoli illustrates this: textile factories were once in England, then in New England, then in southeastern United States, then in Japan, then in Hong Kong.[7] Now subsidized cotton grown in Texas is sent to China to be made into T-shirts and then shipped back to the United States. Second, at the core, globalization is a power concept bearing the seeds of asymmetrical power relations. There is no guarantee of equality or benefit for all. Third, globalization could be perceived as a liberal ideology, with a mind of its own, imbued with postmodernity, dislocations, and hybridity. It is akin to the New Testament concept of *kosmos*: the world order, controlled by an inexplicable and compulsive power, dazzling with allurements, or *kosmētikos*. Some wonder whether friendship with globalization is not enmity with God's design because it breeds poverty at the periphery.

From these perspectives, globalization's pursuit of democratic order is designed to create a friendly political and socioeconomic environment for consumer market economy. But the downside of the democratization process in the third-world countries includes the liberalization of the media space; the increase in the number of discordant voices in the public space; increase in violence, especially ethnic, religious, and political violence; and a chaotic political culture disabling the consolidation that should follow the postelectoral process. On the positive side, the globalization domestic politics has made it possible for intervention into local issues by transnational advocacy groups or diasporic communities. For instance, with detailed information the whole world participated in the debates and negotiations around the recent political violence in Kenya in early 2008.

Similarly, some laud the embedded concepts of economic interdependence and mutual interest without attention to the vulnerability of the third-world countries. The local region is the Cinderella in this global dance and dreads the possibilities of homogenization and Americanization propagated by the ubiquitous multinational companies, which serve as the vanguards of the new global order penetrating into nooks and corners of the globe.

Just as the industrial revolution in nineteenth-century England had negative side effects and bred enormous social problems, which Charles Dickens chronicled in his novels *Oliver Twist*, *Bleak House*, and *David Copperfield* and whose victims were etched in Hogart's paintings, so have the socioeconomic impacts of globalization become a disaster for the marginalized and created poverty, health problems, and other unsavory consequences. Globalization has exacerbated the center-periphery concept of international relations. Livelihood studies theorize that the new social and gender identities have transformed families, decomposed households, and increased diversification and multilocality of livelihoods under globalization.

## RELIGION AND GLOBALIZATION:
## A CULTURAL DISCOURSE

On the whole, the globalization discourse has taken three routes through cultural and economic issues to sociopolitical and global concerns. Some describe what is on the ground while others explain or decipher the impact of what appears to be happening. The weak link perhaps is the application of the concept to religion in general and Christianity in particular. A few illustrations on applying the model in studying religious systems will suffice.

We make the point chronologically from the works of Roland Robertson, Peter Beyer, Karla Poewe, Mike Featherstone, David Lyon, Rosalind Hackett, Brigit Meyer, and Ruth Marshall-Fratani. In the early years of the discourse, Robertson drew attention to the worldwide resurgence of religion, contrary to the earlier predictions about the death of religion and ethnicity in the insurgence of modernity. Jeff Haynes analyzed the contrary trend in the third world and especially in Africa, while Peter Beyer demonstrated the failure of the prophecies on secularism, as shown with the insurgence of religious fundamentalism and ecological spirituality in many parts of the globe. Karla Poewe reinterpreted the resurgent, charismatic forms of Christianity as the new global Christianity, contradicting those who imaged these as the religion of the disoriented or locked them into the fundamentalist mold, pigeonholed as a form of American cultural imperialism or, worse, as part of American right-wing insurgence. Rather, she argued, charismatic religiosity reflected the journey of a spiritual flow, with an ancient source, coursing through various impulses into the interior of the globe. "What is global are traditions that reach across national boundaries, take on local color, and move on again."[8]

Interest soon shifted to the conjuncture with modernity and postmodernity, probing the impact of media and technology as they empower religious crusaders; the cultural discontinuities that must follow; and how new religious forms become agents in spreading the psychology of modernity: the understanding of the self, the Other, and perception of the past. Globalization, it was argued, valorized the democratization of religion and the explosive growth of religion in the Global South. New religious entrepreneurs flourished in the public space, abandoning and reinterpreting old missionary foundations. Some analysts insisted that the Christianity of the South merely fed on the resources of externality and attacked communism by legitimating individualization and the nuclear family or by liberating members from the burden of the past.

These efforts explored the cultural discontinuities caused by the globalization process because of certain characteristics: contraction of space, tearing people from perceived traditions, reorienting them to the wider world, and undermining universal claims and particular identities. However, charismatic religiosity did not always originate from the Western world.[9] More crucial is an analysis that privileges how transnational cultural forms are appropriated, set on wheels, and domesticated; how local cultural lenses shape hermeneutics and determine modes of appropriation; and how global cultural transnational contexts gestate and appropriate external cultural resources.

The hint comes from Robertson, who unwittingly proposed a cultural discourse in the understanding of globalization. He first applied the concept of *glocalization* to deal with the global-local theme, borrowing from the Japanese *dochakuka*, a micromarketing technique for adapting a global outlook to local conditions. Long before them, traditionalization was the favored concept, also using the example of Japanese pattern of industrialization along the grooves of traditional mores. For instance, factories operate as families, using the deference system and loyalties derived from traditional ethics. Those engaged in agricultural development in third-world contexts explored the traditionalization strategy that exploits indigenous knowledge in mediating innovation.

A cultural discourse is more helpful because it does not ignore the dynamics and process of culture contacts and asymmetrical power relations. It shows how economic, financial, and technological resources of externality are domesticated. Viewed from several perspectives at once (and with mixed metaphors), it focused attention on the relationship between the encoder and the decoder, and the interconnectedness of local distinctiveness and global generality. This is akin to the biblical understanding of the "indigenous" and "pilgrim" principles. As the gospel (which is universal) travels as a pilgrim through many cultures, it is experienced and translated into pathways.

This inculturating potential cautions us against homogeneity because hearers interpret with the lenses of their indigenous worldviews. Such a perspective privileges indigenous agency: the initiative and creative responses by local actors. Third-world contexts are not a tabula rasa on which foreign culture—extra space bearers—wrote their scripts. Hidden scripts abound at the level of infrapolitics.

By contesting the blurring of boundaries and identities in the globalization discourse, it becomes possible to demonstrate how global cultural flows are mediated in everyday lives of ordinary people in local places. Finally, the emphasis should be placed on the sense of fluidity and flux in social analysis by restoring the initiative to the underdog and taking wind off the hubris of the presumed top dogs in this dog's life of ours! Globalization has usually been defined with the ideological and power biases of where one is located in the process. But local conditions and cultural patterns do still filter global flows. As Marshall-Fratani puts it, "Appropriation of the new occurs in an endless inventive process of cultural bricolage."

This raises a methodological issue. Most third-world contexts sport three interlocking public spaces: the rural/village/barrio; the emergent urban; and the modern/Western public represented by multinational corporations, agencies, and educational institutions. Both the rural and Western publics catalyze a new, emergent culture that is neither fish nor fowl but a mélange culture. This space generates a popular culture that weaves the indigenous and external resources. It avidly and creatively consumes Western and indigenous cultural ingredients. Cultural influences flow in and from all directions. The urban dweller is still rooted in the rural culture because rural-urban migration, while dislocating people, is often circulatory.

Analysis of globalization must reckon with the resilience of rural culture and its capacity to provide the inculturating pathway for modern/Western values and resources. The rural public is embattled as stronger cultural forces from the urban and Western publics assay to overawe indigenous values, social control models, and structures with new production and consumption habits and gender relationships. In *Broken Hoe*, D. U. Iyam captures the changes in rural Nigerian community.[10] New states in the Global South also struggle to adjust to external demands, technologies, economic structures, and power relationships. Many fail and soften as victims of corrupt, counterfeit modernity and leave a scourge of poverty in their wake.

## THE GLOBALIZING IMPULSE IN CHRISTIANITY AND WORLD MISSION

What connects globalization to mission, especially in contemporary Christianity? Globalization appears as the contemporary response to the human dilemma at Babel: human families, whose language became mixed or "confused" (Hebrew: *bālal*, Gen. 11:9) so that they were dispersed to cover the face of the earth, are now regathering and communicating in cyberspeak. The forces unleashed by globalization shape the terrain or cultural context of contemporary mission and provide tools, resources, and opportunities for doing mission. The negative side effects inform the emphases in the content of missiology and the various challenges that confront the gospel as it encounters various cultures. The fortunes of the gospel are determined by the capacities of cultures as they negotiate the massive transformation caused by global forces.

Two caveats: first, change could come from internal processes as well as from external causes. Globalization could not be blamed for all ills but is here perceived as a change agent. Second, the connection between globalization and Christianity is ironic because the missionary enterprise nursed the seed of globalization. Mission is the heartbeat of the church, and the globalization impulse is embedded in the heart of Christianity. Mission is more cross-cultural expansion, but it is dynamic and contains the mandate to proclaim, convert, and expand territorial boundaries. New technology, easy travel, and enormous wealth created by changing economic structures shape the texture, structures, and strategies of mission.

The story begins with the period when the concept of *Christendom* strained the globalizing impulse in Christianity by raising the problem of representation of the movement. Embedded in the concept of Christendom was a restraint on the expansionist motif in the Christian message and strategy. As the tide of the Jesus movement flowed from Palestine into Europe, rulers employed it as cultural signifier and national identity. Some posed as *defensores fidei*, situated the faith in the domain of the state, exploited it as the compelling rationale, and used it for commercial expansion and assertion of national pride. Thus, Iberian Catholicism, which initiated the incredible European migration of the fifteenth and sixteenth centuries, wove the evangelization of the heathens into the more obvious reasons for the voyages that scoured over the Atlantic and into the Indian Oceans.

The quest for an alternative sea route to the Far East was more a creative European response to the challenges posed by Islam, which had blocked the Levant land route to the sources of spices, seized the breadbasket in the Maghrib, initiated a lucrative trans-Saharan gold trade, and taken over the ancient centers of Christianity. Crusades could not dislodge them, but the discovery of a sea route did and enabled Europe to regain the upper hand. Unfortunately, Christianity became a social ornament in the project; soon conversion of the heathens was overawed by commercial allure, and the evangelists found it more lucrative to enslave prospective converts. The winds went out of the sails of the evangelization movement before the enlightenment worldview put paid to the Christendom concept.

This is the significance of the intense European migration and evangelization project that surged afresh between the years 1875 and 1925 to shape modern Christianity. The Protestant factor predominated, moved by the engine of abolitionism that wiped the slur off the face of the gospel. The enlargement of scale in the missionary enterprise created a new vista because of the number of people, organizations, nations, creeds, races, gender, and class who participated. The voluntarist principle changed the strategy and mobilized a greater range of classes into the missionary endeavor.

At different points in time and as the tides changed under new cultural forces that shaped the world, protagonists have expressed the universal, expansionist thrust of the movement differently. For instance, when the resources and impulse for missionary expansion were challenged by the aftereffects of the First World War, which lasted longer and was more brutal than anyone had imagined, the ideology of *internationalism* emerged to spur evangelism through the interwar years and to the 1950s. The militaristic language of mission resonated with the temper of the times, redolent with the collusion of altar and throne.

The globalizing impulse within Christianity and its practice in the missionary movement could be illustrated with the many missionary slogans, policies, and strategies through time. Each century crafted a new driving ideology, and these driving slogans tended to display the reigning spirit of the nations. It has been argued that internationalism supremely bore the exuberant American imprint.

Germans were chagrined because their role in spreading the first flames of the Protestant missionary enterprise in the eighteenth century went unacknowledged as the American tide deluged the enterprise in the nineteenth century. German scholars complained that the new slogan confused human efforts with God's initiatives. For the leading German missiologist, Bruno Gutmann, the *Volkskirche* ideal was the bastion of protecting local identities from the battering ram of global processes. He argued that primal cultures served as points of contact, containers, and the soil in which the Spirit of God works. Primal ties must be redeemed but not destroyed, replaced, or ignored; those ties should be converted and received into the new reality of Christ's body.

The irony is that though the Germans accused the Americans of westernizing the mission field, the Germans were just as parochial and installed a folk ideology that was native to the German soil and became implicated in the support for the National Socialist cause. Gutmann's ideas were hijacked by the Nazis. Equally notable, internationalism as an emotive globalizing impulse, symbolized by the Christian missionary movement, changed the character of Christianity and resulted in immense diversity of cultural expressions, theological emphases, rituals, and social practices as Christianity gained many heartlands.

The debates at the conference of the International Missionary Council held at Tambaram, Madras, in 1938 were a good example. This conference was planned to take place in China but was moved because of the Sino-Japanese war. It was very important for the third-world Christians for a number of reasons, including its location in Asia within a context of a strong Hindu religion and Hindu-dominated politics. The backdrop consisted of both the insurgent nationalism of India and the use of Christianity as a liberating force by the *Dalit* lower caste.

The organizers created the opportunity for third-world voices that had not been heard, such as Africans, who had been totally absent in Edinburgh in 1910.[11] Above all, it raised the dilemma of globalizing Christianity through mission; the problem of Christ and culture, which has been at the core of evangelization and conversion; and how the church should evangelize people of other faiths. Europe itself was reeling from geopolitical conflicts, including the emergent National Socialism in Germany, which confronted world Christianity with the problem of culture, national identity, and the gospel.

The conference not only continued the rancorous debate between Barthians and non-Barthians over the relationship of nature and grace, but also dialogued about the lordship of Christ in the new cultural contexts and the use of indigenous structures for building national churches. It was stunned by the new voice of the Madras group, which submitted a counterproposal, *Rethinking Christianity in India*. This antistructural document was the harbinger of third-world theology. It raised the problem of becoming a Christian without social dislocation and the need for flexibility and sensitivity to indigenous contexts in globalizing the gospel. It also harkened back to the contribution by a delegate from India, V. S. (Vedanayagam Samuel) Azariah, during the Edinburgh Conference in 1910, when he urged the advocates of mission to commend not just self-sacrifice, but also Christian friendship. In other words, he counseled a shift from missionary heroism and unilateral transmission to indigenous appropriation and mutual integrity.[12]

Missionary promotion of globalization had unintended consequences. Education was the globalizing ligament that, through the modes of ministerial formation, catechism, and theological curricula, bonded the periphery to the center and ironically nurtured the matured voice of protests from Southern Christians. Internationalism gave birth to ecumenism as another means of reinvigorating the global impulse within Christianity. The ecumenical spirit among Protestants in the 1960–70 era was challenged by the refurbished denominational identities in the next decade. The propagation of the concept of "Anglican Communion" is only one example; other bodies such as the Lutheran World Federation sought to bind their adherents into a global ecclesial identity.

Yet, like a seasonal flower, ecumenism blossomed at the end of the second millennium with unblushing petals of interfaith talks. In the United States, for instance, the new organization Churches Working Together ensured that Roman Catholics worked together with Protestants. Mariology won a hearing outside the Roman Catholic fold as evangelicals reprinted the Apocrypha. Why the outbreak of ecumenism? Some conjecture that the impact of globalization bartered away the narrow boundaries of faith, and ecumenism was seen as a bulwark against eroding secularism, which knows no faith boundaries. Perhaps new theological resources relativized the old doctrinal divide and recognized the vitality of diversity and differences.

## GLOBALIZATION AS RESOURCE AND CHALLENGE IN CONTEMPORARY MISSION

Globalization as a descriptor of contemporary culture has imbued the context of doing mission, supplied the tools and resources, and enormously enlarged the scale and opportunities for doing a different type of mission. Yet globalization's negative side effects certainly constitute the modern challenges for missionaries and the content of missiology as a discipline. Thus, power issues such as gender, social justice, ecology, racism, education, migration and diasporic communities, poverty and wealth disparities—these constitute forces that shape contemporary patterns of missions at local, national, and cross-cultural terrains. The growth of Christianity in the Global South, and in Eastern and Central Europe, combined with the emergence of new cultural trends—all have influenced global processes to scramble the old modes of Christian expressions, ministerial formation, theological education, and missionary structures and strategies. The imperative of mission for healing and rebuilding relationships, communities, and the world of nature has not only become urgent; the relevance of Christianity is also at stake amid a broken world.

Perhaps the cumulative effects of the resources of globalization, as well as emergent socioeconomic and social justice issues created by globalization, jarred prominently against doctrinal obscurantism in the face of threats to life. Theology of life therefore trumped other concerns. Interfaith talks, sensitivity to humans' dignity, liberation struggles, and the integrity of the whole earth became more important concerns for the mission of the church and its relevance in the new public space. Lamin Sanneh argued that the old globalizing Christianity that stirred passions in yesteryears has come to an end and is being replaced because now

> "World Christianity" is the movement of Christianity as it takes form and shape in societies that previously were not Christian, societies that had no bureaucratic tradition with which to domesticate the gospel. World Christianity is not one thing, but a variety of indigenous responses through more or less effective idioms, but in any case without necessarily the European Enlightenment frame. "Global Christianity," on the other hand, is the faithful replication of Christian forms and patterns developed in Europe.[13]

World Christianity affirms the integrity of all believers in the face of the gospel mandate. It shifts the focus to Christianity as a lived faith and explains the ferment, varieties, renewals, and plurality of voices in the movement. As the internationalists of yesteryears argued, indigenization is a prerequisite for the power of the Word to act in bonding people across races and nations.

However, the emergent patterns of Christian missionary responses privilege social activism to an extent that has threatened proclamation as a form of witnessing. Perhaps the Pope's encyclical *Redemptoris missio*, in 1998, was responding to this danger. As missionaries of all hues respond to the untoward social problems of a globalized world, the tendency has been toward instrumentalized managerial models, which may lose a strong theological mooring or attention to the role of the Holy Spirit in mission. Stephen Bevans makes this point by imaging perichoresis as a dance of God. Imagine the divine community, he said,

> moving through the world in a great conga line, gathering up into the dance, led by the "Lord of the Dance," . . . caught up in that movement, that embracing, that dance in God's mission. God is a missionary God; . . . the church is missionary by nature. The Trinity is precisely what leads to the process of the inculturation of our faith. Through the Holy Spirit, who pervades all things, and through the

Incarnate Word, who is immersed in creation and in human flesh, we know that all things are holy, and so anything and everything can be a vehicle for the communication of God's gospel. Culture, history, experience are the *stuff* of theology, of preaching, of sacraments.[14]

It is the Trinitarian faith that calls us to enlarge the public space because *missio Dei* is rooted in the relationship within the Trinity, and human *missions* are echoes or participatory footsteps in the conga dance. But the church's mission should be holistic by its *being*, *saying*, and *doing* as the church stands as the sign, representative, foretaste, and witness to the presence of God in communities.[15] It must be a powerful presence in the mundane world, but must neither lose the eschatological perspective nor become reified. Worship and proclamation remain central in mission.

## A CASE STUDY: MEDIA, POPULAR CULTURE, AND TWENTY-FIRST-CENTURY MISSION

Under this tension is the crucial point that mission must perforce embrace ingredients of globalization as empowering resources, but must also be attentive to the potential challenges to the integrity and witness of the gospel. A reflection on mission, popular culture, and media serves as an example of the Janus-faced impact of globalization because media usage is a key emerging theme in twenty-first-century mission. Since the 1990s, following the outbreak of democratization politics, the media landscape has been radically altered in many of the third-world countries due to deregulation and the emergence of new communication and information technologies. There has been a rapid increase in the numbers of privately owned radio and television stations, newspapers and magazines, computers, and mobile phone networks.

With this media diversification have come new opportunities for ownership, production, and participation. Religious leaders, especially evangelical and charismatic Christian groups, and social activists have been the most avid consumers, strengthening and expanding their communities and gaining public recognition for their organizations. In some cases, this resource has been deployed to create competition, marginalize others, and incite conflict and violence. In a few cases, religious groups have used media to promote interfaith dialogue. All these point to the new connections between the resources of globalized technology and Christian mission.[16]

Given the fact that media technology has an innate culture and that popular culture is driven by a different spirit, how do these serve as resources and challenges in Christian evangelism and representation? The argument is that evangelical/charismatic Christianity has reshaped the religious landscape by using media technology and popular culture and has, in turn, been shaped by both popular culture and the media technology. The valorization of the mode of communicating the gospel has created a new culture, values, and meaning system. It had enormous impact on doctrine, polity, liturgy, and ethics. For instance, the prosperity gospel grew wings because it came with an elaborate media representation, including electronic communication designed to reshape religious consciousness and theologies. The electronic synthesizer trumped all musical instruments, and televangelism dominated the muscular practice of mission.

There are certain dimensions of the increased deployment of media that should be spelled out: first, every transcendental idea must be mediated. So, religion is intrinsically woven into various forms of media representations. Communication is essential for building community. It is at the heartbeat of the church's existence and mandate to communicate the gospel, reveal itself to the world, dialogue, and guide through a creative use of symbols and media. Thus, each new form of media provides the church with new language. Second, the new consumers were not the early adaptors of modern media technology but actually were late consumers. Third, religious broadcasting is shaped by the technology and the industrial values and culture that sustain it. Electronic media has its own version of reality, reshapes the contact environment, and concocts a culture for the consumption of images that support life structures understood as patterns of choices and ways of living.

In addition, the media system and field (context) may harbor democratic deficits: It may fail to constitute a democratic public sphere because of the centralization of symbolic political power. The ownership by the wealthy may create unequal representation, homogenized value, declining sense of community, fragmentation of the public sphere, and elitism because of the secrecy of decision-making processes. Corporate agendas may enforce gender, racial, and religious biases. In some cases, state censorships and values of journalists shape the product. Therefore, we should expect that media could be both a resource and challenge to the gospel message and mission of the church, whether evangelism, discipling, Christian nurture, or inculcation of family values. Religious users could try to shape media to their needs, but media could reshape the religions, trivialize the content, and create a counterreligious culture.

Fourth, there is often a thin line between religious and secular techniques in the use of media communication. Improved technologies define the style. Finally, in the third world in this period, religious media were produced from a certain religious and cultural context, by neoevangelical and fundamentalist revivals of recent years in America, and were tied to the conservative mainstream, which shares common symbols, values, and moral culture.

This profile raises several questions about the process of appropriation by local actors and new cultural contexts. The technology is characterized by a culture of packaging, merchandizing, and competition in a cost-intensive market. It tends to legitimate popular culture and reshape the message of Christianity, perhaps distorting its authenticity, its capacity to speak prophetically to power, and its source of salient moral values. Sometimes the message is cut to a size and format that fits the tube, applause is canned, and certain ethics of electronic media such as cults of personality, individualism, and commercialism are privileged; on the other hand, ritual agents neither advertise nor emphasize fees.

Close by is the market theory built around the rational-choice concept that profiles the religious space as similar to a marketplace; this concept examines the commercialization of religion as a commodity because messages are packaged as products in a competitive market. It argues that marketing strategies enable religious businesspeople to dupe gullible consumers by selling their books, videotapes, audiotapes, and all manner of wares, using sales techniques honed in the secular marketplace. It adds that the glitz mixes religion with entertainment, and observes a reciprocal influence that religion and popular culture have on each other in creating a Christianity wherein it is difficult to distinguish popular entertainment from religion. The preacher and television star become inseparable. Media pander to materialism, financial gain, and focus on the individual's desires and quest for prosperity.

Bruce Forbes and Jeffrey Mahan identify four models of relationship between religion and popular culture: first, the *religion in culture* model emphasizes the use of religious themes, languages, images, characters, and subjects in film or music, sports or television. It supports the rebuttal that entertainment appears crucial for the survival of religion in the marketplace of culture.[17] It is an inculturating pathway for touching youthful audiences, who are already enmeshed, wired in the electronic culture, and bored with the equally packaged institutional religion. Religion and popular culture must be geared to attract youth, just as mainline churches experiment with new liturgies and music.

Others note the *popular culture in religion* model evident in initiatives that employ the tools, strategies, resources, language, and media of popular culture for the purposes of transmitting particular faith traditions and communities. This model images the primary goal of media as an enabling, valorized strategy for making disciples; it proffers advice on how to counter its dangerous dimensions. The Web site of the Living Projects Media Network, Nigeria, intones that they are "using timely technology to preach the timeless truths to a dying world." The American magazine *Charisma* carries many articles on how ministry can use media resources to launch, grow, make over, face-lift, maximize presence, become a household name, build brand strategy, evangelize, and find and reach "the most powerful audience on earth," women! The Affiliated Media Group (founded in 1989) promises to serve as media consultants that will assist ministries to access more channels and also join in the fight against the government interference and regulations that hinder Christian programs.[18] Sometimes it runs into problems such as the debate over the use of hip-hop as an evangelical tool. Imani Perry pointed to the expressions of rage, violence, pain, criminality, relationship dysfunction, and abuse of women in a music genre that focuses on how the hip should hop.[19]

Jeremy Carette and Richard King deploy the *popular culture as religion* model to argue that secular corporate interests have taken over spirituality to subvert individuals and seduce them into consumerism, and that advertisements utilize religious cultural cachet and brand products by associating them with personal fulfillment, inner peace, happiness, and success in relationships. Management efficiency is packaged as providing religious paths to enlightenment. Michael Warren concurs: "Merit is a cigarette, *True Life* is cereal for breakfast, *Joy* and *Happiness* are fragrances for the body. Unlike the human values they are drawn from, these names are all of products available for a price."[20] The market has taken over the responsibility of religion, and neoliberalism tries to revalue all values and define the goal of life itself. The convert and consumer are one. The entire communication industry produces, reproduces, creates, and fosters a commodity culture. All communication production is under the economic control of the production and orchestration of consumption, whether used by Christians or others. Should Christian missionary strategies contest and avoid electronic media as a satanic realm?

Some advocate another model, *religion and popular culture in dialogue*, which sees both as linked and requiring mutual accountability.[21] The dialogue is more compelling because of critical scholarship on the popular culture in religion model. Marla Frederick of Harvard University draws attention to one of the challenges: how televangelists respond to the spiritual needs of people and help them grow and absorb Christian spirituality into everyday life. Television programs serve as a counseling discourse for individual transformation, as motivational self-help, teaching resources that change lifestyles, achievement of progress, and social uplift. But, she asks, do televangelists encourage the people to engage society? Or do they merely encourage listeners to contribute to their own individual social and spiritual advancement?

For an answer, she avers that conversionist theology (with emphasis on sanctification) tends to be apolitical, focuses on the emotional and spiritual needs of individual believers, and suppresses a focus on social ills. She states that though televangelism entertains and constructs an integrationist multiculturalism, it may psychologically create self-empowerment by pointing inward because the new individualistic faith is a matter between the individual and God and does not foster community.[22] Does this lead to an apolitical posture? Put differently, what is the impact of the edited worship and thirty minutes of individual-centered clip on the authenticity of the gospel, the message, and the believers? Packaging the message does a number of things: it could distort the gospel, promote the creature instead of the Creator, and encrust a certain interiorized ideology. This, argues Frederick, has an enormous ideological import for the black church, which has served as the forum for civil rights agitation. Privatized spiritual ethics could emasculate the political relevance of Christianity in an environment that needs a strong prophetic voice.

But there is still another dimension: How effective is television medium as a mission tool? Is the allocated television time too short to achieve much? Berit Brethauer responds about the inherent limitations of media evangelism and the ineffectiveness of evangelism via media by arguing that effective recruitment follows the warm lines of personal contact and trusted networks of family and friends. Therefore, "televangelism is hardly an effective way to provoke change in religious identity. Nor do religious media often bring about radical personal transformation from a born-again experience."[23]

However, Martyn Percy rebuts that advertising is not necessarily selling: it does not convert but rather persuades people to take a second look, and it is a legitimate option given the pluralistic nature of the modern world characterized by freedom of choice and competition. He revisits the advertisement theory in posters, handbills, billboards, domestic goods, clothes, and television spots and argues that advertisements can inspire, evoke affection, and impart useful public information; therefore, they may be beneficial to religious groups in a pluralistic age. Asonzeh Ukah follows Matthew Ojo to focus on the use of posters among evangelical/charismatic Christians. He concurs that posters are accessible and adaptable because the technology builds around the plot (problematic), actor, mood, message, and a resolution offered with certitude and authority.

Kwabena Asamoah-Gyadu brings together the two dimensions about the media resource and challenge. He argues that increased media use has reshaped the structure and ethos of contemporary mission, shaped a youth-oriented culture, and encrusted modernizing tastes in ethics and liturgy while dispensing with the old missionary taboos that were used to inculcate frugality and asceticism. Media exposure has changed attitudes to create order, and given the leadership and their organizations' high public profile, sometimes this is to their detriment. Its mood shapes the doctrinal emphases and fosters a transnational image. Indeed, the prosperity theology is moored to the upbeat mood and glitz of television for nurture, expression, representation, and propagation. It has literally transformed the religious culture of Christianity in many places, including Africa, where it created a pentecostalization or charismatization of Christianity and Latin America, which explains the growing impact of Protestantism there.[24]

In conclusion, globalization may be imaged as an external force or change agent that has elicited a variety of local responses and thereby created a dynamic cultural force that has reshaped both Christianity and its mandate to mission. A case study of media, mission, and popular culture is only one of the ways to demonstrate the complex character of the encounter between global processes and local forces. They have created a certain Christian culture shared all over the globe, yet appropriated differently in many cultural idioms. But its many dimensions encapsulate the most powerful assets and challenges to contemporary mission.

# 4

# Many Tongues, Many Practices

## Pentecost and Theology of Mission at 2010

AMOS YONG

On this centenary of the world mission conference at Edinburgh in 1910, the question of what it means to do mission remains even if the world has changed. In 2010, we live in a post-Christendom and postcolonial world. What does it mean to do mission in such a time as this? In this essay, I sketch a response from a Pentecostal perspective in two broad steps. First, I will give an overview of Pentecostal models of mission as they have developed over the course of the last century vis-à-vis the emergence of the postcolonial paradigm in mission. Second, I will sketch a post-Christendom, postcolonial, and Pentecostal theology of mission, wherein I argue that the many tongues of Pentecost open up to many different Spirit-empowered missionary practices that include, minimally, testimony/proclamation, dialogue, and social engagement.

Two caveats need to be registered, however, before we proceed. First, at one level we risk mixing categories in shifting from missiological discourses utilizing the rhetoric of colonialism and postcolonialism (part 1) to historical and theological discourses utilizing other categories such as Christendom and post-Christendom (part 2). I think that the risk is one worth taking since

An expanded version of this essay was presented as one of two keynote lectures at the Chicago Center for Global Ministries' World Mission Institute 2008 meeting, at the Lutheran School of Theology at Chicago, April 17–18, 2008. I am grateful to CCGM for inviting my participation in this event. Thanks also to my graduate assistant, Bradford McCall, for helping with shortening a much longer paper for publication in this volume.

I believe that the insights to be gained from such a cross-fertilization of conversations will be mutually beneficial. Second, however, I will explore how colonialism might be the other side of the one coin that we call Christendom. In this case, then, a post-Christendom theology of mission could be informed by postcolonial commitments, even as the reverse also holds: that a postcolonial theology of mission would in turn be enhanced by post-Christendom perspectives. Yet throughout this exercise we will still need to be sensitive to the nuances at play in both discourses since some differences should not be elided.

## PENTECOSTAL-CHARISMATIC MISSIOLOGY: COLONIAL AND POSTCOLONIAL PARADIGMS

From its beginnings in the early twentieth century, Pentecostalism has been first and foremost a missionary movement.[1] Yet when viewed from within a postcolonial framework, it is unclear exactly what kind of missionary movement Pentecostalism has been over the course of this last century. In this first part of the essay, I will explore this question through three lenses: that of the colonial character of classical Pentecostalism as it has developed in North America, that of the wide range of Pentecostal missiological strategies as they have unfolded in the second half of the twentieth century, and that of postcolonial forms of Pentecostal missions emanating from the Global South in the last generation. In the course of this survey, I will suggest that insofar as Pentecostal missiologies have always been related in some way to the colonial project, they have been part and parcel of colonialism in some respects, postcolonial in others, and perhaps also not easily definable according to the categories of colonialism at all (in that sense forcing an alternative noncolonial frame of reference).

### Classical Pentecostal Missiology: Perpetuating the Colonial Project?

Classical Pentecostal missions, from their beginnings in the early twentieth century, have been in many ways unavoidably intertwined with colonialism. To be sure, as Bible-believing Christians focused on living out the Great Commission, to take the gospel to the ends of the earth, Pentecostal missionaries in general did not critically reflect on the many ways in which their missionary work was complicit with the colonial project. Their own theological resources emphasized not the political and cultural aspects of the missionary task but, rather, the spiritual and theological dimensions. Thus, most Pentecostals embraced the promise of Jesus: "You will receive power when the Holy Spirit has come upon you; and you will be my witnesses in Jerusalem, in all

Judea and Samaria, and to the ends of the earth" (Acts 1:8); they understood their own contribution to be part of the fulfillment of this Spirit-empowered work of covering the earth with the gospel. For these early Pentecostals, the whole point of Spirit baptism was to empower believers to proclaim the gospel, to work signs and wonders. According to the longer ending of Mark, which early Pentecostals universally accepted, "These signs will accompany those who believe: by using my name they will cast out demons; they will speak in new tongues; they will pick up snakes in their hands, and if they drink any deadly thing, it will not hurt them; they will lay their hands on the sick, and they will recover" (Mark 16:17–18). Thus Pentecostals would fulfill the conditions that will hasten the day of the Lord's soon return.[2] In each of these respects, the Pentecostal focus was neither on colonial expansions nor imperial control, but on evangelism and the propagation of the gospel.[3]

At the same time, these early Pentecostal missionaries were also undeniably children of their times. Their missionary sensibilities were thus shaped by the wider missionary beliefs and practices characteristic of their era.[4] For the most part, they were insensitive to the indigenous cultures among which they worked, as well as rather uncharitable in their views of local populations as "pagans" or "heathen." Hence, the missionaries brought with them not just the gospel from the West, but also in many instances believed and then imposed their Western version of the gospel on those being evangelized. Somehow, the supremacy of the gospel was translated also to mean the supremacy of Western (Euro-American) culture. Along the way, then, converts were socialized into rejecting their cultural heritage: this was presented as the essential meaning of Christian conversion. Such approaches surely had not only cultural but also social, political, and economic ramifications. Though most missionaries did not spend much time defending the details of the colonial project, they did believe that the colonial enterprise was providentially arranged by God for the purposes of worldwide evangelism, and this led them to oppose alternative economic and political structures, which they felt inhibited them from carrying out the missionary mandate. Hence, Pentecostal missionaries were patronizing, imperialistic, and even racist, oftentimes without even being conscious of either their attitudes or their concomitant actions.[5]

Some of the ways that Pentecostal missions developed in collusion with the colonial agenda can be seen in the Assemblies of God (AG).[6] Although as early as the 1920s some AG missionaries were recognizing the need to train indigenous leaders to do the work of the ministry, in all too many other instances they "followed the mission-station pattern of the earlier established Protestant missions,"[7] which was based on the colonial model. Even after the effects of colonialism were increasingly recognized and when a more indigenous-centered model was adapted (on which more in the next section), the AG introduced the "Global Conquest" missionary campaign in 1959.[8] The imperialism and militarism embedded in this theme was slowly recognized, but even then only slightly softened when the *Global Conquest* magazine was renamed *Good News Crusades* in 1965, and not finally repented of until the periodical was further renamed *Mountain Movers* in 1979. Meanwhile, the "Global Conquest" theme was also changed to "Good News Crusades" in 1968, and this shaped AG missionary ventures for the next decade. Yet from then to the present—the AG theme for the 1980s was "No Other Name," in recognition of the denomination's unwavering christocentric convictions, and for the 1990s it was "Decade of Harvest"—the commitment to global mission and evangelism has not wavered.

By the end of the twentieth century, AG missionary projects had morphed in keeping with the times. Following the collapse of colonialism was the emergence of what has been called the neocolonial order of global market capitalism. Against the former imperial regimes often promoted via military conquests, the neocolonial and neoliberal agenda was driven instead by the globalization of the market economy, especially since the collapse of the socialist alternative in 1989–91. In this new situation, some scholars suggest that new forms of Pentecostalism, in many ways continuous with the classical Pentecostal denominations such as the AG, have adopted new modes of missionary imperialism congruent with the global economy. Hence, Pentecostal complicity with the colonial project is being transformed so that what is being "exported" by the missionaries and its global media are various forms of the prosperity gospel (with its market individualism, consumerism, and materialism) and polemical rhetoric (e.g., anti-Islamism, anti-Catholicism, antifeminism).[9] It probably does not help the Pentecostal cause when some of the movement's respected theologians are quoted (even if out of context) as saying, in line with the views of earlier generations regarding colonialism as God's means for world evangelization, "We speak about the divinely ordained globalization because the gospel of Jesus Christ is a universally valid, globally relevant message of hope and salvation."[10]

## Pentecostal Missiological Pluralism: Para-Colonial Models and Practices

The preceding survey surely raises questions about how, if at all, Pentecostal missions have been able to buck the colonial paradigm. In this section I review intuitions, internal to the dynamic of the Pentecostal experience, which have invited noncolonial approaches to the missionary task. More specifically, I explore how an emerging Pentecostal missiology has within it the resources necessary to critique and even circumvent the colonial approach.

Beginning in the 1920s, some Pentecostal missionaries had begun to pay attention to Roland Allen's proposals regarding the development of self-supporting, self-governing, and self-propagating mission churches.[11] Since then, there have been two developments in Pentecostal missiology that have either incorporated or provided a more robust theological foundation for Allen's principles. On the one hand, Pentecostals have reframed Allen's ideas in their own words and within their own Pentecostal framework. The AG missionary Melvin Hodges's theology of mission featuring the idea of the "indigenous church" is one expression of this reappropriation of Allen's "three-self" approach.[12] Hodges's Pentecostal experience led him to take his missiological cues from the book of Acts. From this he discerned not only that the church is God's missionary agency to the ends of the earth, but also that the Spirit empowers the church for the ministries of the gospel in various contexts. At the level of the individual, all persons, including nominal Christians, are to be brought into an experiential knowledge of the gospel and "into the fellowship of the life in the Holy Spirit."[13] At the corporate level, the Christian mission is to establish self-propagating, self-governing, and self-supporting local congregations and ministries. These would be the dominant features of what Hodges calls "the indigenous church": established, overseen, and developed by local (i.e., "native") leadership with Western missionaries serving only the role of consultants. The concept of the "indigenous church" certainly opposes the entire colonial enterprise. To be sure, local leadership experienced significant resistance from the missionaries, including Pentecostal missionaries, when it came to asserting their local initiative and vision. However, the point is that theologically and missiologically, at least, Hodges's call for an indigenous church helped Pentecostal mission agencies to take the important first steps away from a colonial paradigm.

Now although Hodges's definition of the indigenous church is congruent with the Pentecostal narrative of the diversity of tongues, which gave testimony to the mighty works of God on the day of Pentecost, Hodges nowhere makes the explicit connection, nor does he fully develop the ecclesiological and missiological implications of this Pentecostal perspective. Further steps toward this end, however, were taken by the next generation of Pentecostal missiologists. Former AG missionary, Paul Pomerville, for example, has combined Allen's three-self model and nascent pneumatological insights with Hodges's indigenous church vision in trying to articulate a more consistently integrated and systematically developed Pentecostal theology of mission.[14] Pomerville's key move is to correct what he calls the "pneumatological deficit" in mission theology, and he does so by formulating what he calls a Trinitarian and pneumatological missiology.[15] The central elements of his proposal include recognizing (1) the diversity of the global Pentecostal and charismatic renewal movement (which simply replicates the diversity of God's intentions in salvation history and corrects the distortions of theology and mission theory as they have been developed in the West), (2) a connection between the work of the Spirit and the arrival of the coming kingdom, (3) and an explication of the shape of the kingdom according to the Trinitarian revelation of God.

Although Pomerville's Pentecostal missiology does not explicitly address the issues regarding colonialism, it is anti-imperialistic in at least two respects. First, it is intentional about minimizing the tendency for Western Pentecostal missionaries to impose their own conceptualizations on the "mission field." Second, what compels Pentecostal missions is the Holy Spirit's work, even as the luring force of the mission of the church is the kingdom of God that is ahead of us; in this framework, the roles, attitudes, and activities of the church cannot be absolutized since the work of missions will be superseded by the coming reign of God.

This focus on the kingdom of God reflects the growing recognition, even among Pentecostal missiologists, that the mission of the church is better reconceptualized as the mission of God (*missio Dei*). This concept has become increasingly popular in the last half of the twentieth century among theologians of mission and has also been adopted by Pentecostal missiologists.[16] The Pentecostal distinctive, however, has often been registered in terms of its pneumatological focus: the *missio Dei* is also the *missio Spiritus* since it is through the person and work of the Holy Spirit that the gospel is made known to the ends of the earth. More specifically, it is the power of the Spirit that produces the indigenous churches, and it is the many tongues of the Spirit that legitimate and invigorate each one, in anticipation of the coming kingdom.[17]

Now it should be clear in all of this work that rarely have Pentecostal missiologists confronted head-on the questions of Western colonialism and imperialism. A few authors have briefly but only descriptively discussed "the decline of colonialism" or recognized the historic interface between colonialism and mission.[18] Hence, I have subtitled this section "Para-Colonial Models and Practices," since the proposals of Hodges, Pomerville, and others contain within themselves the theological ingredients necessary for such a postcolonial task, but the fleshing out of such a postcolonial and Pentecostal theology of mission remains to be done.

## Pentecostal Missions from the Global South: Emerging Postcolonial Paradigms

Perhaps a postcolonial and Pentecostal theology of mission will emerge not out of the Euro-American West but out of the Global South. That is precisely the region of the world where Pentecostalism in particular and Christianity in general is expanding at its greatest rates.[19] Note, however, that the growth of the church in the majority world has also brought with it the reversal of the Christian missionary enterprise: although missionary projects continue "from the West to the rest," there are also an increasing number of missionary movements reaching back "from the rest to the West."[20] Some of these have emerged due in part to migration patterns, but others are due to intentional mobilization according to the missionary mandate.

Of those fueled by migration, we can briefly consider the Afro-Pentecostal diaspora, which has not only carried Africans to the "new world" (primarily through the slave trade), but also, in the last few decades, moved especially West African Pentecostals to Europe and North America, as well as Afro-Caribbean Pentecostals particularly to the United Kingdom.[21] In migratory processes, inevitably churches are established and transnationalistic linkages and networks mediate the exchange of ideas, commodities, personalities, religious practices, and so forth across international and intercontinental lines.[22] Along the way, at least by default if not intentionally, African Pentecostals have begun to conceive of their presence and activity in the Euro-American West in missionary terms,[23] yet not at all according to traditional missionary approaches. Instead, the emphasis has been on establishing Christian beliefs and practices on Afro-Pentecostal terms, even if such has of necessity had to take account of assimilationist forces in the immigrants' locales.[24] In short, the new forms of Pentecostal missions emanating from Africa and motivated by the processes of globalization are shaped essentially by postcolonial factors.

In some cases, however, globalization and migration have also brought forth explicit missionary organization. One such heavily mission-minded church is the Igreja Universal del Reino de Dios, or IURD (Universal Church of the Kingdom of God) in Brazil.[25] Central to IURD's ministry is its commitment to embracing, proclaiming, and living out the prosperity gospel. Whether it has been in terms of financial wealth, physical health, psychological wellness, or family and marriage success, the ministries of the church are oriented toward the attainment of material comforts and social affluence. In the Brazilian context, all of IURD's activities are enacted against the backdrop of the region's spiritist religions; they therefore include central features such as ritual exorcisms and spiritual warfare beliefs and practices designed to deliver people from the evil spirits believed to keep them impoverished, sick, and unsuccessful.[26] These aspects of IURD beliefs and practices differentiate its version of the prosperity gospel from those propounded by the faith teachers in the North American context.

Founded in 1977 by Edir Macedo, today the IURD is present in more than eighty countries throughout the world. Part of the reason for its rapid expansion is that the church not only has an entrepreneurial mentality, but also expertly deploys the latest media and communication technologies to market its message. Not without reason, then, IURD is said to have "adopted the transnational corporation as a model."[27] At the same time, the church adapts some aspects of both its cosmology and emphases, depending on the missionary context. Thus across the Global South, exorcisms may target demons or fallen angels in Brazil, witchcraft and ancestral spirits in West Africa, the "spirits" of HIV/AIDS in South Africa, or "the very tangible evils that afflict the liminal, urban, 'illegal' poor" in the Euro-American West.[28] In developed nations, the spirits to be expelled are less those that possess bodies or souls, but are more afflictions of the mind or psychosocial demons of depression, migraines, envy, jealousy, sexual abuse, alcoholism, unemployment, addiction, gangs, and so forth. In these varied contexts, the message of IURD has caught on, even amid charges both of the church's doctrinal and praxiological heterodoxy and of its being only a quasi rather than genuinely Pentecostal movement.[29] Regardless of how one sees IURD's Pentecostal (or even Christian) credentials, the phenomenology of the church clearly fits the global Pentecostal and charismatic renewal movement even as, just as clearly, IURD's mission strategies also contrast with traditional Pentecostal mission theology and practices.

More conventionally Pentecostal may be missionary ventures from South Korea. While the South Koreans began missionizing close to home—sending missionaries first to Japan[30]—over the last two decades South Korean Pentecostals have begun to mobilize for missionary projects to the rest of the world. We can observe the unfolding of the South Korean Pentecostal missionary movement in three stages. First, we have the establishment of an indigenous South Korean Pentecostal identity around the "Fivefold Gospel" (of Jesus as Savior, sanctifier, baptizer with the Holy Spirit, healer, and coming king) and the "Triple Blessing" (which involves the prosperity of the soul, of the body, and of all material aspects; cf. 3 John 2b). Both have to be understood against the post-Korean War stresses of an impoverished society.[31] These developments have led, second, to a ferocious church growth movement that blankets South Korea with the "Fivefold Gospel" and the "Triple Blessing." Church growth strategies include cell groups (essential for megachurches like the Yoido Full Gospel Church, which has over 700,000 members), lay training programs, and emphasis on signs and wonders (power evangelism), which connect with the masses. With this, however, has emerged also a holistic witness so that the "Triple Blessing" is understood to include social relief activities, social welfare initiatives, shaping of public opinion by using mass media (rather than working specifically on sociostructural changes as in Minjung theology), and environmental ethics.[32] The third phase has been the explicitly foreign mission tasks in which the local church growth strategies have been implemented abroad.[33]

At one level, because of the close ties between South Korean Pentecostals and North American Pentecostalism, there is a question about whether or not its mission orientation is basically Western and therefore colonial in character.[34] Three points need to be made in this regard. First, the ties between South Korea and the West are informal rather than formal; in many respects, South Korean Pentecostalism has nurtured its own distinctive forms of orthodoxy, orthopraxis, and orthopathos, each tied to the specifics of its own national and cultural history, and each more or less independent of Western influences. Hence, second, if there is any "imperialism" in the South Korean missionary venture, it is the reverse one in which South Korean nationalism manifests itself among its missionaries. As Leo Oosterom suggests, "National pride and a deep sense of divine calling and responsibility for the salvation of the world are inextricably intertwined in most Korean missionary thought."[35] And finally, although South Korea has made tremendous strides economically in the past generation, its inhabitants nevertheless find themselves between East and West, rather than simply as part of the first world; in that sense we have at best a form of reverse colonialism, if not an emerging postcolonial sensibility.

## MANY TONGUES, MANY PRACTICES: PENTECOSTAL THEOLOGY OF MISSION IN A POSTCOLONIAL AGE

So far, in this essay, I have suggested that perhaps a postcolonial and Pentecostal theology of mission will emerge not out of the Euro-American West, but out of the Global South. I now want to argue that a viable contemporary Pentecostal mission theology will be informed not only by the postcolonial perspectives from the majority world, but also by pre-, para-, and post-Christendom locations at the margins of the empires in the Latin West. Such a Pentecostal theology of mission was in some ways already heralded by the Lukan account of the early Christian witness empowered by the Holy Spirit in the matrix of the Roman Empire. My thesis is that the Lukan narratives witness to how the many tongues of Pentecost open up to, tell of, and are sustained by the many practices of the Holy Spirit; that these many tongues and practices of the Spirit remained vibrant on the underside of the emergence of Christendom in the West; and that they continue to be viable in our post-Christendom and postcolonial situation.

I will proceed first by looking at the early Christian mission against the backdrop of imperial Rome, then by rereading the history of Christendom from a postcolonial and missiological point of view, before concluding with some central theses for a Christian theology of mission in a post-Christendom and postcolonial age. Admittedly, we will be covering a great deal of ground quite quickly in what follows. Hence, the following sketch should be considered as no more than a down payment for a more extended and elaborate discussion.[36] I only wish to identify the basic biblical, historical, and theological framework for articulating a contemporary Pentecostal theology of mission.

## The Witness of the Spirit: Sketching a Lukan Missiology amid Empire

Pentecostal theological reflection has typically begun with the book of Acts;[37] hence, I want to begin our own constructive thinking there, but will do so in dialogue with the postcolonial perspectives. I suggest that there are congruencies between missiological perspectives derived from Pentecostalism in the Global South and that which are seen among the earliest Christian communities in the book of Acts. More to the point, just as Pentecostal missions have been anti- or even postcolonial (with regard to the colonial enterprise) in some respects, so also were early Christian missions anti- and even non-imperial (with regard to Rome) in many respects. Let me propose at least the following three points as a springboard for teasing out a postcolonial but yet Lukan theology of mission forged within the matrix of the Roman Empire.[38]

First, many scholars assume a "diaspora" or "colony" mentality, in which Christians are a minority group amid and within empire.[39] However, while some then insist on seeking the peace of the city within which Christians find themselves, others advocate a more oppositional posture toward the wider culture and society.[40] But which is Luke's point of view? Scholars debate this question, with arguments either that Luke sees Christians working symbiotically and strategically with imperial leaders, forces, and mechanisms in order to further the project begun by Jesus, or that he actually views the empire in demonological terms as hostile to Christian faith and practice.[41] Within the Acts narrative, both approaches can be found. On the one hand, there are certainly confrontational episodes in which the fledgling Christian group is assailed by the political and religious leaders of their regions, and against which their witness is borne to the point of persecution and even death. On the other hand, there is also a wide range of incidents featuring Christian cooperation with the ruling elite as well as Christian reception of protection from the various forces of empire, whether centurions, governors, proconsuls, town clerks (e.g., at Ephesus), or communal leaders (e.g., Publius of Malta). In short, the Acts narrative presents no homogeneous stance toward empire.[42] Yet rather than this being a liability, the diverse experiences of the early church lead us instead to adapt a both/and approach that recognizes various resources in the early Christian experience to draw from in formulating a contemporary stance toward the forces of empire. What is consistent in the Lukan witness is that Christians lived amid empire, even if they never fully accommodated to the imperial forms of life.

This leads, second, to the recognition that there are contextual circumstances that may elicit a more dialogical versus kerygmatic, or oppositional, approach toward the wider culture and society. Most often we see the apostolic witness testifying to the lordship of Christ and inviting repentance and conversion. In some cases there is explicit reference to the commission of sins (e.g., Acts 2:22–23; 3:13–15), although this is usually followed by the declaration about the forgiveness that is available through the grace of God (e.g., 2:38; 3:19). There is no avoiding the fact that proclamation of the gospel is sometimes politically incorrect, that to speak the truth in love is often a painful task, and that at some levels there is no inoffensive way to bear Christian witness. In other cases, however, we see the apostolic witness operate in ways that are sensitive to various local situations. Thus Paul adopts a more philosophical approach at Mars Hill (Acts 17), or a more dialogical attitude in Ephesus (cf. 19:9, which indicates that Paul interacted [διαλεγόμενος, *dialegomenos*] daily and patiently with the residents of Asia for a period of two years), and a more hospitable posture in Rome (28:30 mentions that while under house arrest in Rome, Paul "welcomed all who came to him"). Also distinctive is Paul's shipwreck on Malta: as a guest of the islanders (28:2 calls them βάρβαροι, *barbaroi*), his response was only to receive their hospitality and to pray for the sick, who were cured![43] Hence, we see various responses to the ideologies (philosophies) and forces of the world, not just a one-size-fits-all approach.

Finally, however, regardless of the means and contexts of the Christian mission, Luke's portrayal shows the mission of the church as best accomplished by its faithful discipleship, by simply being the body of Christ. In Acts, besides the standard forms of missionary activity such as proclamation and evangelism, the expansion of the church was also accomplished through faithfully living out the way of Jesus. Hence, life among the earliest believers involved the day-to-day gathering together, breaking of bread, praise and worship, and the sharing of all things. These practices can be seen as a form of discipleship that shaped Christian character, nurtured Christian virtues, and constituted Christian life as a whole. And through these practices, Luke records that "the Lord added to their number those who were being saved" (Acts 2:47). While some might conclude that Christian mission is a by-product of ecclesial life, a Pentecostal and pneumatological perspective would insist instead on their equivalence: Christians bear witness to and are missional agents of the gospel precisely through their Spirit-empowered following after the life and teachings of Jesus.

Our brief survey of the missionary project of early Christianity amid empire so far confirms, in broad strokes at least, the leading intuitions of postcolonial thinkers. This includes the Radical Reformation's insistence on nonviolence as a fundamental Christian conviction: in no instance do we see Christians availing themselves of the powers of empire in coercive ways. From a Pentecostal point of view, I propose framing the entire preceding discussion in pneumatological terms: all that the apostles and disciples did by way of Christian life and witness was empowered by the Holy Spirit. It is the Spirit who enables nonviolent resistance, who empowers kerygmatic proclamation, who sustains believers amid imperial persecution, who shapes Christian solidarity and *koinōnia*, and who opens up Christians to hospitable interactions—as guests and hosts—with those "outside" the colony. In effect, I suggest, the many tongues of the Spirit at Pentecost prefigure the many practices of the body of Christ in a world of empire.

## Deconstructing Christendom: On the Tongues and Practices of World Christianities

I now will further develop the Pentecostal theology of mission begun in the preceding discussion by exploring how the anti- and nonimperial workings of the Spirit persisted in the postapostolic periods of Christian history. In doing so, I want to see if the modalities of the Spirit's empowerment during the apostolic period can be discerned even amid the rise and fall of what we have come to call Christendom. My thesis is that the many tongues and many practices of Spirit-empowered witness indeed have manifested themselves most clearly in enabling resistance to the encroachments of empire/s. If that is the case, as I hope to sketch, then any theology of mission post-Christendom will always be one that is also postcolonial precisely in its proceeding from the margins and underside rather than from the centers of empire.

I have neither the time nor expertise to chart the rise of Christendom in the Latin West. Most scholars, however, agree that what we now call Christendom arose slowly over the course of the fourth through ninth centuries, ebbing and flowing from Constantine through Charlemagne.[44] Regardless of the details, I suggest that our reification of Christendom has covered up the diversity of tongues and practices through which the church has interacted with the world. With regard to the rise of Christendom, for example, Peter Brown convincingly demonstrates that there has always been more local diversity than generally realized.[45] The "Christianization" of the empire after Constantine actually empowered local leadership and local expressions rather than imposed a monolithic template on the various sees.[46] So, while relics were transferred, styles of art and buildings emulated, and ecclesial customs/practices were transported around the empire, local agencies did so and received such on their own terms. Rather than "peripheries" being subjected to the Roman "center," various little centers of Christianity emerged instead, each in touch with Rome, but each also cognizant and conscious of the directly experienced powerful presence of God. This "enabled the local society to establish a 'vertical' link with an overarching cosmos, which was shared by center and periphery alike," so that there grew an interregional "inter-connectivity . . . among a loosely spread constellation of centers."[47] My point is that the rise of Christendom, while imposing the rule of law in various respects, also empowered local creativity in unpredictable ways.

Even during the centuries of undeniable (so far, anyway) Christendom in the Latin West, highly ambitious popes were never able to completely control what I would call local resistance projects. These can be seen in the various monastic experiments, the emergence of countless missionary orders, and the flourishing of a wide range of spiritual, religious, and reform movements. Then later, the Anabaptists of the Radical Reformation were themselves part of a much larger group of dissidents ("protest-ants") who spoke in a plurality of languages, unleashed with the invention of the printing press and the vernacularization of the liturgy during the late Renaissance period; they ministered through a diversity of missionary practices. These protesting and reforming movements can be understood as a part of what historian Stanley Burgess has called "peoples of the Spirit":[48] groups that resisted the institutionalizing mechanisms of church and state in the quest to allow God to turn the world upside down in their own days.

The emergence of a post-Christendom and postcolonial world has also been facilitated by the rise of such resistance movements. As Lamin Sanneh has recently shown, anti- and postcolonial forms of Christianity in the Global South can be understood to be part of this lineage of locally empowered agents, who have always acted against the center.[49] In Sanneh's retelling of the Christian history from the underside, there have always been a variety of Christianities—even under the tent of the one Christendom—each of which has been a product of indigenous agency, of vernacularly formulated and articulated practices, and of thoroughly diversifying processes from start to finish. In fact, Christendom is what it is precisely because of Christianity's translatability, mutability, and adaptability.

I am suggesting, then, that when heard through the sounds of the many tongues spoken on the day of Pentecost and when seen through the many practices empowered by the Spirit poured out on that day, Christendom itself must be understood in a much more pluralistic fashion. If Christendom really is a unity constituted by plurality, then from a Pentecostal point of view, what is crucial will be charismatic discernment of the local contexts within which the church is what it is and does what it does. In some cases, "Christendom" encroaches and needs to be resisted; in other cases, "Christendom" can actually aid in the church's mission by producing local constellations of power that can offset any hegemonic impulses. Christians may also find themselves in pre-, non-, and anti-Christendom contexts, and in these situations, will need to be discerning about other tongues and practices that will signify its faithfulness and energize its missionary witness. In such a pluralistic world, what may be a form of resistance in one context might turn out to be imperialistic in others, and vice versa.[50]

## Tongues/Practices of the Spirit:
## Toward a Pentecostal-Political Missiology of Resistance

It is now time to tie the threads of the preceding discussions together. Our goal throughout has been to formulate a Pentecostal theology of mission. Such a mission theology, as should now be apparent, will be both post-Christendom and postcolonial, in various respects. Hence, the following might serve also as a proposal for a general consideration of a Christian theology of mission, albeit rendered in Pentecostal perspective. I now sketch the contours of such a missiology in three theses.

*Thesis 1*: A post-Christendom, postcolonial, and Pentecostal theology of mission is pre-, para-, and post-Christendom and pre-, para-, and postcolonial in various respects. My claim here is both historical/empirical and theological. Historically, we have seen that Pentecostal missiologies are not easily classifiable according to the categories of colonialism (part 1), and that Christian missions have also colluded as well as resisted the encroachments of empire and of Christendom in various ways (part 2). The distinct thread we have observed in this historical pluralism, however, can be understood pneumatologically: the Spirit can be seen as empowering resistance among the early Christians, throughout the history of Christianity (and of Christendom), and even among Pentecostal movements. When put together, I suggest that a Pentecostal theology of mission will have to be discerning about its social and political locations amid the empires of this world. Christendom and colonialism may be finished as historical projects, but new forms of empire are arising and indeed already present. Pentecostal discernment requires nothing less than vigilance so that the Christian witness can be appropriate to the complexities of the empire, as well as its complicities with it, until the Parousia.

*Thesis 2*: A post-Christendom, postcolonial, and yet Pentecostal theology of mission always depends on the church being a body of Spirit-empowered people who embody and invite an alternative way of being in the world. There will always be empires, Christian-based (allegedly) or otherwise, and it is the work of the Spirit to form pockets of resistance that not only oppose the godlessness of the powers that be (if that is actually the case, since sometimes the powers that be are not entirely godless), but also serve as oases (colonies) for rest, nourishment, and formation. Such a missiology of resistance will seek to discern the Holy Spirit's leading about when to speak prophetically, when to interact dialogically in truth-telling exchanges, and when to engage in practices of social justice. Let us be mindful that resistance takes different shapes, sounds, and works of service in different contexts, depending on whether we are close to the center, located on the periphery, or anywhere in between. Yet resistance is also never for the sake of criticism and opposition alone, but in order to invite the world to give the gospel an opportunity. Even so, the shift from a politics of resistance to a kerygmatics of resistance risks transforming resistance into violence, prophetic criticism into coercive rhetoric, proclamation of the universal gospel into a universalizing of a Christian vernacular. This quandary, therefore, leads to the next thesis.

*Thesis 3*: A post-Christendom and yet Pentecostal theology of mission is empowered by the many different tongues and practices of the Spirit-filled people of God. This prevents both a monopoly of the "center" (of Christendom, or empire, etc.) as well as the fragmentation of the periphery; it also guards against one dominant voice, a single set of mission strategies, or a politically correct (or corrupt or contaminated) missiology. Instead, it requires the orchestration of the Spirit to check the center from the periphery and vice versa, and to provide a contrast to the status quo from the underside. These workings of the Spirit ensure that the church's mission will be politically engaged rather than politically complicit. Proclamation, dialogue, and social action will proceed from any and many points of the global renewal movement, and in a post-Christendom and postcolonial world, each will have its own tasks, means, and alien colonies to engage in a variety of ways. At the same time, each will also be confronted with its own seductions and challenges, but will in turn be equipped to handle these precisely because of its accountability to and linkages with the diversity of the missiological tradition.

Hence, a Pentecostal missiology of the many tongues and practices of the Spirit insists that missionary beliefs and practices are intertwined, as are proclamation, dialogue, and social action. Such a pneumatological theology of mission holds together the center and the periphery, as well as empire and its constitutive parts. In this framework, translations occur in many directions, through many venues, via many tongues, and amid many practices. Herein can be discerned the multicentered, multifaceted, multilinguistic, multicultural, and perhaps even multireligious work of the Spirit to turn the world to

Christ, so that all can be returned to the Father. In the end, there is no way to deny that this is also an imperialistic vision, but its articulation represents the attempt of only one fallible tongue to preserve and value the plurality of human expressions, perhaps much of which may be the product of the many works of the Holy Spirit.

# 5

# Mission from the Rest to the West

## *The Changing Landscape of World Christianity and Christian Mission*

PETER VETHANAYAGAMONY

We are in the midst of one of the most dramatic demographic changes in the history of Christianity. For the last half century or so, the Global South, with the former "mission frontier regions," is experiencing a rapid growth of Christianity, while in the Global North, especially in Western Europe, the historic "Christian heartland," Christianity is in a steep decline. At the beginning of the twentieth century, 80 percent of the world's Christians lived in Europe and North America. However, as the century closed, 60 percent of the world's Christians were living in Africa, Asia, and Latin America.[1] Until very recently, Christianity has been perceived to be a European and North American religion and identified almost exclusively with Western civilization. Conversely, at the turn of this new millennium, Christianity is not only predominantly a non-Western religion but also vastly pluralistic and diverse. Whether or not we are ready to acknowledge it, there is a major shift in the epicenter of Christianity, and the future of Christianity seems to lie not in the West but rather in the non-Western parts of the globe.

Another new fact of our time, one that has momentous consequences for mission in the twenty-first century, is that the Great Migration has reversed.[2] On account of wars, famines, political and military displacements, globalization, advancements made in education and technology, economic oppression, and related factors, people from the developing countries immigrate to Western nations, making the Global North diverse in terms of religion, race, and culture; by all indications this pattern will continue. Thousands of Christians immigrated with their particular ethnic identity intact, and some even retain distinctive characteristics of conservative spiritual and theological orientation. A host of mission-minded laypeople from third-world churches who come into contact with the older, established forms of Christianity end up becoming instruments of their rejuvenation. Yet others, who have immigrated to the West and transplanted their church and congregational life, have begun to conceive of their presence and activity in the West in missionary terms.[3] Though some restrict their ministry to members of a particular ethnic group, functioning as diaspora or expatriate congregations for that community, others see their function in purely evangelistic terms of having a calling to bring the gospel to the local people.[4]

However, the territorial "from the West to the Rest"[5] model, which predominated the Western missionary movement (1492–1950), still holds sway in the thinking of Christians, though Christian mission has been rethought substantially during the past half century. The economic strength of the West and the U.S. hegemony in international affairs lead many to take for granted that the initiative and leadership in Christian mission lies with the West.[6] At the same time, growing evidence mounts that Christian mission is proceeding in the opposite direction: non-Western Christians are becoming the agents for reevangelizing the West. These developments present a number of conceptual and practical challenges. This essay explores this shift in the center already occurring for the Christian missionary movement and its implication for Christian mission today.

## THE ALTERED LANDSCAPE OF WORLD CHRISTIANITY

The rise of non-Western Christianity has come as a huge shock to the secular West. In the 1970s, Christianity outside of the West was thought to be a product of European imperialism, and it was expected to collapse and die in the postcolonial era.[7] However, one of the great ironies of our time is that Christianity grew swiftly after the end of colonialism, suggesting Christianity in the "rest of the world" is a grassroots people's movement rather than a product of Western colonialism. As Dana Robert observed, "[t]he process of decolonization and independence began severing the connection between Christianity and European colonialism. The repudiation of missionary paternalism, combined with expanding indigenous initiatives, freed Christianity to be more at home in local situations."[8] In 1900 there were only about 9 million Christians in all of Africa. By the middle of the century, this number had tripled, to about 30 million. By 1970, however, this number has nearly quadrupled, to over 117 million. Today, the number has more than tripled again, to an estimated 382 million Christians in Africa. This massive shift to the Christian faith in Africa, Asia, and Latin America, a fact pointed out by missiologists, was recently brought to the attention of the larger public by Philip Jenkins in *The Next Christendom: The Coming of Global Christianity*. In a succinct summary of current statistics, Jenkins stresses the increasingly global character of Christianity as follows:

> According to the respected *World Christian Encyclopedia*, some 2 billion Christians are alive today, about one-third of the planetary total. The largest single bloc, some 560 million people, is still found in Europe. Latin America, though, is already close behind with 480 million. Africa has 360 million, and 313 million Asians profess Christianity. North America claims about 260 million believers. If we extrapolate these figures to the year 2025, and assume no great gains or losses through conversion, then there would be around 2.6 billion Christians, of whom 633 million would live in Africa, 640 million in Latin America, and 460 million in Asia. Europe, with 555 million, would have slipped to third place. Africa and Latin America would be in competition for the title of most Christian continent.[9]

Some white people find it difficult to accept that these Christians are more likely to be people with darker skin color and from poor nations, as opposed to the stereotypical white person in rich Western nations.

On the other hand, one of the ironic features of the major shift taking place in world Christianity is the sudden and dramatic collapse of Christian faith among the Western Europeans. The Western Christianity that to a great extent was responsible for the epic shift in the demographic, and had every reason to celebrate its achievement, went through a crisis[10] and began to crumble at a faster pace. Historian Callum Brown, in his recent book *The Death of Christian Britain*, describes how organized Christianity in Britain has been sent on "a downward spiral to the margins of social significance":

> In unprecedented numbers, the British people since the 1960s have stopped going to church, have allowed their church membership to lapse, have stopped marrying in the church and have neglected to baptize their children. Meanwhile, their children, the two generations who grew to maturity in the last thirty years of the twentieth century, stopped going to Sunday school, stopped entering confirmation or communicant classes, and rarely, if ever, stepped inside a church to worship in their entire lives. The cycle which had for so many centuries tied the people however closely or loosely to the churches and to Christian moral benchmarks, was permanently disrupted in the swing sixties. Since then, a formerly religious people have entirely forsaken organized Christianity in a sudden plunge into a truly secular condition.[11]

Christian faith has become peripheral, sectarian, and irrelevant to the construction of reality in which the British population is engaged. In Great Britain only about one million of the twenty-six million members of the Church of England attend Sunday services. The church loses 1,500 people every week, losing not only people on the edge, but also those at the heart of the church, leaders and those involved for twenty to thirty years. A new genre of Christian literature during the last decade is all about why people are leaving the church.[12] How long can someone believe without belonging to a specific faith community? Some of these people are ending up in the emerging churches. What is said about the United Kingdom is true of the other Western European nations too.

## THE IMPLICATIONS OF THE DEMOGRAPHIC SHIFT

What does this mean to world Christianity? Has it lost the West, the former heartland of Christianity, forever? The lesson one may draw from the history of the church seems to offer some prospect rather than despondence. Though most other religions have continued to be organized around their historic centers, Christianity has proved to be a sojourner sort of faith.[13] In its early history, neither the fall of Jerusalem, the fall of Edessa, the fall of Rome, nor the fall of Constantinople resulted in the extinction of Christianity. Although these had been significant centers, and certainly played a critical role in shaping worship, spirituality, and theology, the Christian faith was already advancing across new frontiers by the time they were in peril. As Kenneth Ross, the chair of "Toward Edinburgh 2010," puts it:

> It could be readily argued that it is quite typical of Christianity that, when its long-time European home is becoming inhospitable, it has already set off on a fresh journey and has been embraced by the people of the great Southern continents on an unprecedented scale. On this analysis it could well be that modern Europe will share the fate of such earlier centers of Christian influence as North Africa or Turkey, which nurtured the faith in its early centuries but which today are largely bereft of Christian presence.[14]

There is, however, another possibility. The renewal on the environs will prove to be the source of rejuvenation for today's Western church just as the church at Philippi was for the church in Jerusalem.[15] It is quite possible that vitality experienced in the Global South will become contagious.

In other words, if Christianity is becoming predominantly non-Western, then what happens in Africa, Asia, and Latin America will have a growing influence on what Christianity will be like worldwide. It is not only the numerical strength but also the passion with which Christianity is lived out in the Global South that is making an impact on world Christianity in terms of theology, ethics, and spirituality. The Global South Christians are far more conservative in terms of both beliefs and moral teachings. They hold fast to a strong supernatural orientation, and are usually far more interested in personal salvation than in social justice issues and radical societal changes. Jenkins sketches the scenario as follows:

> These newer churches preach deep personal faith and communal orthodoxy, mysticism and Puritanism, all founded on clear scriptural authority. They preach messages that to a Westerner appear simplistically charismatic, visionary, and apocalyptic. In this thought-world, prophecy is an everyday reality, while faith healing, exorcism, and dream visions are all basic components of religious sensibility. . . . On present evidence, a Southernized Christian future should be distinctly conservative.[16]

This is certainly true of the churches of Pentecostal, neo-Pentecostal, and indigenous origins. The key issue for Christianity in the Global South is the prevailing worldview that subscribes to a belief in direct divine intervention in the daily lives of people. The divine power that is mediated through Christianity can provide healing for mind, body, and soul, and these three entities of a person cannot be separated. Besides, the age-old local beliefs about visions, prophecy, and healing have also contributed to Christianity's distinctive supernaturalism in the Global South.

The phenomenal growth of Christianity in the Global South has also brought with it the reversal of the Christian missionary enterprise: while missionary projects continue "from the West to the rest," there are also an increasing number of missionary movements reaching back "from the rest to the West." The great missionary movement is not over, but it has become omnidirectional, mission in and to six continents, and the leadership in mission is increasingly shaped and led by the Global South. This is evident in the fact that though the United States still leads the world in mission sending, it also receives the largest number of foreign missionaries.[17] There are 400,000 missionaries in the world, but most are not from Europe and North America. Welcome to the new world of global missions. In 1990, in Nigeria alone, 900 missionaries were serving sacrificially in rural Northern Nigeria, and in Niger, Cameroon, Chad, Burkina Faso, and "darkest London." Robert Eric Frykenberg estimates that there are more than 40,000 indigenous missionaries sponsored by more than 200 indigenous missionary societies currently involved in evangelism in India.[18] Indian Christians are involved in evangelizing the neighboring nations too. Indian Pentecostals are founding rapidly growing churches in Nepal. Korean Christianity, besides becoming a significant force in the United States, has produced thousands of international missionaries to serve in various parts of the world. According to the Korean Research Institute for Missions, in the year 2006 there were 14,905 Korean missionaries sent by 175 mission organizations serving different regions of the world.[19] Then there are the Brazilians who head to Portugal, Angola, and Boston.

Mission as evangelism and church planting is taken seriously by the Global South. The Second International Congress on World Evangelization, often called "Lausanne II" or "Lausanne '89," met in Manila and concluded the following:

> "Mission" is no longer, and can no longer be, a one-way movement from the "older churches." . . . Every local church is and cannot but be missionary. . . . [It] is responsible for its mission, and co-responsible for its mission of all its sister churches. Every local church, according to its possibilities, must share whatever its gifts are, for the needs of other churches, for mission throughout mankind, for the life of the world. . . . The Spirit of the Lord calls each people and each culture to its own fresh and creative response to the Gospel.[20]

Since 1963 we have been speaking of mission in six continents.[21] Mission is no longer in the South and the East, but also in the North and the West. This is evident in the change in Roman Catholic missiology, from mission *ad gentes* to mission *ad extra*, international mission.[22] "As a matter of fact," as Indian theologian Amaladoss claims, "mission is more urgent in parts of the world where people do not seem to believe in anything at all than in areas where people are still very religious."[23] Given this reality, the massive migration to the West seems to offer the hope of reevangelizing the secularized West.

African, Latin American, and Asian Christians from former traditional mission fields are now evangelizing and forming new congregations in Europe. They have been set up by overseas "mother churches."[24] These mother churches, as in South Korea, for example, provide resources, pastors, or pastoral workers, especially in the first phase of establishing a new congregation in Germany. Once the new congregations become more independent, members of these churches tend to find their own way with regard to theological and organizational issues. Reverse missionary congregations put much effort in evangelizing immigrants of the same origin, with Koreans evangelizing Koreans. All over Europe, independent churches, the majority of which are Pentecostal/charismatic, grow and are reflecting a worldwide phenomenon. "The marginal, the lonely, the displaced, the refugee find these churches a home for the homeless and they experience *koinōnia*."[25]

The migrant churches in the West no longer take a backseat but steadily gain in self-confidence, assertiveness, and evangelism in societies that lost their faith during the two World Wars. Independent churches have begun to attract white Christians who, in an experience of crisis or exclusion, find little comfort, healing, and belonging in the established churches.[26] In Cologne the largest worshiping congregation is Korean. The largest congregation in London is an African-founded one. The largest congregation in Europe is in Kiev and founded as Nigerian.[27] It is estimated that more than three million Christians of African origin are living in Europe.

Bishop Newbigin in 1984 identified the assistance of Christians from the non-Western world with these words: "We need their witness to correct ours as indeed they need ours to correct theirs. At this moment, however, our need is greater, for they have been far more aware of the danger of syncretism, of an illegitimate alliance with false elements in their culture, than we have been. But we imperatively need one another if we are to be faithful witnesses to Christ."[28] Asian, Latin American (in the case of Spain), and African-influenced Christianity in all its diversity and contextuality can provide a model for reshaping religion and the Christian faith into a holistic undertaking in the Western world.[29] However, the issue is whether the Western churches are ready to embrace the opportunity available at their doorsteps. The remark of Hollenweger that "Christians in Britain prayed for many years for revival, and when it came they did not recognize it because it was black"[30] seems to suggest that Europeans are not ready yet.

On the other hand, missionaries from the Global South are faced with several challenges. They do not have the economic and political clout that those from the West had in the past. Christianity was once the religion of the confident, technologically advanced, and rising affluent, and sometimes those things were seen as a mark of God's favor. Christianity, now increasingly, is associated mostly with rather poor people and with some of the poorest countries on earth. Just like the Pauline mission, their mission is powerless in worldly terms and therefore dependent on the Holy Spirit. It not only lacks economic and political might; it also lacks the big organizational structure of the modern missionary movement. "More and more the agents of Christian mission come from among the weak, the broken, and the vulnerable. . . . More and more it is the poor who are taking the gospel to the rich. . . . Many migrants come from the new heartlands of Christianity and bring the flame of faith to the old centres in the north where the fire is burning low."[31]

Nonetheless, non-Western Christianity has carried itself across the continents by strong cross-cultural forces. Already the impact of this new missionary movement is beginning to be felt in Europe, as Andrew Walls observes:

> It is clear that [African and Afro-Caribbean] churches are among the few expanding sectors of European Christianity. It is also clear that they are beginning to have an impact on the indigenous Western population, for some of whom, being untouched by traditional

culture—Christianity, immigrants from Africa or Asia (and in Spain, from Latin America) provide the first contact with Christianity as a living faith.[32]

African church leaders begin to see evangelizing the West as part of the mission of their churches. As archbishop of Abuja in Nigeria, John Olorunfemi Onaiyekan remarked: "I believe priests from places like Nigeria can re-evangelize Europe. One hundred and fifty years ago, it was Europeans who were doing the evangelizing. Now we should have two churches at work—African and European."[33] Several Asian, Latin American, as well as African-descent immigrant churches reach out to the local people. For instance, "the mission of the Church of the Lord (Aladura) in Europe and other parts of the world is mainly to spread the good news, . . . the message of our Lord Jesus Christ, to every nook and corner of this world, irrespective of the hearer's nationality, race or political leaning. It is also to show the world one other way to worship God in truth and spirit, in which the worshippers may feel the presence of God." Commenting on the mission further, Ositelu adds:

> The main goal of this mission is to gain new people for Christ Jesus and to receive the lost souls which have been carried away by the material things of this world, so that they may come to the knowledge of Christ as their savior and the redeemer of humankind. . . . The mission of the Church of the Lord (Aladura) in Europe is therefore to win all new, lukewarm, and lost souls for Christ. The mission has been reversed because those to whom Christ Jesus was once preached are now back on the territory of the former preachers to preach Christ Jesus to them in all his goodness. What a "mission reversed" indeed![34]

The Western churches are confused as well as enriched by the presence of these vibrant immigrant churches. The diversity, flexibility, spontaneity, easy adaptation to new circumstances, and joy and encouragement in response to the specific cultural and socioeconomic situations of the non-Western churches—all this was seen by the European churches both as enrichment, concern, and confusion, as is evident in the following statement of the Evangelical Church in Germany (Evangelischen Kirche in Deutschland, EKD):

> How should EKD member churches and local congregations deal with the variety of these churches? Pentecostal and charismatic congregations, . . . especially from Africa, are . . . a steadily growing group of worldwide ecumenism. However, their shape is very difficult to describe and their strength not to be put into exact figures. . . . Their West African leaders are little-educated evangelists and missionaries who approach and gather their country-people through street-missions and evangelism. Their conduct toward the Church in

Germany oscillates between the wish to cooperate and the pretension
to form an alternative to European confessional Christianity.[35]

To many native Europeans the recent foundation of African Christian congregations is an anomaly.[36] However, various European churches are making
efforts to work in cooperation with the immigrant churches, though the task
appears to be complex.

   In May 2001, the United Evangelical Mission organized a conference
under the theme "From Reverse Mission to Common Mission," in which
it brought together missionaries from Africa and Asia and church workers
from Germany who wanted to explore ways of doing mission together.[37] The
challenges faced by both the neo-Pentecostal churches of the immigrants
and the established churches of Germany include learning about each other's
culture and coming to appreciate the differences as adding to the witness of
the body of Christ, not taking away from it. Many German churches remain
quite critical of the reverse missionary movement. The reason can be racism
(Why should we be evangelized by Blacks?) as well as theological rejection
(Why should we be evangelized by the Pentecostals?). Difficulties also arise
from the different concepts about what the mission of the church is and how
evangelism should be conducted—or even whether it is needed at all.[38] For
a united mission, it is important to build mutual trust and understanding, as
Claudia Währisch-Oblau rightly points out:

> The mainline churches had to realize that Pentecostals are not a sect,
> even if they drive out demons during their night prayers. Conversely,
> the Pentecostal churches had to learn that mainline churches are not
> necessarily dead, even if nobody there speaks in tongues. Such toler-
> ance also means that both churches abstain from crude attempts to
> "convert" the other church to its own theology and practices while at
> the same time they acknowledge that their contact and cooperation
> will eventually change them both in ways they may not foresee yet.[39]

Such acceptance is formed by the understanding that each church is a mixed
body of saints and sinners, that each church falls short of its calling in certain
ways, but that the Spirit nevertheless works through them in unexpected ways.
   Besides the above-mentioned bewilderment from the European churches,
there are issues from within the immigrant churches that become great imped-
iments for a common mission. Foremost among them is the competition and
antagonism among immigrant churches and church leaders. Unity, even
among immigrant churches of shared background and culture, often remains
intangible as individuals set up new churches and steal members from exist-
ing congregations. Churches and church leaders who feel threatened by such
competition are usually not open to cooperation. To achieve mission in unity

among immigrant and indigenous churches in Germany, these stumbling blocks need to be rolled away one by one. Some immigrant religious leaders' lack of knowing the local European language is another factor to be addressed. It is heartening to know that the Evangelical Churches in Germany (EKD) are taking some serious steps to remedy the situation. The "Program for Cooperation between German and Immigrant Congregations," which tries to build bridges, was set up by the United Evangelical Mission in 1998 for its German region. Participants are listening to Others carefully and seeking to understand what Others are saying. The journey for mission unity, the coming together as the colorful and multicultural body of Christ, has just begun.

As far as the U.S. churches are concerned, there has been little if any missiological reflection upon the significant impact of ethnic church life in the United States.[40] The October 1991 issue of the journal *Missiology* devoted its contents to the topic "The Gospel and Our Culture." Writers incisively pointed to issues that are crucial for envisioning proper cross-cultural evangelization for the twenty-first century. Third-world churches have been quite aggressive in planning missionary deployment to the United States. The U.S. churches have yet to reckon with these reverse missions in their midst. For all the talk about "reciprocal mission" or "mission in reverse," it is hardly feasible that any North American Protestant church would do anything but laugh if it were suggested that an African or Asian be called to be the founding pastor/evangelist for a project to plant a new church in an area inhabited by white middle-class folks.[41]

Let me close with some practical suggestions for the Western churches to be hospitable to "the mission from the rest to the West." First, they should recognize that mission and mission fields have completely changed. For centuries the Western church has been the repository of Christian faith and its authoritative expositor; now it must undergo a mental revolution if it is to recognize that Christianity's center of gravity has shifted to the South. It is quite unfortunate that many Western churches are too perplexed to come to terms with the fact that the real center of Christianity is now located in the non-Western world. This conceptual shift involves not only a new humility on the part of the church in the West but also a new form of missionary engagement. The missionary task must be done by Christians from all the churches acting together and no longer by one-sided initiatives from or within the West.

Second, the Western church should recognize that we are always the recipients as well as the agents of mission. A critical point to recognize in the new missionary paradigm is that all are addressees as well as agents of mission.[42] It is God's mission, and human involvement is always first as addressee and only then as agent. The recession of Christianity in the West can in all probability be addressed by migrants who have come from countries where the church is being renewed and expanded. They could be used as a source of spiritual renewal. The old "mission fields" of the "third world" could provide the springboard for a fresh evangelization of the West.

One of the most fascinating features of this new missionary paradigm is that, mostly, it is mission from the poor to the rich. What excites the Christian imagination about this development is that after the long years when the gospel was compromised by being intertwined with imperial power and economic exploitation, it is now restored to the poor and marginalized, who are its original agents. This is how it was with apostolic Christianity. The initially despised Galileans, who first preached the gospel, eventually won the allegiance of the mighty Roman Empire.[43] Mission is "from everywhere to everywhere." "Indeed, responsibility is increasingly falling to the churches of the non-Western world. . . . The Western sense of ownership of the missionary enterprise must give way to an appreciation of the worldwide church as the base for Christian mission."[44] David Bosch's suggestion for the appropriate tone needed for authentic missionary witness is still relevant to our time. The tone of our missionary witness should be "a bold humility—or a humble boldness. We know in part, but we do know. And we believe that the faith we profess is both true and just, and should be proclaimed. We do this, however, not as judges or lawyers, but as witnesses; not as soldiers but as envoys of peace; not as high pressure sales-persons, but as ambassadors of the Servant Lord."[45]


## CONCLUSION

The church's center of gravity has shifted substantially during our generation, thanks to the endeavors of the Western Christian missions of the last five centuries. Though Europe no longer is the Christian heartland, the heartening news is that, in the world as a whole, Christianity is not in decline. The West will matter less and less in Christian affairs as the faith becomes more and more associated with and marked by the thought and life of Africa, Asia, and Latin America. The current situation in the West can be understood as a challenge, a new opportunity, providing new possibilities rather than a dangerous situation. As we appraise the remains of a once-strong church in the Global North and monitor the enthusiastic new growth of Christianity in the Global South, we ought not to anguish or be disheartened by this contrast. On the contrary, we can see this as a renewing force channeled from the rest to the West.

One of the most common claims today is that dominant Western churches need to listen to hitherto marginalized non-Western voices. The prevalence of globalization calls Christians, especially in the United States, to focus on the world church, engage in Christianity as a global fellowship, and promote it locally. A new way of being a global Christian community is possible today through the growing strength of Christianity in the non-Western world, the migration of a section of these Christians to the Western hemisphere, and the easy interconnectedness made possible through the modern phenomenon of globalization. Mission is no longer a one-way street; we need to learn from each other and be enriched by each other.

# 6

# Expanding the Boundaries, Turning Borders into Spaces

## Mission in the Context of Contemporary Migration

GEMMA TULUD CRUZ

## MIGRATION EXPLOSION: AN INTRODUCTION

Eleanor Wilner writes, "There are always in each of us these two: the one who stays, the one who goes away."[1] Journeys are, indeed, part of humanity's story. Borders have been redrawn and histories have been rewritten because individuals or large groups of people moved. Clearly, migration is not a new phenomenon. People have moved from one place to another over the ages for various reasons: out of fear of invasion, to escape political or religious persecution, in search of better pasture, to establish new commercial links, or in pursuit of a vision to (re)create a new mode of society. In recent times, however, migration is capturing people's imagination and fascination primarily due to its explosion. Spurred by globalization's marginalization of third-world economies and sophisticated developments in communication and transport technology, more and more people today move from place to place at an increasingly faster pace.

Consider the following statistics: In 2005 the United Nation's (UN's) International Migration Report says that the number of people living outside their country of origin (the technical definition of a migrant) increased from 120 million in 1990 to more than 191 million in 2005. One in 35 persons in the world today is a migrant. On the worldwide scene, migrants (as of 2005) now account for approximately 2.9 percent of the world population; if they were to constitute a country, theirs would be the world's sixth most populous.[2] The fact that more than 60 percent of these migrants are in developed countries, accounting for as much as two-thirds of the population growth in these countries, is not surprising. That about 75 percent of all migrants live only in 28 countries is probably not surprising as well. But there are some interesting points and developments that ought to be noticed in this UN report. For instance, 48.6 percent of the migrants are women, which is a far cry from traditional trends and conventional assumptions, whereby migration is overwhelmingly associated with men.

The details of this UN report also challenge old trends and traditional thinking that the West is the destination of all migrants. The specific intake of migrants by continent in 2005 (Europe, 34%; North America, 23%; Asia, 28%; Africa, 9%; Latin America, 3%; and Oceania, 3%) actually shows Asia receiving more migrants than North America. The distribution also shows that even stereotypical migrant-sending continents such as Latin America and Africa (and Asia) also served as hosts to migrants. In the United States, undocumented immigrants are also traditionally stereotyped as Mexicans, if not Latin Americans. In a report by CNN's Anderson Cooper in August 2007, however, the breakdown of undocumented immigrants' places of origin reveals that 9 percent come from Asia and, perhaps more interestingly, 6 percent come from Europe and Canada.[3]

Most recently, the January 5, 2008, issue of *The Economist* devoted its fifteen-page special report on the issue of migration. It offers some compelling statistics and prognostications that illustrate how the growing density in people's mobility in contemporary times is bringing a tremendous diversity that is fascinating and, at the same time, challenging. The report points out that the global stock of migrants has more than doubled in the past four decades and that the number of migrants in the world today, both legal and illegal, is thought to total perhaps 200 million. At the last count in 2005, for instance, foreign-born immigrants made up 9.7 percent of the British population. Arguably, this pales in comparison to the American landscape. Annually, particularly from 2002 to 2006, the United States has accepted about one million legal immigrants, which is more than all other nations combined. Not surprisingly, the number of minorities in the United States reached the 100 million mark for the first time in 2006, making them now a third of the U.S. population. Moreover, the Census Bureau predicts that minorities will account for half of the U.S. population by 2050.

## CONTEMPORARY MIGRATION'S CHALLENGES TO MISSION

To be sure, the above-mentioned situations merit thoughtful reflection as they definitely put forward a few critical questions. For instance, what do these tell us about the contemporary human condition? Where is God in all of this? Most important, how could we create spaces for experiencing the sacred as well as create and nurture faith communities amid all of these migrants? To arrive at possible responses to these questions, let us first explore what appear to be the challenges that the conditions inherent to contemporary migration pose to Christian mission.

## A Question of Justice

Migration, as we are witnessing it today, is largely born from and bred by global economic injustice.[4] On the one hand, it is true that contemporary global integration has created a different breed of "desirable" migrants: the "skilled transients" (the corporate managers, consultants, and technicians who hop or get transferred from one international branch of a transnational company to another) and the "transnational migrants" (the elite group of rich entrepreneurs who can "buy" citizenship and shuttle or split their time between two or more countries).[5] On the other hand, current global patterns have also spawned a more dependent underclass. Because global economic integration has increased the economic divide between rich and poor countries (according to the World Bank, more than 1.2 billion people live on less than a $1 a day), more and more people see international migration as the best if not the only way out of poverty. Though migrants are arguably not the poorest of the poor, desperation and survival still impel countless people to risk life and limb as high levels of unemployment and underemployment and its attendant social ills—poverty and hunger—plague third-world countries. Impoverished nation-states, whose political and economic powers are further limited by transnational companies and institutions, then capitalize and exploit their citizens, not only by legitimizing migration but even promoting it.

Today, migrants are the primary "exports" of many poor countries that are saddled by debt—the same countries where much of the national budget often ends up being used for debt payments or, worse, for paying just the interest rate. Consequently, they have become contemporary globalization's flexible, expendable, and disposable capital. Because there is a vast labor reserve from the ever-increasing millions of poor people from third-world countries, migrant workers (especially women) are today's "hot commodities" that can be "acquired" at "cheap prices" and may be exploited and abused in many ways. This is true particularly of those who resort to or fall prey to irregular/undocumented migration where migrants are kept in bondage or forced into prostitution.

What makes this a worse malaise today is that there is a discernible chain of injustice. As painted in broad strokes above, this chain of injustice begins in migrants' home countries as influenced by global inequalities. These inequities are then exploited by a host of transnational individuals, networks, and institutions—such as recruiters, smugglers, traffickers, banks, and lending institutions—who viciously prey on the life savings and very bodies of hapless migrants. Then comes the complex and sometimes humiliating immigration process or, for the undocumented, perilous journeys. Whether by boat or on foot, via the merciless sea or the unforgiving desert, the thousands of undocumented migrants who perish while trying to cross increasingly policed border controls are a testament to the brutal spiral of death-dealing conditions inherent in contemporary migration.

Unfortunately, migrants' misery does not end if and when they make it through the journey. Many of the jobs they often end up with are the 3D (dirty, dangerous, and disdained) and SALEP (shunned by all citizens except the poor) jobs. On top of this, migrant labor is not integrated into the global economy; hence comes its reputation as needed but not wanted, cheap labor. It is often rendered "invisible" since it is not usually reflected in labor statistics and is marginalized, if not excluded altogether, from labor laws. If it is accorded some kind of legislation, such as a minimum wage, theirs is not only the lowest-paid but also the first to be victimized in times of economic slowdown. Most of all, migrants are easy targets of problematic stereotypes. They are cast as the ones who take away local jobs, drive wages down, and commit crimes. Migrants' struggles against these injustices, coupled with their active efforts to have higher profiles in receiving countries, then heighten social tensions and fuel the rise of a problematic brand of nationalism. In several European countries, for instance, this struggle has led to the emergence and relative success of anti-immigrant political parties, many of which associate immigration with social ills such as unemployment and crime.[6]

## The Gift of Struggle

Nevertheless, migration today also offers a critical point of reflection for Christian mission in the way it has offered paths to some form of economic salvation, not just for migrants and the receiving countries, but also for the sending countries. To be sure, money sent by migrants keeps the economy of migrant-sending countries afloat or steady. Put together, the money sent by migrants worldwide in 2005, according to the World Bank, is estimated at U.S. $232 billion, even surpassing the U.S. $167 billion development aid given to poor countries.[7]

Today, as well, migrants' economic contributions go beyond remittances since they have become their home countries' social capital. They invest; help build and maintain vital infrastructures like schools, wells, and health centers (even churches); put up funds for scholarships; or raise money for calamity victims. Indeed, migrants today have higher profiles (they can even vote in their country's elections while abroad) and are more likely to demand stronger legal rights and formal recognition than previous waves of migration.[8] Mexican migrants, for example, gained the right to vote after threatening to withhold remittances, which has become Mexico's second most important source of foreign exchange after oil. The riots by second-generation African (particularly Algerian) immigrants in the suburbs of France in 2004 and 2006—purportedly to draw attention to their marginalization—illustrates this as well. Lastly, migrants today are also more organized as well as more open, insistent, and defensive about their religious and cultural identity.

This higher profile, which gives contemporary migrants deeper agency or subjectivity, is bolstered by transnationalism, whereby migrants create a worldwide migration chain on the basis of family, clan, language, region, religion, and country; utilize a wide array of global communication and technology tools to maintain familial and other social relations; and develop or engage social networks within the migrant community and abroad. They literally and figuratively create some kind of virtual barrio (neighborhood), town, or country.

## The Challenge of Diversity

When people move, they come not only with their clothes or backpack, but also with most things that remind them of home, particularly their cultures and religions. Hence, social diversification inevitably comes with migration. Many cities, especially megacities around the world, for instance, are characterized by a host of ethnic food stores and restaurants, a plethora of cultural styles, and a sea of people with different physical features, language, and skin color. As of 2006, for instance, London's population had ballooned to more or less seven million, and more than 250 languages are spoken on its streets on a daily basis.

Dealing with diversity is not only challenging for the host society, but also for migrants, especially the newcomers from third-world countries. For example, the highly urbanized landscape of Hong Kong and the typical congestion in its living and breathing spaces present constraints on Filipina domestic helpers, most of whom are from the Philippine countryside, with its wide open spaces. Though poor, they are used to living in houses that have ample space. Hence, the cramped space that characterizes most of their workplaces, which they compare to an "icebox," "prison," or one of the constricted tenement buildings in poor urban areas in the Philippines, create feelings of claustrophobia and forced confinement among them. Consider the following lament of one of the domestic workers:

It's okay for the employers. They were born in a flat. We Filipinos
are different. We're used to a much different style of life. Our home
is not halfway to heaven. It's right there on the ground. It's fully air-
conditioned 24 hours a day. When we want to know what's happening
in the community, we just open the window and let all the news blow
in. Filipinos live in freedom. Living on the 44th floor of an apartment
is like being in a prison. . . . After spending 144 hours a week trapped
inside an icebox I need to get out, to spread my wings, to meet my
friends. Otherwise, I'll go crazy.[9]

The Filipina domestic helpers in Hong Kong even have a caricature, "Maria
the stupid DH [domestic helper]," which serves as an icon of their travails in
adjusting socially and culturally in Hong Kong. Many of the so-called "adventures" of "Maria the stupid DH" are enshrined in jokes. One joke has it that
Maria keeps on mishearing or misinterpreting her employer's instructions to
"fry" the chicken as "fly" the chicken.[10] As a result, she throws the chicken out
of the window and ends up being terminated. When the Immigration Depart-
ment asked why she was terminated, Maria put down "starvation."

To many DHs, jokes are their way of getting back at their employers in a
covert manner. Most jokes, especially chicken and cooking jokes, make fun of
the employer's English. An example is that of Maria's employers going out for
dinner, and the conversation goes like this:

> **Sir**: (*in broken English*) Maria, come—eat outside.
>
> **Maria**: Sir, you mean you're going out for dinner?
>
> **Sir**: Yes, come . . . you like?
>
> **Maria**: Thank you, sir. But I prefer to eat here.
>
> **Sir**: All right. Just cook yourself![11]

Many cases of miscommunication, indeed, occur between the DHs and
their employers because of language differences. The inability to speak Cantonese also severely limits the DHs in their daily interaction with the local
people, especially where they inevitably have to go to certain places, such as
markets and shops. It intensifies, as well, their vulnerability to abuses since
they are often made the butt of jokes and objects of insults and malicious
talk without their knowledge. All in all, the DHs' sociocultural, economic,
and political power is reduced by the language difference because it is not
taken into account in Hong Kong society and is even taken advantage of by
unscrupulous employers, public officials, and other locals. Domestic helpers
are often shortchanged, cheated, and given a raw deal without their consent.
In some cases in interactions between the employer and the DH, Hong Kong

officials and employers are known to deliberately switch to Cantonese so the foreign DHs are made linguistically helpless.

Migration has also drastically changed not just the cultural landscape, but also the religious demographics of many cities and countries around the world. Arguably, nowhere is this more deeply illustrated than in the United States. Described by Diana Eck in her 2001 book, *The New Religious America*, as "the most religiously diverse nation in the world," the United States is now home to many religions that were not present only a few decades ago. Gregg Easterbrook, in an article titled "Religion in America: The New Ecumenicalism," directly attributes the rise of spiritual diversity in the United States to the influx of immigrants, particularly through the current wave of non-European immigration. Riding on the much-vaunted freedom of religion and/or religious expression, most Asian and African immigrants, says Easterbrook, bring along with them and do not give up the religions of the East and the subcontinent—Hinduism, Buddhism, Islam—and the African interpretations of Christianity. They celebrate their own festivals and build their own places of worship, so much so that, in Easterbrook's situation, a Hindu temple, a Sikh *gurdwara*, a Mormon temple, and several Muslim mosques are all within driving distance from his home.[12] This is probably the experience of many an American, and if not now, certainly in the near future.

On the one hand this diversity has brought positive changes to host communities. In both North America and Europe, for instance, new immigrant Christian groups embody a fresh spirituality, particularly since they reproduce or exhibit the same dynamic, creative, and celebratory character of religious rituals in their homeland. Moreover, they bring new life and vitality, not just in worship and spirituality but also with evangelistic zeal.

But then again, this does not come free of challenges. First, there is the challenge within the different Christian denominations to more fully accept or embrace their (immigrant) sisters and brothers in faith who exhibit differences in terms of culturally based religious beliefs and practices. As it is, the prevailing approach or practice could be construed as token integration since immigrants or immigrant congregations are allowed to use church spaces, albeit with conditions or limitations. Indeed, while it is true and good that immigrants can use most local churches for their own services, Martin Luther King's statement that the most segregated hour of the week is at eleven on Sunday morning still rings true in places of worship worldwide as cultural differences inhibit the formation of integrated churches. In some cases immigrants encounter certain levels or degrees of explicit dissociation by local religious communities, especially when class or socioeconomic differences enter the equation. Take the case of the following Mexican immigrant community in the southwestern part of the United States, which had to ask the bishop for its own church because its members were rejected by the members of the local Roman Catholic church:

> It was really hard work and long days, still we were happy to have our Sundays free. Yet, even then we could not feel at home in the Catholic Church since we were denied pews at Our Lady of Perpetual Help (pseudonym). The Italians would tell us, "All seats are taken." No matter how early we arrived, the pews were always reserved for Italians. That is why we asked the Bishop for our own church.[13]

Second, all people face the challenge of learning to live with peoples of other religions. The sharing of a Hindu about the experience during the early years of their temple in a southern suburb of Houston reflects this:

> When we first built the temple there were feelings of animosity toward us by members of the surrounding community. They were a farmland community that had never seen such a structure before in their life. It was a conservative community, and a few miles before the temple there is a church located on the left side. We were not worried about any harm that would come to us, but we were a little apprehensive about how the community would treat the temple. One day, a crazy man came running into the temple. I believe he was a Christian fanatic, but anyway, this person came in telling us that we would all go to hell, and that we should leave before any bad thing came to us.[14]

## EXPANDING THE BOUNDARIES, TURNING BORDERS INTO SPACES: REIMAGINING MISSION IN THE CONTEXT OF CONTEMPORARY MIGRATION

So what are the missiological implications of the religious (dis)continuities and transformations brought about by contemporary migration? What are the facets of a Christian mission that takes into account the new or more pronounced issues and questions put forward by contemporary migration? Moreover, what are the areas in theology of mission that need reelaboration, redefinition, and reorientation if it is to dialogue with the human community's experience of migration today? More specifically, how could we talk about God in a context where isolation, alienation, and discrimination constitute the very fabric of one's living conditions? How could we speak about the Divine in a situation where the community spirit is tested by the challenge of more deeply integrating a sizable number of fellow believers who look, speak, and worship differently? How could we minister to immigrants whose faith is challenged by exposure and immersion not only to unbridled secularization and urbanization but also to religious and cultural pluralism?

From the dehumanizing poverty that drives millions to brave the perils of migration, the countless number of migrants who go home in coffins or lie buried in the desert in unmarked graves, the limitation of the practice of one's cultural and religious identity, to the vibrant liturgical celebrations in the once-dying churches of Europe, the megachurches in the United States, and the gyms as well as auditoriums in Australia and Hong Kong—we have to admit that these phenomena are creating a new or nuanced context for mission. If we truly listen to this complex situation, I see two possible missionary responses to these issues.

## Liberation and Mission

Obviously, contemporary migration is riddled with unfair conditions. These problematic conditions demand more just and right relations between and among countries and churches, as well as between immigrants and citizens. Having said this, I argue that mission in the context of contemporary migration, first, has to be contextually liberative. In a situation where poverty and alienation rips the very fabric of people's dignity, even when one is outside the country, mission needs to be done with primary consideration of the context and from the perspective of liberation. Empowerment is the ultimate goal. It should not just be pastoral in the sense of giving stopgap solutions, such as counseling and legal assistance, which are not really long-term solutions because they only take care of the effects of the problem, not its causes.

There is a need to conscientize and strengthen more than just the socioeconomic and political institutions of the immigrants' home countries. Conscientization and conversion are also needed on the part of government leaders who have become quite vulnerable, if not gullible and willing victims, to the elitist economic globalization. An equally strong stance and action should be taken as well against unscrupulous traffickers, employers, transnational companies, and financial institutions that prey on immigrants. The global and structural inequality that has driven millions of people to take on dangerous journeys demands that we, as responsible Christians, must also respond both on the local and global level in a collaborative and preventive manner if we are to combat the roots or sources of the oppression. There not only has to be critical and continuous international collaboration between and across religions or religious denominations; religious groups and institutions should also actively seek and fight for the transformation of the very structures that contribute to the oppression and migration of migrants themselves.

Mission, as it is in the biblical tradition, has inescapable social implications. It entails social justice. As Justice in the World—the document from the 1971 World Synod of Catholic Bishops—says: "Action on behalf of justice and

participation in the transformation of the world fully appear to us as a constitutive dimension of preaching the Gospel, or, in other words, of the Church's
mission for the redemption of the human race and its liberation from every
oppressive situation."[15] So, if mission is to be rooted in the biblical tradition,
especially in Jesus' mission, it must be contextually liberating.

The various ways in which migrants deal with their oppression also prompt
mission theology to articulate struggle as a face of liberation. Although pushed
to live on the borders of their host societies, many migrants refuse to do so
completely and have created strategic spaces to survive. Their street demon-
strations and public and private gatherings, such as Sunday rituals and fellowships, illustrate this creative and strategic use of spaces. In the United States,
Hispanic migrants' occupying certain sidewalks in their search for work has a
revelatory quality since sidewalks are highly public and core spaces. In some
ways this is reminiscent of the parable of the Workers in the Vineyard, where
the vineyard owner goes out to the market at various times during the day to
look for and hire day laborers. While today's day laborers, the migrants, have
been pushed to what could be construed as an imposed shrunken space, on the
sidewalk, I consider that the parable's fundamental message rings louder and
clearer today: the justice of God is mercy.

In any case the migrants' reconfiguration of borders into spaces brings
a new dimension to missiological reflections. For one, it gives us a glimpse
on how pushed-to-the-fringe or marginalized existence can be transformed
into spaces of presence. Their transnational families, networks, and communities, for example, strike at the heart of traditional missiological reflections
on home, power, identity, and subjectivity. The barrios or neighborhoods
they create, whether literal or virtual, challenge mission theology to articulate
home not as a place "but a movement, a quality of relationship, a state where
people seek to be 'their own,' and [to be] increasingly responsible for the
world."[16] It also means reassessing the adequacy of "land" as a category for
missiological reflections on "home" and "identity."

## Interculturality and Mission

I also believe that mission in the context of contemporary migration has to
be intercultural. The Filipino diaspora, for example, has put one out of every
five Filipinos in a more multiethnic and multireligious milieu. Hence, it is
imperative that migrant Filipinos who come from a predominantly Roman
Catholic country and are usually rural in origin be equipped with the disposi-
tions and skills needed for living in societies marked by cultural and religious
pluralism. The Philippine church, for instance, tries to minister to migrant

domestic helpers by giving a predeparture orientation seminar (PDOS). Together with a few students of mine, whom I brought for an exposure, I attended one such PDOS run by the Religious of the Good Shepherd. While the nuns' efforts are laudable in that they have taken on what is supposedly a government responsibility, yet only a short time was devoted to learning to live in a different place with people of other cultures and religions. Moreover, this part of the orientation session only dealt with extreme cases, particularly Saudi Arabia, where migrants are prohibited from bringing any non-Islamic religious materials and where even Muslim Filipinos could encounter difficulties because of the puritanical brand of Islam that is enforced in the kingdom.

In Hong Kong, where most of the domestic helpers go, the Roman Catholic Diocese of Hong Kong has created the Diocesan Pastoral Center for Filipinos in recognition of the tremendous need for an apostolate for the Filipina DHs. Here the approach and strategies are more substantive and exhaustive. For the DHs' religious needs, for example, there are weekly religious services, prayer groups, Bible studies, theology classes, and opportunities for volunteer activities. For their social, emotional, intellectual, and psychological needs, the DHs are organized into small groups akin to basic ecclesial communities, which gather regularly for parties and all kinds of celebrations. Through the pastoral center, the DHs can also take free guitar and meditation lessons, borrow books for free, and share their thoughts, dreams, stories, and consequently their writing talents in the magazine (now defunct) that the center created and regularly published for them. There is also free counseling and legal assistance, as well as ministry for those who land themselves in jail for various reasons. More significantly, they are given language and cooking lessons in Chinese (especially Cantonese) and taught a variety of skills. Thus they can utilize such skills as means of livelihood so they do not have to migrate again after they go home to the Philippines.

The church is needed not only in helping migrants to deal with their experiences of injustice, but also in showing them how to witness to and celebrate their faith amid different cultures and religions. As could be seen in the experience of the Mexicans with their fellow (Italian) Christians, immigrants experience not only cultural alienation but also religious alienation even within their own religious communities. The Hong Kong Roman Catholic Church, for example, says that though they appreciate the contribution of the Filipinos to the church of Hong Kong, there are difficulties in establishing a church that is both Filipino and Chinese. They identify what is at the heart of the problem: "We are aware that we still need to inculcate among our Chinese people that the Church is universal and that two cultures can proclaim the same faith in the same Church, in different ways and languages, . . . and [that] the Diocese of Hong Kong would like to see the Chinese and the Filipinos join one another at Mass and gatherings, as equals and as friends."[17]

On the other hand, Christian mission is also challenged to creatively draw from the richness that comes from this migration-induced cultural and religious pluralism. This is so especially since, by virtue of their deep and steadfast witness, many migrants also become missionaries.[18] Religious rituals and sacred places like churches are the principal site of celebration of immigrants' identity and community. Immigrant churches themselves are often veritable centers and sources of socioeconomic needs for immigrants, making migration a potent source of missionary activity today.

Take the case of the Chinese Gospel Church in Houston, Texas. It started in 1972 with about thirty students and young professionals from Taiwan and Hong Kong who came together for Mandarin Sunday worship services after an immigrant-founded church (Chinese Baptist Church) willingly hosted them. When cultural and social disparities became evident between the newcomers and the earlier Cantonese-speaking and upwardly mobile immigrants, the newcomers moved and founded their own church. Like most immigrant churches, their number fluctuated as immigrants came and went. Like most immigrant churches, they also imported their own pastors from Asia and created various social services, which included language classes, welcome parties for new Chinese students, charity as well as special crisis funds to help members during emergencies, scholarship funds, and a bulletin board that displays important ads and information, such as used cars for sale, real estate and insurance agents, jobs like babysitting, food donations, and so forth. Classes on critical issues such as applying for a job and how to get various kinds of insurance are also conducted. They have also formed fellowships made up of fifty people, which hold religious meetings and go on picnics, camping trips, potluck dinners, thereby becoming formidable sources of intimacy and mutual support. Like a considerable number of immigrant churches, they have also developed an evangelistic ministry that did not only create a daughter church, but also actively supports missionary work in China (with a $50,000 annual donation). They also send missionaries to South and Central America, to various Asian nations, and to Britain and other European countries, as well as work at the Houston Port with Chinese seamen. Fellowship meetings include regular training workshops and Sunday school classes for doing one-on-one evangelism, singing, praying, Bible studies, and religious lectures on topics such as married life, children's education, and workplace relationships.[19]

Immigrants arguably bring some kind of ecclesiogenesis to their receiving communities. They bring diversity and breathe new life into the faith communities of their host countries at a level that the Hong Kong Church even calls "missionary." In the words of the Hong Kong Church:

Our churches are very alive on Sundays because of their presence. The Filipinos have brought their religiosity and faith to the Church of Hong Kong—they enhance the faith of our local people with their presence, witnessing hospitality, joy, and love for music. The diocese is truly blessed in many ways because of the Filipinos, and their dynamism will keep alive the faith in the territory. . . . In short, *the Filipinos are to be called missionaries first before they are labeled as domestic helpers.* [emphasis added][20]

Migrants today arguably witness to new ways of being church and new ways of understanding and doing mission. For example, Gerrie ter Haar maintains that there is a link between the evangelistic zeal of African immigrants and colonial Christianity. She says that African Christians in Europe themselves see their evangelism as a form of a reversal of colonization. Thus ter Haar states:

> Just as European missionaries once believed in their divine task of evangelizing what they called the dark continent, African church leaders in Europe today are convinced of Africa's mission to bring the gospel back to those who originally provided it. Thus, many African Christians who have recently migrated to Europe, generally to find work, consider that God has given them a unique opportunity to spread the good news among those who have gone astray.[21]

At the heart of the biblical tradition and Jesus' missionary vision is the gift of a "home," a place and space where justice is done and respect and compassion unite everyone. Today death-dealing and life-giving conditions inherent to contemporary migration are redefining all our notions of "home" and challenging our very understanding and approach to mission. The call, therefore, is to engage in a mission that brings about contextual and borderless liberation. Moreover, mission in the face of contemporary migration should not only be a mission beyond inculturation, but also a mission of interculturation: a mission that more deeply respects, embraces, and transcends differences and enables people to live in harmony with diversity. Only when mission is both contextually liberational and interculturally dialogical can mission truly respond to the cry of today's stranger par excellence: the migrant.

# 7

# Short-Term Missions as a New Paradigm

ROBERT J. PRIEST

## HISTORY OF SHORT-TERM MISSIONS

In 1910, missionary service normatively expected lifelong career commitment. But sometime around the middle of the twentieth century, a gradual change commenced. For example, in 1949 the Methodist Board of Missions approved a revolutionary new program[1] in which recent college graduates, traveling in groups of 50, were appointed for 3-year terms of service in specific countries such as Japan or India. After six weeks of training, these "45-day wonders" (as veteran missionaries sometimes called them) served as rural development workers, mission secretaries, and office staff, teachers at MK (missionary kids) boarding schools, staff at medical hospitals, and so on. Such two- or three-year terms of service became common for Mennonites and increasingly for other agencies.

By at least the early 1950s, traveling music evangelism teams (comprised of one or two speakers with a music group) or sports evangelism teams from America were traveling through Europe or the Orient. By the late 1950s and early 1960s, new agencies like Operation Mobilization (1957) and Youth With A Mission (1960) appeared on the scene, agencies organized entirely around new paradigms of short-term service ranging from a few weeks to a

I want to thank the Faculty Reading Group at Trinity Evangelical Divinity School for reading an earlier version of this essay and providing helpful feedback and critique.

couple of years. The U.S. Peace Corps (1961), a parallel secular organization, was also founded about this time. Beginning in the 1950s and 1960s, Christian colleges increasingly began to organize summer mission trips, as did campus ministries (like Campus Crusade and Intervarsity Christian Fellowship). Gradually even shorter terms of service, lasting as little as one week, became normal. By the 1980s whole new organizations developed, such as STEM International (1984), Teen Mania Ministries (1986), or Adventures in Missions (1989), specializing in such short-term mission trips. Local church youth pastors increasingly made an annual mission trip core to their youth ministry, with destinations either domestic or abroad. Larger congregations increasingly included on their staff a designated "mission pastor," who would help lead their own mission projects, projects often organized in partnership with sister congregations abroad and sustained through regular groups of traveling short-term missionaries.

## SIZE AND SCOPE OF SHORT-TERM MISSIONS TODAY

By 2005, approximately 1.6 million adult U.S. church members were traveling abroad every year on short-term mission (STM) trips, with the average (median) amount of time spent in service abroad per trip (not counting travel time) now being eight days.[2] Less than a third of STM trips for young people are currently longer than fourteen days.[3] One indication of the increase in the numbers of STM participants comes from Wuthnow's national random survey data, where he reports:

> Only two percent of those who had been teenagers during the 1950s, 1960s and 1970s said they had gone to another country on a short-term mission trip while in high school, whereas the proportion increased to five percent among those who had been teenagers in the 1990s and 12 percent among those who had been teenagers since the 1990s.[4]

A 2002 national random survey by Christian Smith (n = 3,370) of 13–17-year-olds in the United States discovered that 29 percent indicated that they had traveled at least once on a mission or religious service project (either domestically or abroad), with a follow-up survey in 2005 (n = 2,604) of the same population—now 16 to 20 years old—which found that 41 percent reported having gone on such mission trips or religious service projects.[5] This survey did not ask specifically about trips abroad, and thus this data includes domestic service trips as well. Yet what this data indicates is that youth participate in STM trips at quite high rates, suggesting that Wuthnow's 1.6 million figure for annual adult STM trips abroad significantly undercounts the total number of individuals traveling abroad on STM trips in a given year. Thus the total number of U.S. Christians traveling abroad on STM trips is likely to be somewhere between two and three million per year. Wuthnow (2009) calculates that at current rates, the lifetime "probability of a particular church member going abroad on a short-term mission trip could reasonably be 20 to 25 percent."

My own survey of 2,208 seminary students in required master of divinity (MDiv) courses in U.S. seminaries (across denominations and including Roman Catholic seminaries) discovered that 48 percent had traveled abroad on one or more STM trips. Among 562 students in required courses at 10 Bible colleges, 62 percent had done at least one STM trip abroad.[6] In core general education courses at 31 Christian liberal arts colleges (CCCU schools), 47 percent of 2,790 students reported having traveled abroad on STMs. This contrasts with 7 percent of 246 students taking general education courses at 5 Roman Catholic colleges (NCCAA) who had taken mission trips abroad. Again, in my survey of 591 adult members of Sunday school classes or Bible Studies at ten megachurches, 32 percent of respondents indicated that they had traveled abroad on an STM trip at least once. In short, STM is today an enormous phenomenon, central to the ministry practices of a high proportion of American Christians.

Although it is often claimed that STM is primarily practiced by Christians in the United States, STM is actually increasingly practiced by Christians around the world. For example, in my survey of 672 Protestant pastors in Thailand, 55 percent reported that their current congregation has hosted a visiting group of short-term missionaries from the United States. But almost the same percent (51%) report that their congregation has hosted a visiting group of short-term missionaries from South Korea. Furthermore, they report that they themselves and some of their congregants have also traveled on STM trips. From Peru to El Salvador, Paraguay, Singapore, Thailand, South Korea, or Kenya, one finds Christians not only partnering with visiting short-term missionaries, but also sending out STM teams themselves, either abroad or to destinations within their own country. In a survey of 1,086 MDiv students in Korean seminaries, fully 68 percent had traveled abroad on STM trips—suggesting that Koreans may surpass Americans in their STM involvements.

## JUSTIFYING SHORT-TERM MISSIONS

From the beginning, career missionaries have sometimes criticized the new paradigm. In 1949, for example, an old missionary to India wrote a letter to the Methodist Mission Board, complaining about the two groups of fifty recent college grads that were soon to arrive in India for three-year terms. She described a gathering of veteran missionaries in which

> *not one of us* could think how we could put them to work at all! . . . They will not have the language and will not be trying to get it. Neither will they have any proper preparation for any particular type of work which they could do without the language. WHAT CAN they do? We don't know! On the other hand, it's no wonder they "take it into their heads and ask to be sent out" in this way! It's a wonderful trip for them, why wouldn't they want to come out?[7]

Today short-term mission trips typically last under two weeks, not two or three years. And with an average cost per international mission trip of $1,400,[8] an amount raised in the name of "mission," there are naturally questions raised about the stewardship involved in short-term missions.

## Strengthening the Career Mission Enterprise?

During the decades of the 1980s and 1990s, as short-term missions exploded, most STM leaders justified short-term missions, not in terms of a strategic contribution that short-termers were supposed to make on the field, but by claiming that short-term missionaries were likely to become career missionaries and/or were more likely to financially contribute to career missions. The larger career missionary establishment was thus asked to relinquish its former monopoly on the right to use missions rhetoric and funding strategies, and to allow the STM movement to support itself through missions rhetoric and funding strategies. Why? Because STM would strengthen the career mission movement. Today the results are clear that the explosion of STM coincided with a plateauing and decline of career missions,[9] and that the STM expansion reflected or at least coincided with a redirection of resources away from career missions rather than an increase in the amounts given in support of career missions.[10]

## Having a Positive Impact on Short-Term Mission Participants?

Alternatively, as short-term missions has become central to youth ministry and congregational formation activities, some youth leaders and mission pastors acknowledge the limited value of their activities to recipient communities, and instead justify STM in terms of how it positively benefits the short-termer and the sending congregation or youth program. Thus in the *Youthworker* magazine, Scott Meier explains that the "real reason" for STM is to benefit the short-term participant spiritually.[11] Paul Borthwick acknowledges the limited value of STM to recipients and bluntly states, "The number one purpose of a short-term mission trip is to change the lives of those who participate," the lives of the short-termers.[12] And indeed, if one asks financial supporters why they are helping fund a young person to go on a mission trip, they typically answer in terms of its hoped-for impact on the young partici-pant, rather than in terms of this ministry pattern being particularly strategic to mission impact in the receiving community.

Mission trips have largely replaced summer retreats or youth camps as the annual youth event for church youth groups, with many camps reporting that there is today a shrinking or even nonexistent market for them to host youth retreats. Back in the early 1980s, when I served as a youth director, we took our high school youth on an annual retreat to the beach, with thousands of other teenagers at "Fun in the Son." Outstanding youth speakers powerfully focused our attention on witness, service, community, social justice, missions, racism, materialism, hedonism, stewardship, and vocation. We were called to witness to an unbelieving world that needed Christ. Then we headed out to socialize with other church kids. We were warned not to live self-indulgent hedonistic lives. Then we headed out to enjoy the sun, the sand, and the sea. Speakers powerfully spoke of racism, discrimination, and the need for social justice. Then we headed out to surf or play volleyball with other white kids from the suburbs. We were called to live lives of servanthood for others. Then we headed to the cafeteria, where ethnic minorities served us delicious food.

Today youth pastors are more likely to make the annual youth event a mis-sion trip. This may be part of their job description. Youth pastors will focus on similar themes. But now when servanthood is talked about, it is also being practiced. When racism or prejudice or poverty and wealth are considered, the issues are not distant, abstract reflections from the suburbs or the beach or a retreat center. Rather, reflection occurs in the very context of relationship with people of other ethnic or racial groups, people themselves often strug-gling with poverty. When our materialistic and hedonistic lives are critiqued, it is away from the taken-for-granted home suburban setting. When vocation is considered, it is in the context of human need, both physical and spiritual.

Not surprisingly, students treasure pictures from these times, pictures dis-played on walls, screensavers, or Facebook—pictures that capture and display a desired self-image, an image of the self who is loving and serving those in need. John, for example, is a medical student. On his desk is a picture of him-self and his dad serving in a Mexican slum with Mexican friends. When asked about the placement of this picture on his desk, he replies that this picture is there to remind him every day while he is in medical school why he is there. Rather than inspire himself to study hard with images of money, prestige, or wealth, John inspires himself with a symbol of human need and a reminder to live his life in service to others.

Today STM is a core part of youth ministry. The very job description of youth pastors, and indeed of many associate pastors or mission pastors, includes the requirement of organizing and leading short-term mission trips at home or abroad. So STM ministry is a core part of the internal discipleship ministry of local churches, participated in because of its spiritual benefits to the sending church and its own members. Like pilgrimages, these trips are rituals of intensification or spiritual renewal where one temporarily leaves the ordinary, compulsory, workaday life "at home" and experiences an extraordinary, voluntary, sacred experience "away from home"—in a liminal space where sacred goals are pursued, physical and spiritual tests are faced, normal structures are dissolved, *communitas* is experienced, and personal transformation occurs. This transformation ideally produces new selves to be reintegrated back into everyday life "at home," new selves that in turn help to spiritually rejuvenate the churches they come from and inspire new civic virtues at home.

## Mission for Whom?

Those with more traditional understandings of mission have responded that activities designed to further the internal discipleship ministries of one's own church are valuable, but they should not be done in the name of missions. Under the older paradigm, youth pastors funded their annual youth events either through the church youth budget, through car washes, or through individuals paying their own way. Now youth pastors have a new way to pay for their youth events. By calling them "missions," participants are allowed to appropriate (some would say "hijack") the sacred rhetoric and funding strategies historically reserved for career missionaries (with the use of prayer letters, requests for support, etc.) in order to pay for something that is ultimately for the good of the short-term missionary and the sending church. Critics sarcastically comment, "For the first time in history, Christians have figured out a way to give to themselves and call it missions."[13] That is, *if* the fund-raising rhetoric explicitly appeals to mission, i.e., asks for support to travel to another country and (altruistically) serve people there, but where the partnership project primarily uses other people as a rhetorical ploy and staged backdrop to something really primarily (and narcissistically) focused on the well-being of the short-term missioner and the sending church, *then* there are good reasons to reject this justification as adequate.

The question remains: In what sense may the STM paradigm be thought of as a genuine good for recipient communities, and not merely for the travelers?

In my own surveys of hundreds of pastors in Thailand and Peru, a majority of pastors indicated that they sometimes wondered about the motivations of short-term missionaries they had hosted. But though there doubtlessly are a wide array of possible self-serving motivations in STM (ranging from a desire to travel, experience other cultures, add global volunteering to one's résumé, grow spiritually, grow closer to others in your church, escape from ennui, feel that one's life matters), most of these pastors who had worked with visiting STM groups nonetheless indicated that these groups had made contributions that were of strategic value to host partners and/or recipient communities. Most were enthusiastic about having further opportunities to work closely with visiting STM groups. Thus there is evidence that the energy for STM partnerships comes not merely from the side of the travelers; there also is often a great deal of energy and effort and vision on the part of recipient communities to attract and inspire visiting missionaries.[14] In what way, then, does the STM paradigm reflect a significant new way of doing "mission," of making a strategic contribution that benefits others?

## Evangelizing the Least Evangelized?

As we explore this question, one clue for us is to observe where short-term missioners from the United States go. David Barrett has divided the countries of the world into three groups: World A includes countries that are least evangelized; World B, countries that are somewhat evangelized; and World C, countries that are most evangelized. Taking data on 4,671 mission trips that I've collected from thousands of Christian college and seminary students, and organizing it in accord with these categories, I find that 3.5 percent of short-term missionaries travel to the least evangelized world (World A), with 12.5 percent traveling to the somewhat evangelized (World B), and fully 84 percent of short-term missionaries going to the 33 percent of the world that is most evangelized (World C). Hence, the vast majority of short-term missionaries are going to the regions that Philip Jenkins, in his book *The Next Christendom*, identifies as the new centers of global Christianity. The point here is not to suggest that the STM enterprise ought to be redirected toward World A, that high school summer teams ought to flood Afghanistan or Saudi Arabia rather than Peru or Kenya, but rather to empirically draw conclusions about the nature of the STM enterprise by recognizing where it actually focuses. There are probably quite good reasons why T-shirt-clad monolingual and monocultural STM groups are not normally the best way to evangelize highly sensitive regions of the world. Whatever the STM movement is as a paradigm, it is not, as an empirical matter of fact, primarily a paradigm for reaching the least-reached portions of the world evangelistically.

## A Movement to Transfer Religious Knowledge to New Believers?

Alternatively, upon observing that STM groups are going to places where Christianity is already numerically strong, one might hypothesize that STM groups, traveling from older centers of Christianity to newer ones, are involved in teaching and discipling, transferring deeper biblical knowledge and understanding to new and untaught believers. The problem with such a hypothesis, again as an empirical matter, is that STM is composed of participants lacking the linguistic skills to effectively communicate such knowledge; perhaps more important, it is a lay movement whose participants have no unusually high levels of biblical knowledge. I recently spoke with a Protestant pastor in the Yucatán, who told me that his church with its own large youth group was a regular recipient of high school mission groups from the United States. When I asked if his youth knew their Bibles as well as the gringos from up the North, he laughed. He explained that youth groups in his association of churches regularly competed in sword drills, Scripture memory, and Bible knowledge contests—and that his youth group loved to engage the visiting groups in Bible knowledge contests, typically held on the last evening of the visit, a contest that the visiting short-term missionaries never won. The divide between Christians in the sending communities and the receiving communities is not primarily a divide in depth of biblical knowledge.

Those who read Philip Jenkins's *The Next Christendom: The Coming of Global Christianity* (2002) or the recent book by Miller and Yamamori, *Global Pentecostalism: The New Face of Christian Social Engagement* (2007) are led to imagine Christianity of the Global South as the new center of Christian energy, strength, and influence, not dependent on connectedness with Northern Christianity. But demography does not equal influence and power. Everything from higher education (with its libraries, buildings, leisure time set aside for study) to Christian publications, Christian radio or television, medical facilities, global travel—all directly depend on material resources. And the vast proportion of Christianity's material resources is controlled by Christians from North America, Australia, Singapore, Europe, or South Korea. Not surprisingly, it is Christians from these regions who travel to Thailand, Guatemala, Tanzania, or Peru, not vice versa. The single most important difference between the Christians doing global short-term missions and those Christians with whom they partner at their destinations is that the STM travelers come from Christian communities with greater material resources and partner with those having less. And it is new patterns of global connectedness, largely ignored by Jenkins as well as by Miller and Yamamori, that characterize the STM paradigm and is a central element in twenty-first-century mission.

## THE QUEST FOR MISSIONARIES

The agency for such connectedness comes from both sides. The Finnish anthropologist Harri Englund, in his article "The Quest for Missionaries," describes attending a Pentecostal church in Malawi. When he refused their efforts to have him play the role of missionary, they inquired about the possibility of others from Finland coming as missionaries. Englund writes:

> My stories about the weak presence of Pentecostalism in my native Finland prompted the church elders to contemplate sending a small team there. The idea was to launch crusades in Finnish market places, at bus and railway stations and in other places where large numbers of people were present. Some of the (converted) Finns would then come to Malawi as missionaries. Trying to inject realism into this project, I described Finland's snowy winters in graphic detail. This made the church elders restrict their proposed crusade to two summer months. When I observed that my compatriots were unlikely to appreciate preaching in Chichewa and that the elders' English was somewhat halting, I was asked to be the interpreter during the crusade. Undeterred by climate and language, the church elders acknowledged the greatest difficulty was in raising enough funds for the crusade. The congregation's bank account totaled 143 kwacha ($10). The church elders resolved to raise funds "little by little," incurring debt if necessary.

The church elders were able to see humor, even absurdity, in some details of their proposed crusade to Finland. However, the basic idea captured their, and the rest of the congregation's, imagination for several weeks. It bespoke a mixture of zeal and despair, unflagging confidence in the gospel, and profound disquiet over the appalling poverty of the church.[15]

Englund describes how these Malawian Christians were fully confident in their own spiritual maturity, not seeing missionaries as "Christians more advanced than themselves," but nonetheless desperately wishing for the connections and resources that these missionaries made possible.

Two different North American women described to my wife, Kersten, and me their former pattern of going on vacation to the Dominican Republic to all-inclusive resorts. In each case Dominican Christians met them and insisted on introducing them to their pastors, giving them a tour of ministry and human need, and actively recruiting these wealthy North American women to shift from taking self-indulgent vacations buffered from human need in all-inclusive beach resorts, to the use of their vacations for STM service projects. Each of these women, unrelated to each other, have now spent their vacations for several years serving through STM in the Dominican Republic. But it was Dominican Christians who recruited them to such ministries.

Or take the Peruvian AMEN mission, an indigenous mission that mobilizes hundreds of largely Pentecostal Peruvians for missionary service throughout Peru. The missionaries are confident, articulate, and committed, but economically live on the edge. They have no formal links to foreign organizations, but often try to make strategic alliances with short-term mission groups. For example, the AMEN missionaries were trying to begin an evangelistic outreach in the town of Canta but were rebuffed by town leaders who were hostile to Protestants. The AMEN mission learned of a group from Kentucky comprised of Methodists, Presbyterians, and Baptists that was looking for an appropriate place for a medical mission trip. The AMEN mission actively recruited them for a joint initiative and approached the mayor of Canta with an offer to hold a medical mission project with dentists, ophthalmologists with eyeglasses, gynecologists, and pediatricians. They were welcomed with open arms, and a church was planted. Kersten and I visited in the second year, when the same group of 47 Kentuckians joined with 60 Peruvians in a joint one-week project. Every government building on the town plaza was filled with medical teams, and Peruvians did the spiritual counseling in each line. The Peruvian *evangélicos* not only were given access; they also were granted deep appreciation by non-Protestants, because of their role in helping this town establish strategic links with valued resources.

## PERU AS EXAMPLAR OF WORLD C

As indicated earlier, most STM groups travel to regions of the world formerly thought of as "mission fields," but that today are new centers of Christian presence. Since my own research has focused most extensively on Peru, a brief overview of the religious setting, particularly as it relates to Protestantism (which characterizes most short-term groups), is in order if we are to better understand the nature of the links.

A few weeks before the presidential runoff in Peru in June of 2006, a private meeting was held between presidential candidate Alan García and sixty Protestant pastors. The pastors complained that "while Peru proclaims religious freedom, in fact the Roman Catholic Church is privileged and *evangélicos* discriminated against. Protestant church properties are taxed. Roman Catholic properties are not and even receive government subsidies. Roman Catholic priests have full access to hospitals and jails. Protestant pastors cannot even visit their own parishioners in the hospital. Only the Roman Catholic Church has full presidential access—exemplified in the annual Catholic *Te Deum* service where the Cardinal delivers a charge to the president." Alan García reportedly expressed great sympathy and a willingness to work for change.

On July 28, Peru's Independence Day, outgoing president Alejandro Toledo attended the *Te Deum* just before Alan García was sworn in as the new president. On the other hand, as his second public act as president (July 30), Alan García attended rather a worship service at an *Iglesia Alianza Cristiana y Misionera* [a Christian and Missionary Alliance Church]—a service intended specifically as a Protestant version of a *Te Deum*, with Pentecostal pastor Miguel Bardales delivering the charge. Protestant Christianity is currently a key part of the changing religious landscape of Lima.

Before the mid-1970s, Protestant churches in Lima were few, small, lower class, and worshiping in small buildings on marginal streets (in marked contrast to large imposing colonial Roman Catholic churches on central streets and plazas). There were few Protestants and many career Protestant foreign missionaries. For example, the Christian and Missionary Alliance (C&MA) had dozens of full-time missionaries from the United States and Canada in Peru. But a turning point was reached in the 1970s with a major evangelistic campaign [*Lima al encuentro con Dios*] led by the C&MA.

An interesting mix of factors came together. Peruvian Protestant Christians mobilized for evangelism. A major donor from the United States (R. G. LeTourneau) agreed to buy expensive properties on high-visibility, prominent parts of Lima (such as Avenida Arequipa or Avenida Brasil) and to pay for construction of large church buildings.[16] And Argentine pastors were brought to Lima to spearhead these churches, pastors whose accents and identities associated them with middle and upper-middle classes. Soon the C&MA (or rather *La Iglesia Alianza Cristiana y Misionera*) had large churches of several hundred to several thousand middle-class members, worshiping in large buildings on central streets. This church association simply became a part of wider changes, where today there are several thousand Protestant congregations in Lima, with churches ranging in weekly attendance from a couple dozen up to eight or ten thousand. Several hundred Peruvian theological students can be found in the various Protestant seminaries and Bible institutes in Lima. With Lima having nearly a third of the Peruvian population, today there is great energy and vitality among Protestant churches in the city. And today the dozens of foreign C&MA missionaries are completely gone. The C&MA no longer considers Peru a "mission field." Similar retrenchment of foreign career missionaries in Peru has occurred with numerous mission agencies and denominations, contributing to a loss of connectedness with resource-rich churches in other parts of the world. This connectedness is now established through new patterns of global mission.

During the summers of 2005 and 2006, I had numerous opportunities to visit Lima's Jorge Chávez International Airport. On each occasion I hung out for a few hours to observe arrivals and departures. Invariably there were STM groups—identifiable by T-shirts, groups ranging in size from 5 or 6 up to 50 or 60, and on one notable occasion, a group of 198 from a megachurch in Minneapolis—coming to partner with a large C&MA congregation of 2,000 members in Callao (seaport city just west of Lima and part of its metropolitan area). There were Baptists, Lutherans, Presbyterians, Nazarenes, Seventh-Day Adventists, Methodists, Pentecostals, and Mennonites. During my three months in Peru, I saw STM groups of many sorts: high school youths with their youth pastors, university students with Intervarsity Christian Fellowship, adult professionals, and mixed family groupings. I encountered STM groups from England, Scotland, Germany, South Korea, Canada, and the United States. There were STM groups from Chinese-American congregations who came to minister to Peru's Chinese diaspora community. There was one STM group of Paraguayan Mennonites. On one evening I met a group from a Korean congregation in Spain, arriving to meet a group of Korean-American Christians to jointly participate in a collaborative project under the supervision of a career missionary from South Korea. Some groups were there to join a sister congregation in an evangelistic outreach activity. Some were there to do construction or medical work. Others came to serve in an orphanage or to work with homeless street children. There were drama groups, music groups, sports groups (soccer, surfing, and skydiving), groups that taught English or gave cooking classes. Some came to learn how they could lobby for justice (related to issues of free trade or to lead poisoning in La Oroya), others to help indigenous artisans market their goods in the global economy, and yet others to provide inexpensive wheelchairs for the handicapped.

In a sample survey of 551 Protestant pastors in Lima, a majority (58%) reported that their congregation had hosted a visiting group of short-term missionaries from abroad during their current pastorate. And these pastors were overwhelmingly positive about the collaborative relations. As I've researched the Peruvian side of the encounter with visiting STM groups, it is the desire for *linking social capital* that seems to me to be key.

## LINKING SOCIAL CAPITAL

In *Bowling Alone*, Robert Putnam focuses on the importance of social capital (social connectedness) to the good society; he says that historically, faith communities were "the single most important repository of social capital in America," with half of all philanthropy and volunteering linked to such faith communities.[17] Putnam contrasts two types of social capital, *bonding* versus *bridging*. *Bonding* social capital involves social connections among those who are demographically similar. It focuses inward, "reinforcing exclusive identities and homogeneous groups";[18] it creates strong in-group loyalties and easily "creates strong out-group antagonism."[19] By contrast, "other networks are outward looking and encompass people across diverse social cleavages."[20] *Bridging* social capital establishes relations across cultural and ethnic divides. And certainly traveling STM groups often bond with their fellow church members in the group, and often bond across ethnic and national divides.

But it is a third kind of social capital on which I wish to focus here. Other scholars, such as Woolcock, focus attention on *linking* social capital,[21] or what Robert Wuthnow calls *status-bridging* social capital: vertical connections across marked differentials of wealth, status, and power.[22] These scholars stress that people who are economically and socially subordinate or poor may have extensive social connectedness to others who are similarly subordinate; but unless there are social and moral connections upward to those with resources and power, the benefits of social capital are limited. I believe that an analysis of STMs as a part of global social connectedness can be fruitfully explored in terms of *bonding*, *bridging*, and *linking* social capital. Here I focus on *linking social capital*, something that Peruvian *evangélicos* seek through partnerships with STM groups from abroad.

## Resource Sharing

The primary reason STM groups travel from the United States to Peru (rather than vice versa) is economic, not religious. These groups are not bringing a Christian faith that currently is present in the United States or Europe but is absent in Peru. Rather, these groups travel from materially wealthy Christian communities to partner with Christian communities that are often numerically and spiritually as vigorous as their own, but which are, by comparison, materially poor. Peruvian *evangélicos* are part of lower, lower-middle, and middle classes, which—compared with Protestant church members in Europe, South Korea, or North America—live under great economic constraints. The cost of living in Lima is not low. It is difficult to provide healthy diets, health care, or education for one's own children and difficult to pay for expensive church buildings, seminary education, or a church sound system on an income of a $150 to $250 a month. A typical North American or European STM member traveling to Peru and serving for two weeks may expend $1,800 on expenses related to this voluntary service, roughly equal to the average (median) annual salary of Peruvian pastors. These short-term mission groups thus build social connections between Christian communities across marked differentials of wealth.

One function, then, of these STM trips is to create links between Christians with material resources and those with less. One common pattern, for example, is for visiting groups to participate in the construction of a church building—and to bring finances for this. The visiting group may or may not include professional builders, but it will bring resources. For example, I observed one group of Peruvian churches that arranged with visiting church youth teams from the United States to help them build their *templos*. Each team lived in the church facilities and helped with construction and outreach. Each North American high school student asked their grandparents, aunts and uncles, neighbors, and other church members for help. Their parents paid part of it. Each person then raised money for their own costs, plus enough to contribute $285 to church construction. One STM team of 15 provided, in addition to $3,900 toward local church expenses of hosting them, another $4,275 toward the church building. Another group of 33 provided $8,580 toward hosting costs, and an additional $9,400 toward ministry and/or construction costs. The church that received this group of 33 is located on a key plaza, with a building now valued at over a million dollars, built over the years through the collaborative aid of 28 visiting STM teams. This is simply one example of a way in which resource sharing occurs. All over Lima one can find church sound systems or music sets provided by visiting short-term mission groups. Visiting short-term missionaries often decide to help provide more sustained sponsorship of orphans or seminary students.

Two scholars who have explored the role of short-term missionaries in resource sharing are C. M. Brown,[23] who looks at church-to-church partnerships in the Ukraine, and Kersten Bayt Priest,[24] who explores how Chicago-area women serve through STMs as "resource brokers" in South Africa. There surely are major challenges associated with such resource sharing, challenges related to issues of stewardship and power.

In any case, many visiting STM groups do not provide much in the way of material resources, but they are nonetheless desired for a different reason.

## Open Doors, Social Access

Evangelical churches in Peru sustain and propagate themselves through active evangelism. But within a historically dominant Roman Catholic order, *evangélicos* often find doors closed to them, literally and metaphorically. One Peruvian pastor explained, "If I knock on another Peruvian's door, they will see me and turn me away. But if I knock with you, a gringo, standing next to me, they will greet us with a smile, open the door, serve us coffee—and listen attentively to what we say." When Peruvian *evangélicos* join collaboratively with gringos from abroad, as when Peruvian AMEN missionaries tried to plant a church in Canta, they often find that town plazas, government offices, high schools, English language schools, university classrooms, jails, and hospitals that normally limit access to *evangélicos*, now open their doors wide.

Peruvians working with visiting STM groups will often say that they use the visitors as *carnada* (bait) or an *anzuelo* (hook) to pull people in. The STM teams teach English, do drama, provide medical care, teach tennis, or sing songs, and often this provides a means for Peruvian *evangélicos* to establish connections or to open doors for service and witness.

Kersten and I spent three days observing one group of 198 short-term missionaries from a church in Minneapolis, a church with an 18-year partnership with a congregation in Callao, a poor part of Lima. For one week the two congregations collaborated on multiple projects. They put on an evangelistic circus (with the "world champion" unicyclist and a family of magicians from the visiting church), had a large parade to the town plaza (stretching for blocks). The mayor of Callao attended. The police provided escorts. Joint teams of Peruvians and Americans visited jails and hospitals. A team of doctors from the Minneapolis church (including a medical school's provost and faculty members) entered into formal cooperative projects with Peruvian medical school faculty in Lima, implanting pacemakers, and so forth. The North American team spent over $400,000 on travel, hotel, and other expenses for this one-week set of activities. Little of this money was transferred directly to Peruvians involved in joint ministry. But this Peruvian church, made up of lower and lower-middle class members, was able to attract several thousand newcomers to visit their church during that week; it was able to build social connections with police, the mayor, medical personnel, gatekeepers at hospitals and jails—all by virtue of *linking social capital* with North Americans, connections across marked differentials of status, wealth, and power. Later the pastor of this church was given a public award by the mayor of Lima for his strategic work in cultivating valued connections with North Americans. He now has ready access to hospitals, jails, or schools that formerly would have maintained closed doors.

## Leverage for Social Change

Yet in addition to resource sharing and to helping establish open doors and access, visiting short-term groups often help to leverage social change. Christians in the mining town of La Oroya were concerned for their children's medical problems.[25] They connected with an STM group, led by a pharmacist from a poison control unit at a children's hospital in Ohio. This team tested their children, discovering that almost every child was severely lead poisoned. Through repeated efforts of specialized STM groups, which brought in medical, environmental, media, and legal experts, collaborative efforts documented and publicized the problem and pressured the mining company and the Peruvian government to take action to correct the environmental abuse and to address the medical situation for those harmed. Without such strategic links with outsiders, it is doubtful if local Christians (poor, uneducated, and fearful of losing their jobs) would have been able to success-fully lobby for change.

Again, in Kersten Priest's research, when black South African Christian teachers at "The Whip," a run-down public school with broken windows, were trying to get government aid and attention, a visiting group of short-term missionaries from Chicago not only brought help for the school but also joined these teachers in a visit to the South African secretary of education on behalf of the school and its needs.[26] Before the next STM annual visit, the government had given this school a new and state-of-the art building, a ben-efit widely perceived as directly a result of STM interventions by Chicagoans.

## CONCLUSION

For Christians abroad who receive and partner with visiting STM teams, three of the most common benefits of linking capital are (1) shared resources, (2) open doors and enhanced credibility, and (3) strategic leverage for change and justice. Each of these three areas represents goods to which short-term missions can contribute.

The center of Christianity today, in terms of numbers and vitality, has shifted southward into Africa and Latin America. But the center of material wealth and power remains in North America, Europe, and parts of Asia. Short-term mission groups play a key role in bringing Christians from resource-rich portions of the world into collaborative projects of witness, service, and justice with Christians living under conditions of great economic and social constraint. When carried out in healthy and wise ways, these have potential for good.

But insofar as Christian mission includes the goal of communicating the gospel to the least Christian and least evangelized peoples of the world, then it must also be recognized that the STM paradigm is a poor vehicle for achieving such ends. Traveling teams of monolingual and monocultural lay Christians, using brief windows of vacation time, cannot be effective at get-ting the Bible translated into minority languages of the world; they are poorly prepared to present the Christian message in highly sensitive regions of the world. Churches that make short-term missions the sole focus of their global mission involvement are embracing a pattern of mission where the goal of communicating the gospel to the least Christian and least evangelized peoples of the world largely disappears. Alternatively, churches that self-consciously recognize both the strengths and limitations of short-term missions will make short-term missions simply one valued element within a wider array of global mission commitments and strategies.

# 8

# "Do Not Fear: Go"

## The Commission of Theological Feminism in the Mission of the Church

NANCY BEDFORD

## THE COMMISSION GIVEN TO WOMEN BY THE RISEN JESUS

According to the canonical Gospels, women disciples are immediately com-missioned by the risen Jesus on Easter morning to spread the good news. In Matthew's account, in chapter 28, Mary Magdalene and another woman also named Mary go to the tomb early that morning. There they encounter trembling guards and an angel, who charges them to announce the resurrec-tion to the male disciples. As they run to do so immediately afterward, feel-ing both fearful and joyful, they encounter the risen Jesus, who repeats the commission: "Do not fear: go and give the good news" (cf. Matt. 28:10). The language of "Do not fear" and "Go, do as I command you" echoes many call stories known to us from Scripture: leaders and prophets such as Gideon and Jeremiah come immediately to mind. What is remarkable here is that right at the beginning of the events unleashed by the resurrection, events that will eventually lead to the movement that will come to be called the Christian church, women who follow Jesus receive a *commission* to announce the good news. They are specifically told to transmit it to the male disciples, to remind them what they must do in order to see Jesus—in this case, go to Galilee.

This essay was originally presented in shortened form as the 2009 Scherer Lecture of the Chicago Center for Global Ministries. My heartfelt thanks to Yoojin Choi, Lisa Knaggs, and Donna Techau for reading and critiquing an earlier draft.

Commenting on Mark's version of the resurrection story, where the women receive the good news of the resurrection but are afraid to say anything about it (Mark 16:8), Osvaldo Vena makes the point that the way both for them and for the men to become true disciples is to find the courage to follow the risen Jesus to Galilee, overcoming fear and incredulity.[1] Indeed, in the Gospels' resurrection narratives taken as a whole, courage is needed by both groups: the women disciples have to overcome their fear of carrying out their commission, and the male disciples have to be brave enough to hear the women's commission and act upon it, overcoming their incredulity. In the Gospel of John (20:11–18), Mary Magdalene hears what she supposes to be the gardener's voice,[2] then learns that Jesus is the one speaking to her. Jesus gives her a commission: "Go to my brothers and say to them. . . ." Mary then goes and announces to the male disciples, "I have seen the Lord."

This commission is literally a common mission: the resurrected Jesus, by giving these women a commission is sharing with them (and with us) God's mission, the *missio Dei*. That is Jesus' first recorded act upon rising from the dead. Indeed, the Great Commission of Matthew 28:16–20, which many centuries later will become one of the foundations of the modern Protestant missionary movement, takes place as a result of the prior commission given to the women at the tomb. In Amy-Jill Levine's words, this group of "independent, motivated women are both the first witnesses of the resurrection and the first missionaries of the church."[3] The strongest statement of sending or mission in the Synoptic Gospels, where the disciples are sent to share the good news with all peoples and nations, appears precisely in Matthew, where the women's commission is not questioned by the male disciples, but rather is acted upon.

There are indications within and without Scripture, however, that from the very beginning the founding and fundamental commission by the risen Jesus to the women was questioned and resisted by some of the male disciples, to their own detriment and to that of the Jesus movement. In Luke's account, Mary Magdalene, Joanna, Mary the mother of James, and other women encounter God's heavenly messengers, who ask: "Why are you looking among the dead for the One who lives?" (cf. Luke 24:5). The angels remind them of the words of Jesus before the crucifixion, and the women are able to put two and two together. Though in Luke's account they do not receive a commission to announce the good news, they do go and tell the male disciples what they have witnessed.[4] When they announce the news to the group of apostles, it is not well received: "But they [masculine pronoun] considered their words to be madness, and disbelieved them" (cf. Luke 24:11). The RSV translates: "But these words seemed to them [the male disciples] an idle tale, and they did not believe them [the women]."

A noncanonical source, the *Gospel of Mary Magdalene*, reflects this theme of skepticism toward the testimony of women on the part of the male disciples, depicting Peter's unwillingness to take Mary Magdalene seriously as a source for the good news. Levi, however, defends her authority. The text of this apocryphal gospel survives in Greek and Coptic fragments that are quite ancient; the Greek fragments likely date back to the late second century. The Greek text has Levi reprimanding Peter for his angry opposition to Mary. He challenges Peter: "If the Savior has judged her worthy, who are you to despise her?" The Coptic version fills in details about Mary's reaction and adds: "In tears, Mary said to Peter: 'Peter, my brother, what are you thinking? Do you think that this is all my imagination or that I have deceived the Lord?'"[5] This source does not make reference to the commission given by the risen Jesus to the women on Easter morning, but rather to gnostic teachings supposedly given by Jesus to Mary in secret. In other words, it has a particular ideological slant and does not need to be taken literally. Nonetheless, at a descriptive and narrative level, it seems to hit the nail on the head with regard to the attitude of many representatives of dominant ecclesial streams throughout Christian history, particularly that of men with a good bit of institutional power. It depicts an unwillingness to give much credibility to women as we undertake to carry out the commission given to us by Jesus, the commission to share the good news with our brothers—and with the entire world. In an imaginative rereading, Peter can represent the suspicious attitude toward women that appears in much of church practice and theology across the centuries; Levi can embody the male disciples who are willing to believe that Jesus' commission bestows sufficient authority on women to take them seriously as theologians and bearers of the good news. Mary Magdalene, who manifests in her tears the pain of being disregarded by her brothers in Christ, appears as one who challenges not only Peter (a hostile male), but also Levi (a friendly male), to take seriously her personal integrity and the authority of her voice—and along with her, that of all her sisters in Christ across time. She also puts the burden of proof on Peter: it is he who must prove that she does not have a founding commission or the authority to carry it out, not she who must somehow prove herself.

My primary thesis in this essay is that without taking seriously the *commission* of the risen Jesus to women, the subsequent *mission* of the church as a whole loses force and integrity, too often becoming bad news, rather than good news both for those who encounter it and for those involved in its proclamation. The whole body of Christ is damaged when this commission is compromised. Expressed positively, the commission of women lends vitality and veracity to the mission of the church as a whole. And yet, here we must pause immediately and qualify this thesis. Paying attention to the commission of women cannot in itself guarantee that the church's mission will truly constitute good news. The category "women" is not a univocal one, any more than the category "men." As the excesses of "missionary-imperial feminism"[6] show, gender analysis cannot be applied reductively, but rather must be understood in its intersections with colonialism, economic asymmetries, and racism, to name only a few. Women can and do treat other women unjustly. For that reason, *how* the commission that Jesus gives to women is carried out is as important as *that* it be carried out. However, what a healthy, liberating, antiracist, decolonial, joyful, pneumatic theological feminism *can* and *must* do in the mission of the church is to help the church give more of itself, to be more faithful to the good news of Jesus, and to cooperate with God's Spirit in the liberation and renewal of all things for life abundant.

## THEOLOGICAL FEMINISM AS AN IMPULSE FOR MISSION

What I am here calling "theological feminism" is not some recent addition to be grafted into the mission of the church; as the scriptural witness to the commission of Mary Magdalene and the other women shows, it is constitutive of that mission from the very beginning, and necessary to it, even though the writers of the Gospels did not insert a footnote of clarification using this particular term: they simply left us with a story worth telling. The fact that the empty-tomb narratives made it into the Gospels, even though the earlier Pauline list of witnesses to the resurrection omitted the role of women (see 1 Cor. 15:5–7), is a sign of the persistence and importance of their action in the genesis of the church's mission. "Theological feminism" is simply a way of talking about the impulses toward gender equality and empowerment of women that have always existed in the church, despite all attempts to smother them. The church is and has always been a gathering of more women and children than men; it has been a space where the spark of the Spirit can lead women (and men) to imagine and act out audacious and unexpected possibilities.

Theological feminism is rooted in pneumatology, for it evokes the Spirit-infused experience of transformation and empowerment that many women (and men) have described throughout history as a consequence of their encounter with the gospel. In practice, this means that though the church is an ambiguous organism, imperfect and sometimes downright toxic, it is also quite often a site for people on the margins, and women in particular, to learn how to speak with assurance, how to lead, how to organize, how to read and interpret difficult texts, and how to subvert oppressive readings and structures. In these contexts, many women become leaders despite themselves: leaders, though they had not planned it and had not particularly wanted it, and though their leadership may in time lead them to contest the complicity of their own churches in injustice.

Most women who consider themselves feminists or womanists and continue to be involved in the Christian church and its mission have experienced the empowering dimension of the gospel in one way or another, even while they struggle to transform the church and theology. But what I am calling "theological feminism" is not limited to people who confess themselves to be feminists or womanists; many women (and men) would not choose such words to describe themselves, and yet they can relate instances in which the experience of the gospel became truly good news for them as human beings in the world. The testimony of Margarita Canteros, who belongs to the Qom (Toba) nation in Argentina, is a case in point. She speaks about how her encounter with a liberating hermeneutic of the Bible gave her the courage to stand up boldly in the face of white people and of the men in her own indigenous community: "I was very timid. It is difficult for a Toba woman to be talking to white people. . . . But thanks to the Bible, we have been able to discover the value of each culture." Likewise, her friend Hilda Gómez, also part of the Qom nation, tells of how new ways of reading the Bible led the women to speak up in church, organize for their rights, and find a new voice.[7]

The example of these Qom women shows the complexity and ambiguity of how theological feminism functions. On the one hand, the arrival of white Christian people and the invasion of Qom ancestral lands was very bad news for their ancestors. When their communities converted in the last few decades to various kinds of Pentecostal Christianity, this did not mean that their lives became much better or that they were able to recuperate their lands, even land that the government had officially granted back to them.[8] On the other hand, the subversive possibilities of the gospel have lately begun to leaven their struggle, and their desire to read and interpret Scripture has transformed their lives and empowered them in their ability to stand up to gender and racial injustice, defend the value of their language and culture, and insist on their right to the land. Their example points to the importance of interpreting and living "theological feminism" in nonhegemonic ways, so that it may better contribute to the decolonizing of mission and the unmooring of the church from ties to oppression and toxicity.

## GLOBAL FEMINIST THEORIES AS A RESOURCE FOR A MISSIONAL THEOLOGY

Theological feminism, as I have described it here, precedes feminist theology. Feminist theology is rooted in the experience of theological feminism, which means that it is rooted in a movement and praxis of justice, to which it returns in order to be nurtured and challenged. This experience of "theological feminism" is not exclusively—or even particularly—a North Atlantic or a "Euro-American" one. To point out these sometimes-ignored feminist voices is not just a matter of historical justice, but a matter of epistemology. Non-hegemonic feminisms—either those with roots in the Global South or those engaged in resistance to the "common sense" of the world as we know it, even from within the Global North—are able to open our eyes to reality in deeply transformative ways that contribute to a better theology.

One of the biggest potential contributions made by global feminist theorists to a theology of mission is a realization that may at first sound paradoxical: it is simply that gender analysis is not enough and functions in a reductive way when looked at in isolation. Arguments about what is worse—racial injustice, gender injustice, or economic injustice—are not helpful because they simplify reality too much, creating false dichotomies. Rather, what is needed is an agile understanding of what Patricia Hill Collins calls a "theoretical framework of intersectionality." She posits that elements such as sex, gender, or class constitute an interrelated rather than a competing framework for analysis.[9] For instance, advocacy for black women or a critique of sexism within the black church community does not mean remaining silent when black men continue to be jailed out of all proportion to their share of the population in the United States. Thinking of the gender dynamics of migration from Latin America to the United States does not mean that an awareness of economic injustice should be pushed aside. Looked at theologically, this sort of intersectionality allows us as theologians to better understand the breadth and density of oppressions in this world: they are sin. Put theologically, feminist theory is helpful in developing a robust hamartiology—not that we, as theologians, might wallow in it, but that grace might abound even more. Global feminist and womanist theories accord us analytical tools that help us understand reality in its complexity, in order to transform it as part of our mission in the Spirit.

## THE MISSION OF THE CHURCH
## IN GLOBAL FEMINIST PERSPECTIVE

When I speak about the mission of the church, I am trying to think both locally and globally at the same time. First, I think of my own Anabaptist congregation struggling to act faithfully in our economically and culturally mixed neighborhood, amid all the complexities of getting together and getting along as a group of quite diverse human beings with a variety of sometimes divergent theological convictions. It is the place where I am called to account as a theologian, where I am challenged to give coherent and understandable expression to my theological convictions. It is the place where I hope my three daughters will continue to find ways to grow in liberating faith; the place where I pray my husband's deep concerns for social justice and the rights of immigrants will not go unheard. Even as I write, I see new evidence of the force of theological feminism in my church community, where an interim pastoral team that emerged from within the congregation is composed of three women, none of them white—this in a congregation that once upon a time almost split over the matter of women in pastoral leadership. God's Spirit is once again at work among us in unexpected ways; yet for every wound healed, it seems that we are in danger of opening new lesions, even when we proceed with the best of intentions.

When I speak of "mission," though, I am also thinking of mission in a global sense, including the mission of industrialized Northern countries toward the Global South (of which I am literally the daughter, as someone born in Argentina of North American missionaries). I am likewise speaking of the dimension of mission from the Global South toward the Global North as a result of the transformative influence of migrants. This has happened in the Roman Catholic parish in my neighborhood, where the priest is South Asian and many of the congregants are Mexican and Central American. I also think of the mission of countries in the Global South toward each other, as in the case of the mission experiences of some of my former Argentine seminary students in Equatorial Guinea or of Korean missionaries working in Argentina and Paraguay. I think about the good aspects of intercultural Christian mission impulses, and also about the bad aspects: not only about the complicities of Western mission with colonialism, but also about the way in which missionaries from the Southern hemisphere often repeat patterns of paternalism and racism when they go to other countries in the South.

Mission at home and elsewhere is never devoid of ambiguities and complications; at the same time it is constitutive of our call as followers of Jesus and gives material shape to our life in the Spirit. How might a feminist missiology born out of theological feminism help us theorize mission in these various senses? In thinking of mission in each of these ways, some guiding questions come to mind: Are women freely, joyfully, and creatively able to carry out the commission given by the risen Jesus? Is the gospel shown to be truly good news for women in each of these contexts, both for those who announce the gospel and for those who receive it?[10] Why or why not?

Mercy Amba Oduyoye has been persistent in asking similar questions in the African context, often answering them in a rather somber way, one that is disquieting to those who are ready uncritically to celebrate the growth of the Christian faith in that continent. She writes:

In my opinion, it is still debatable whether or not the influence of Christianity has been beneficial to the socio-cultural transformation of Africa—and I am most concerned with its effects on women. It seems that the sexist elements of Western culture have simply fuelled the cultural sexism of traditional African society. Christian anthropology has certainly contributed to this. African men, at home with androcentrism and the patriarchal order of the biblical cultures, have felt their views confirmed by Christianity.[11]

In the face of such testimony—and she is not alone in bringing such concerns to the surface—it seems urgent to explore how Christian mission and ministry might serve to bring life, rather than to drain life, to heal rather than to harm.

Letty Russell, one of the mothers of contemporary feminist theology, has written most perceptively and hopefully about the mission of the church, as an educated Euro-American woman who spent her life in active solidarity with those at the margins. Parting from an understanding of mission as *missio Dei*, she defines "God's mission or action in the world as equivalent to God's liberating action or liberation."[12] Her method leads her to seek for clues to a feminist ecclesiology "among all sorts and conditions of people rather than among feminist communities only."[13] In other words, it is not a reductive approach: rather, she is happy to find conditions for the flourishing of creation no matter where they might appear, and to imagine how they might contribute to a way of being church that is committed to God's mission of healing and liberation.

In order to discover "clues for feminist liberation ecclesiologies," ways forward for communities so that the gospel might truly function as the good news that it is, Russell explores three ministry settings. She focuses on renewed Christian communities that make inclusiveness central to their ministry; on basic ecclesial communities such as those in Brazil and in the Philippines; and on feminist Christian communities or Women-Church in the Global North. What she discovers in her explorations are three deceptively simple principles. First, "the missionary nature of the church as it participates in God's sending and liberation work in the world requires a *justice* connection." Second, "the witness of the church is rooted in a life of *hospitality*." And third, the life of the church nurtures a *"spirituality of connection."*[14] Mission therefore has to do with justice, with hospitality, and with connection in the Spirit. We need to take all three of these factors into account: hospitality will not flourish without connection and justice, justice cannot be served without the compassion and solidarity of hospitality and connection, and connection can easily become asymmetrical and oppressive (not of the Spirit) if justice and hospitality are pushed aside.

We can provisionally test out the relevance of Russell's three factors for a theology of mission by looking at two essays on mission. In the first essay,

Gnana Robinson, a biblical scholar from Tamil Nadu in India, correctly reminds us that followers of Jesus are "called to abandon the broad way of superiority and domination and to enter through the narrow way of solidarity with the suffering people," in order to carry out the Great Commission.[15] I agree with him, and yet it seems to me that a problem arises when those attempting such solidarity are blind to the gender and economic asymmetries in which they are involved. What does solidarity mean for persons who have their basic needs covered? What does it mean for those in dire need? What does it mean for those who are not in a place of "superiority and domination" at present? Robinson adds that "the missionary responsibility demands of every one of us to let loose our own identity and get involved in the struggle of the people for the total liberation of humankind."[16] Again, this is true, and yet such "losing oneself" for the sake of the kingdom cannot happen in healthy ways unless mission is able to critique itself and transform itself, taking into account the intersectionalities suggested by Hill Collins. For women, especially poor women, "losing oneself" can easily turn into just another form of erasure and oppression. Sometimes, what people need is to "find themselves" for the sake of the gospel and of God's kingdom, not to "lose themselves." For Robinson's suggestions to be good news for women, walking the narrow way of solidarity must be empowering and not a path of self-denial that enables abuse. Taking into account Russell's three "clues" of justice, hospitality, and connection helps mission find its balance here.

The same is true for the "relationship missiology" with "permeable boundaries" suggested by Mary Schaller Blaufuss in another essay on mission, also written in India. For mission to operate as she would wish, from "within a web of connections," encouraging a "multi-directional and multi-influential movement" and influence, and facilitating "mutual encouragement and correction," following a Trinitarian pattern,[17] it is first necessary for power asymmetries to be addressed. Otherwise, even a discourse as attractive as that of a Trinitarian mutuality can serve to hide deep injustices, asymmetries, and the silencing of certain voices; it can even lead to the violent permeation of healthy boundaries. For women's voices to be heard in this multidirectional movement, they need to be raised with a certain amount of courage and persistence. Some supposedly "multicultural" situations, for instance, give an illusion of mutuality but in reality are nothing but business as usual, with a few multicultural flourishes. Some white Protestant churches in the United States seem deeply involved in mission to immigrants and have satellite congregations where people worship in Spanish, Cantonese, or Tagalog—but without letting that fact change the ethos of the dominant white congregation. Russell's clue of "justice" here again becomes central if hospitality and connection are also to flourish and movement is to be truly "multidirectional."

The point about women needing to raise their voices (or to use my earlier image, to fulfill their *commission*) is made by Musimbi Kanyoro in another context, that of the church in sub-Saharan Africa. She writes of the mission of the church: "We have been busy binding wounds, but we have not stopped the war. We have prepared bodies for burial, but we have not stopped the killing. I dare ask, is our involvement a sufficient and efficient way of our mission? Do these efforts witness effectively to our being missionaries on this continent?"[18] She adds that what God is calling African Christians to do is to "reread our Scripture with new eyes and see that God is calling us and empowering us to do the more difficult tasks of our mission, that is, to speak out for the truth."

Such speaking out, she writes, is a prophetic task that involves serious risk. Furthermore, it requires credibility: not just preaching the gospel, but also living the gospel. Kanyoro finds examples of such credibility and bravery especially among African women who "are saying *no* to being relegated to the back, women who are saying *no* to cultural practices which dehumanize them and prevent them from having life in abundance."[19] She is not satisfied with the paternalistic praise that she says women in African churches often receive from male leaders; rather, she calls on the churches "to empower us, to nurture us towards maturity, and finally to welcome us as partners in God's mission and ministry." She adds that "the models of women in the Bible teach us that change comes when the personal is made political and when the political is made personal," as in the story of Lydia, who practiced her faith in public and prevailed upon Paul.[20]

We can find a hint of a healthy, Spirit-filled mission impulse in the story of Mizo women vegetable vendors in Northeast India, in an area where 80 percent of the people are Christian. Lalrindiki Ralte tells how these women came together to find ways to protect their livelihood in the face of soil depletion and globalization. They organized to better produce and distribute their vegetables, founded an association, "United Mizoram Grassroots Women," and began pressuring the government to provide assistance and education, as well as interacting with other grassroots women's organizations in India, and beyond their borders in Bangladesh and Pakistan. Ralte points out that by combining "elements of subsistence economy and the system of exchange in the local market," these women "pose a radical critique of modern capitalist economy," with its emphasis on the accumulation of the private wealth of a few.

Ralte then examines the role of the church in this situation and challenges it to push aside paternalistic patterns and join in as a partner with movements such as that of the women vegetable vendors. She observes that many of the vegetable vendors "left the mainline churches and joined smaller denominations or sectarian groups" because they consider the traditional churches "too

elitist, hierarchical and patriarchal" and too interested in financial contributions from their members. They moved to spaces where they could express
their faith more freely, with their voices and with their bodies through dancing.

Ralte's account is therefore one about women who have not only raised
their voices, like Lydia or Mary Magdalene, but have also voted with their feet
and sought out communities of faith where they can express themselves freely.
These women challenge the church to "acquire a new face and new experiences," by entering into the reality of the marginalized, which "can make its
mission work much more effective and relevant for contemporary society."[21]
In their stories we find all the clues mentioned by Letty Russell: hospitality,
justice, and a spirituality of connection. They show us how women today,
even in very difficult conditions, can find ways to fulfill the commission of
the risen Jesus to women, opening new paths toward flourishing in concrete
material ways, and calling the church to a truly life-giving mission.

## THE COMMISSION OF WOMEN
## IN A THEOLOGY OF MISSION

How then does the commission of the risen Jesus to women, in order that the
church's mission might truly bring good news, affect theology as a whole? In
other words, how does the praxis of theological feminism in the mission of the
church shed light upon a theology that takes mission seriously? I will reflect
briefly on three ways in which the commission of women—and especially
the voices of women in the Global South and on the margins of the Global
North—helps theology to give "more of itself": in its pneumatology, in its
theological anthropology, and in its ecclesiology.

That feminist approaches to theology of mission remind us of the centrality of the Holy Spirit and therefore of Trinitarian approaches to theology
seems by now a given among many theologians. Indeed, if one reviews what
women in particular are writing about in theology of mission, a Trinitarian
theme with a strong pneumatological emphasis is easy to detect. In other
words, they pick up the theme of the *missio Dei* but read it in strongly pneumatological terms. Kirsteen Kim reminds us, for instance, that "the mission
of the Spirit encompasses the whole breadth and depth of God's purposes
in the world," to the point that an "overarching definition of that mission"
would be impossible.[22] Mission cannot be narrowly defined, but where the
Spirit is at work, there we will find the mission of God. Katja Heidemanns
likewise emphasizes that "the signs of our times require a mission theology
of the Holy Spirit," one that moves beyond ecclesiocentrism and is able not
only to speak, but also to *listen*. She proposes a "missiology of risk" that values

"finitude, interdependence, and particularity" in all their fragility, to replace the old "missiology of control," which assumed that efficacy could somehow be guaranteed if all the right mechanisms were put into place.[23] Susan Smith agrees that "to seek to understand the Spirit as the principal agent of mission represents an important development in contemporary missiology," one that may provide an alternative to both ecclesiocentric and christomonistic paradigms.[24] She points out that a pneumatological vision of mission "encourages an inductive approach to mission" by which the missionary task is to "discern with others the action of the Spirit within a particular context and culture."[25]

One reason a pneumatological approach to mission gives women literally more breathing space is that it opens up new possibilities for ministry, along the lines of Jesus' promise in John, chapter 14, that by the power of the Spirit his followers would do things similar to those that he did, and things "even greater" (14:12 NIV). This promise both links the mission of the church to Jesus (for the Spirit will remind Jesus' followers of what he said and did; 14:26) and opens up mission by the Spirit to new possibilities in new contexts. By its very nature a pneumatic mission breaks down gender asymmetries and allows imagination to flourish. The *missio Dei* understanding of mission is potentially very powerful precisely because it opens up a Trinitarian paradigm for the work of God and of the church in the world—and if Trinitarian, then pneumatological; and if pneumatological, then subversive of the powers that be, of hegemonic "common sense," and conducive to hearing the cries of all of creation (Rom. 8:19–26). Pneumatology can have a curative and transformative effect on theology, and after centuries of relative neglect, its increasing importance in Protestant and Roman Catholic theologies is a radiant sign of hope to me.

A second theme that comes to the fore when the commission of women is taken seriously in a missional theology is that of theological anthropology. An androcentric understanding of the human condition, an understanding that takes certain privileged and idealized males as the standard for humanity, is shown to be inadequate: the *imago Dei* is best seen in many different human particularities, in many different bodies and personalities and cultures. One of the exciting aspects of mission is precisely learning about how God's image is reflected in so many different ways of being in the world, and how God's Spirit is at work in each of them, to renew the face of the earth. The *imago Dei* only comes clearly into focus if women—all kinds of women, women all over the world—are celebrated as manifestations of the image of God, and if their bodies are cherished as part of that image.[26] As womanist theologian Linda Thomas points out, the *imageo Dei* needs to be taken into account by the *missio Dei*, since all women in Africa and elsewhere are made in the image of

God. Therefore, "oppression of African women is oppression of God's own image and energy."[27]

Once women are understood to be truly (and not only secondarily) made in the image of God—and the commissioning of women by the risen Jesus is a strong reinforcement of the agency that is born of bearing such an image—their abuse should become doubly disturbing to those who say they love God. And yet, violence against women is not decreasing in the world, but rather increasing. Feminicide, rape as a tool of war, and domestic violence are reaching unheard-of levels, and yet this topic fails somehow to be at the center of Christian preaching and mission. A healthy theological anthropology will not be able ever to justify or ignore the fact that women are so often submitted to violence in horrific ways. Silencing the voices of women and suspicion toward their commission in the wider mission of the church ends up justifying violence against them—and this violence is happening as we speak, not only in the feminicide in Juárez and the rapes in the Congo, but also in the fact that women in most societies, rich or poor, are at risk of being raped by men they know. It is only in societies where there is a strong distaste for violence, a good measure of gender equality, and a clear recognition of women's contributions to the society—only there does rape become infrequent or absent. This is certainly not the case of the United States, one of the most rape-prone of all contemporary cultures.[28] A mission that does not engage in resistance to these specific and particular evils is not the *missio Dei*. When a woman is raped, the *imago Dei* is raped, and the *missio Dei* is to help heal the wounds that exist, to do justice, and to work on rape prevention. Because most of the perpetrators of rape are men and most (though not all) of the victims of rape are women, this particular problem shows how important the transformation of both men and women is, if life abundant is to flourish. If the mission of the Christian church does not work to prevent violence against women, how can it be said that it is a bearer of good news? If mission is not working actively and creatively to promote nonviolence, gender equality, and the recognition of women, in church and elsewhere in society, then it becomes complicit with violence against women.

A third theme is ecclesiological: though Christian churches always have been largely populated by women, the concerns of women have often not been central to the theology and ministry of church leadership. In the long run, this indifference can lead to the emptying of Christian churches: when women are faced by persistent indifference to their concerns, they not only may move to churches more open to their interests (as in the case of the Mizo vegetable vendors), but they also may move out of church altogether. This is not only something that happens in the secularized regions of Western Europe, but also in the Global South, even though at the moment many women are engaged in church movements in the Southern hemisphere.

Indeed, the recent growth of Christianity in the Global South can arguably be analyzed in terms of its being a women's movement, as Dana Roberts has suggested. She posits three gender-linked elements that have contributed to women's participation in new Christian movements in Africa and Latin America. First, women find female solidarity and support for their ordinary lives in churches. Second, Christian movements "hold out hope for healing, improved well-being and reconciliation with others in their communities." And third, in the churches they find a context in which female education is valued, at least in venues such as Sunday school, and often beyond that. In this context, they are able to develop leadership skills, which over time (and sometimes generations) can propel women into leadership in the larger society.[29] The impulses that Roberts describe are similar to what I name "theological feminism." However, Roberts asks an important further question: "What happens when women no longer find fulfillment and satisfaction in these forms of participation?" This is a question that a theology of mission can no longer ignore.

Despite this challenge, it seems to be still mostly women taking the "commission of women" very seriously. As I was writing this essay, to test this hypothesis I conducted a brief, unscientific survey of the literature on mission being published in the main academic journals dedicated to the topic, and of some recent books on mission. Their contents seem to indicate that the importance of the agency of women in mission still appears mostly as something of interest to women.[30] Yet, as Korean theologian Nam-Soon Kang points out:

> As long as this question remains a "woman's issue," androcentric theological discourse will consider it a theological non-question. The fundamental theological and missional questions raised by feminists will then continue to be marginalized in missional discourse, and the full potential of the impact they could make on "malestream" theology and discourse on mission of church will be lost.[31]

The truth is, though, that the commission of women is not, as we would say in Spanish, *cosa de mujeres*, "a matter for women only." It is a matter for all of us: children, women, men, and nonhuman creation. If we are serious about the mission of the church as truly good news on this earth, we have a lot to learn and a lot of listening to do; we have a lot to relearn and a whole lot to undo, lest our mission become toxic and bad news. And yet, the Spirit of life has not given up on us; the Spirit beckons us to get over our fears and our incredulities, even as the first witnesses of the resurrection were asked to do.

The risen Jesus did not say to Mary Magdalene and the other women: "Go, be good little girls and don't bother the grown-ups"; or "Go, be fearful and silent, making sure you don't speak up in church"; or "Your ideas are good but the time just isn't right to innovate"; or "You aren't qualified to continue on with my work because you have the wrong gonads"; or "Don't worry your pretty little head about anything because we men have you covered"; or "Be quiet and smell the burial spices"; or "Go talk among yourselves about women's issues." The risen Jesus gave women a commission. Jesus said: "Do not fear: Go! Announce the good news!" The words of Jesus still resonate today, and they affect every one of us. May all of us who believe that the message of the gospel can indeed be good news in this world—may all of us believers learn to heed Jesus' words and act upon them, wherever the Spirit of life leads us.

# 9

# Defining "Racisms"

## Understanding Our Globalized, Terrorized, Ecologically Threatened World

### Dawn M. Nothwehr

## INTRODUCTION

I have *always* understood "ethics" in relation to "mission." Indeed, I learned to "do ethics" from Jack Keagan, a moralist who was also a member of Maryknoll, the foremost Catholic Mission Society in the United States. It was during my MA studies at Maryknoll School of Theology, in a milieu steeped in mission, that I was introduced to the work of Daniel C. Maguire. Significant for our purposes, at the heart of Maguire's work, as well as my understanding of the relationship of ethics and mission, stands the "Foundational Moral Experience": reverence for persons and their environment.

My understanding of mission is also shaped by more than twenty years' experience of working side by side with a wide variety of peoples who were also often marginalized—poor folks of ecologically ravaged Appalachia; Native Americans of urban Minneapolis; munitions workers with "mystery illnesses" in Colorado; refugees from Guatemala, El Salvador, Nicaragua, and Southeast Asia; and persons with HIV disease, schizophrenia, or Alzheimer's disease.

From these experiences, I have learned that the starting point for mission must be the unequivocal recognition of the *imago Dei* in each and every

Permission to publish this material, taken from the first chapter of the author's book, *That They May Be One*, published by Orbis Books, Maryknoll, N.Y., 2008, was granted by the publisher.

human person, and that without it, attempts to practice the Christian tenets of love and justice are quite worthless.

Thus, all mission efforts must be rooted in justice and guided by the reality that it is not only *that* one practices love and justice, but also *how* one practices these virtues that makes the good news appealing and relevant for the thriving of humankind. True love and justice require more than pallid liberal charity that patronizingly gives alms or blindly and passionlessly renders empirical judgments, altering the lives of those considered Other.

Rather, true love and justice require impassioned radical empowerment, exemplified by the incarnation, where Jesus' choice to become powerless encountered our poverty. Such action first demands a full identification with poverty and abjectness, then cries out for the relinquishment of power by the powerful and a taking up of power by the poor and the marginalized. This exchange of power needs to be based on the common recognition of the full personhood of the Other, the concomitant valuing of the Other, and a common regard marked by trust, respect, and affection. In other words, the practice of love and justice requires mutuality. Mutuality as a formal norm for Christian social ethics stands at the heart of mission, especially the mission of working for racial justice in a globalized, terrorized, and ecologically threatened world.

The 1910 Edinburgh World Missionary Conference that CCGM is commemorating accomplished many good and righteous things. However, for our purposes, there was a singular defining moment at Edinburgh. As Stephen Bevans reminded us in his 2008 Scherer Lecture, attitudes of arrogance and illusions of superiority blocked these fine Christians from a stance of empowering mutuality.[1] At best, their mind-set obstructed the extension of good news to the poor; and at worst, it enslaved those they considered "Heathen Others."

Fortunately, there was at least one challenging voice from Edinburgh that can guide us today. That voice was the definitive prophetic witness of Bishop V. S. (Vedanayagam Samuel) Azariah, who "unmasked the racism and superiority of many foreign missionaries in India." He defined the racism that the conference was not able to recognize, exposing "a certain aloofness, a lack of mutual understanding and openness, a great lack of frank intercourse and friendliness. . . . [He asserted that] too often you promise us thrones in heaven, but will not offer us chairs in your drawing rooms."[2] His address reached a climax with the following words: "Through all the ages to come the Indian Church will rise up in gratitude to attest the heroism and self-denying labours of the missionary body. You have given your goods to feed the poor. You have given your bodies to be burned. We also ask for *love*. Give us FRIENDS."[3] Sadly, as Bevans explains, "his words at the end were greeted with stunned silence and cries of disagreement."[4] I daresay that in that silence, insidious racism was allowed to define the church's mission. We must not be equally struck dumb or repeat the sins of our forebears. Instead, we need to recognize ourselves as also capable of such error, but then consciously and proactively sharpen our moral sensitivity to the signs and symptoms of the dynamics of power that define the racial injustices of our day and hone our social analytic skills to defeat them. In what follows, we will explore some key notions involved in such processes.

I will first make the claim that the definition of racism given by Tunisian-born French philosopher, educator, writer, and essayist Albert Memmi is foremost among those adequate for our day. Second, in light of Memmi's definition, I will explore three forms of racism that require our particular attention today: color-coded racism, tribalism or ethnocentricity, and xenophobia. Third, while fully acknowledging the church's egregious complicity in racist activity (past and present), I will raise to high relief two key factors within the church that allow for its potential return to the moral realm as an agent of racial justice. Finally, because I am a Roman Catholic and cannot presume to speak for other Christian traditions, I will briefly unpack some key ideas from two little-known Vatican documents that define racisms. I will highlight the importance of those ideas for mission.

## THE IDEA OF "RACE"

Human beings are hardwired to distinguish differences.[5] Thus, there is a perennial need for us to assign meaning to those differences, distinguished among fellow humans, and then to act accordingly.[6] However, "race" is a relatively new idea that has signified a variety of things, depending on the historical period and context. For decades, it has been widely agreed that there is no scientific basis for setting any absolute boundaries that determine the inferiority or supremacy of any one group of humans over another.[7] Scholars concur that before the thirteenth century BCE, "race" simply indicated distinctions of difference.[8] However, especially from the medieval period, through the age of discovery to the Enlightenment, "race" took on increasingly more connotations of a deterministic classification of humans in hierarchies of superiority. Developments in defining "race" in Europe, China, and Japan likely had the most extensive impact, and taken together, those ideas established the basic framework for the major constructs of "race" and racisms around the globe and across time.

A fatal step toward deterministic interpretations of difference was taken when, in the early sixteenth century, the term "race" ("racial stock," as in breeding animals) entered the vocabulary for describing traits of human beings.[9]

The characteristics distinguishing different "races" grew to include skin color, eye color, types of hair, customs, language, religious beliefs, and more. In the racist mind, these determined whether or not a people was "civilized" or qualitatively equal to those making the judgment. Thus, when we speak of "race," we are dealing with a "social construct" that takes many forms.[10]

In the seventeenth century, "civilized" Europeans questioned if other people (not "civilized") of particular "races" could "progress" or "advance." Human monogenesis or polygenesis was debated, though the majority of scholars supported monogenesis, as indicated in the biblical stories of Genesis 1 and 2. Most held that because humans could interbreed, human differences are within the same species and do not isolate different species. Of mixed significance was the fact that, influenced by Baron Montesquieu (1748), most scholars held that environmental and historical factors accounted for human differences. Thus it was possible to accommodate differences through education.

Sadly, by 1758 the thought of Carolus Linnaeus already began to take its toll. He included humans as a species of "primates" and then divided the "primates" into different groupings of creatures based on physical structures, emotional temperament, and intellect, ranging from mythical monsters to *Homo afer*. Subspecies were distinguished by skin color, hair color, eye color, behavioral propensities, and biological traits. Such deterministic categorization made some peoples irreparably inferior.

From the eighteenth century to the present, equally insidious pseudoscientific notions such as social Darwinism and the eugenics movement were developed. Such thought culminated in three predominant, prototypic, and ethically egregious systems for interpreting how human differences stunted human life around the globe: (1) U.S. chattel slavery, (2) South African apartheid, and (3) Nazi Aryan white supremacy. These systems crossed a line by legally establishing racism in the structures of the entire societies.[11] This short review gives us but a glimpse of the understanding of race and racism that was available to those at Edinburgh in 1910.

## FROM RACE TO RACISMS: DEFINITIONS AND DYNAMICS

I contend that the most adequate definition of racism for the twenty-first century is given by Albert Memmi. He holds that racism is fundamentally a structure and a set of social relations, not only a feeling of prejudice toward an Other. Racism is a generalizing definition and valuation of differences, whether real or imaginary, to the advantage of the one defining or deploying them [*accusateur*], and to the detriment of the one subjugated to the act of definition [*victime*], whose purpose is to justify (social or physical) hostility and assault [*aggression*].[12]

Further, Memmi claims, the archetype of this oppression is colonialism, in which

aggression against a weaker society requires the disparagement of the other to justify itself, to legitimize having appropriated others' land and homes, and having benefited from truncating others' lives and social dignity. Racism is indispensable to the colonist mentality, to make its domination appear reasonable to itself.[13]

Memmi distinguishes four moments that, when occurring together, constitute an absolute and timeless occasion of oppression called racism.[14] Racism is first an instance in which one recognizes that a "difference" exists between persons or among groups. Second, a negative value judgment is imposed on those persons who bear or manifest certain characteristics and who are different, and a positive valuation is given to the correlative characteristics born by the one(s) providing the judgment. Third, the difference and its value are generalized to an entire group, which is then depreciated. And finally, the negative value imposed on the group becomes the justification and legitimatization for hostility and aggression.

Accordingly, Memmi has shown that racism has no real content, and therefore it can change at the will of the oppressor. Indeed, it is not the nature or the kind of difference that matters, only that a negative difference is perceived to exist. "What counts is the form, the self-approbation that emerges from the assumptions and disguises inherent in any negative valuation of the other group."[15] It is illogical that racism can be only a personal matter because to make a generalization requires the presence or consideration of a group; thus, racism is a social matter. Racism as a social system relies on its ability to define the Other. The act of definition requires the exercise of the power of one group over another. The fact of definition sets up a dependency of the dominant on the Other for their own social identity and on the hostility engendered by that dependence. Only legitimization of the dominance as a relationship provides any semblance of content.

Critical for understanding racism in its many forms is to see the integration of the biographical, the historical, the personal, and the analytical in the mind of the racist. Memmi defines racism in two senses. In the narrow sense, racism is the focus of biological difference or specific traits that are given to devised paradigms called "races." Biology, or the criterion given for the discriminating category, acts as a pretext or an alibi. The function of racism is "both the rationalization and the emblem for a system of social oppression."[16] Memmi elaborates:

> Racism subsumes and reveals all the elements of dominance and subjugation, aggression and fear, injustice and the defense of privilege, the apologetics of domination with its self-justifications, the disparaging myths and the images of the dominated, and finally the social nullification of the victim people for the benefit of the persecutors and executioners—all of this is contained in it.[17]

Racism in the broad sense is self-valuation through the devaluation of the Other, and the justification of verbal or physical assault or abuse. Racism in the broad sense is more prevalent than it is in the narrow sense. As Memmi explains, "It would seem reasonable to consider biological racism, which is a relatively recent phenomenon, as a special case of the other, whose practices are more widespread and much older."[18]

Memmi and others also warn of the danger of an illusional insistence that there is actually no difference among peoples.[19] He cautions that some psychoanalytic theories "affirm that racism is built on heterophobia, a fear of difference, of those who are different, that is, a fear of the unknown. But the psychoanalysts ask, 'What is this "unknown"?' and, they respond, it is our own unconscious, which is frightening because it is strange, and we wish to project it on[to] others."[20]

Clearly this and any other purely theoretical approaches avoid dealing with the concrete realities of human differences that do, at least initially, spark discomfort because they are unknown to us. Heterophobia, fear of difference, or xenophobia, fear of strangers, is each rooted in particular concrete experiences and contexts. Any "cure" for such fears needs to be dealt with in equally concrete and experiential ways. One deeply embedded myth—strongly reinforced by Western education, colonial, and slave mentalities—is that it is bad to be different.[21] This stance fully undergirds neoliberal "color-blind" approaches to resolving racism in the United States and the xenophobic violence involving immigrants in Europe and elsewhere.[22] It would thus be a huge mistake on the part of any antiracist effort, particularly by the church, to stress the universal without also acknowledging the particularity of differences that exist among all peoples. The real task for the church is not only to assist people in developing their intellectual capacity, character, and spirituality, but also to teach them the skills and strategies necessary to draw on "difference" as the occasion for empowerment of all and celebration of the presence of God's grace in all people, rather than as the basis for fearful exclusion or even violence.

# FROM RACE TO RACISM
# IN THE TWENTY-FIRST CENTURY

In light of Memmi's definition, today three forms of racism require greater attention: color-coded racism, tribalism, and xenophobia.

## Color-Coded Racism

Color-coded racism is most viperous in that it presents the criteria for the inferiority of the Other in biological and phenotypical terms such as skin color, bodily shape, cranial structure, and Negroid, Caucasoid, or Mongoloid features. Through a process of racialization, one group (the white majority, for instance) targets the Other as inferior, formulating a mythical or ideological construct to support and provide rationale or justification for legal, social, political, and unjust discrimination and oppression.[23] The particular characteristics defining inferiority or superiority are indelibly stamped into the very body of the Other and thus cannot be changed through any form of assimilation into the "superior" way of being or culture.[24]

## Tribalism or Ethnocentricity

Tribalism names a form of racialized relations between ethnic groups. A tribe is "a social organization or division comprising several local villages, bands, or lineages or other groups sharing a common ancestry, language, culture, and name."[25] A general sense of belonging that comes through membership in a tribe or some group is necessary for human well-being. But tribalism is the attitude and practice of harboring such a strong feeling of loyalty or bonds to one's tribe that one excludes or even demonizes those Others who do not belong to that group. This exclusion is manifested in engaging or failing to engage with the Other in obtaining the necessities of life, education, employment, just and fair governance, healthy political and economic relations, membership in social and religious groups, or equitable opportunities for rising to positions of authority or leadership.

Tribalism or ethnocentrism is a universal human tendency rooted in the reality that people are most comfortable with those familiar to and like themselves. However, people prosper and thrive best in a way of life that allows all groups to sustain themselves within a stable social, political, and economic order. The legacy of colonialism is the deep disruption of such systems among those colonized.

Significantly, colonizers needed to justify their takeover of the property and persons of those they conquered. Justification required demonizing tribal peoples, exaggerating any conflicts among them. The most common technique used to gain control (of often powerful groups) was that of "divide and conquer." One of the colonizers' most egregious practices was to arm one tribe, set that group up against their neighbors, and then employ them to "catch" their "enemy" and sell them to the slave traders. The colonizers' act of eliminating one group or favoring another over against the Others was a genocidal activity.

The effects of this damage live on in the postcolonial world in many ways. As the recent postelection events in Kenya showed us, the most devastating effect that has plagued newly independent nations is that divisions remaining among peoples threaten formation of any positive cohesive national unity. Tribalism and ethnocentrism infect all aspects of life with corruption, graft, incompetence, and injustices, resulting in a general sense of distrust and disenfranchisement among all citizens. Such an unstable political situation, when combined with dire economic poverty, has frequently been volatile, even to the point of genocide, as in Rwanda and Burundi (1994).

## Xenophobia

Literally, "xenophobia" means "fear of the stranger" (Greek: *xenos*, stranger, foreigner; *phobos*, fear). It is

> a somewhat vague psychological concept describing a person's disposition to fear (or abhor) other persons or groups perceived as outsiders. Xenophobia may have a rational basis to it, such as when it refers to a worker whose job is threatened by the intrusion of migrants whom he labels as outsiders and therefore fears. It may also take an irrational form, for example, when someone fears Sikhs because he or she believes they carry knives for use as potential weapons. But to call a person xenophobic does not necessarily say anything about the rationality of that condition. Nor does it entail examining the underlying causes of their disposition.[26]

Xenophobia is so lethal because, rational or not, it is easily manipulated and fueled toward mass hysteria, which can fling even the most levelheaded and altruistic persons into aggressive oppression of the Other.[27] Evidence for this development is found in emerging political parties: the French Front National, the Dutch Centrumdemocraten and the Centrum Partij, the Austrian Freiheitlechen, the German Republikaner and Deutsche Volkunion, the Belgian Vlaamis Blok and the Front National.[28] In the United States, as recently as 1989, a well-known Klu Klux Klansman, David Duke, ran as a Republican and won a seat in Congress.[29]

In recent years, especially in Europe, three interrelated phenomena have combined to feed xenophobia and xenophobic behavior. Neil MacMaster exposes them as

> the skillful elaboration and diffusion of a "New Racism" that offered a powerful [1] ideological revision of traditional biological racism; [2] the concurrent emergence and electoral challenge of xenophobic "National-Populist" parties that made use of the new current of thinking on cultural racism and national identity; and lastly, [3] the tendency of the "New Right" conservative parties, as well as socialist and all mainstream parties, to play to the same gallery, particularly through the construction of "Fortress Europe" and the scapegoating of refugees.[30]

The New Racism plays on latent xenophobia by lauding the importance and natural necessity of cultural difference. A typical statement of the proponents of this position is "I'm not xenophobic, nor does the fact that I like the French and France best mean that I hate foreigners or hate other countries."[31] Here the vocabulary of "culture" is the code word for the language of "race." Antiracists' efforts toward affirming the values of cultural diversity and creating "multicultural societies" are manipulated to exaggerate and emphasize the impending loss of a comfortable, predictable homogeneous society. These manipulations are supported theoretically using Italian Marxist philosopher Antonio Gramsci's claim that the state depends on material force, economic relations, yet also on a cultural hegemony enforced by controlling people's worldview, through managing ideas, language, and their discourse, and thus creating meaning.[32] The New Racism supporters also rely on sociobiology, reasoning that certain ways of doing things are right because they are natural, and if they are natural, they must be true. Such reasoning argues that people live in particular countries, just like fish thrive in certain habitats, or wolves live in packs.

Further support is garnered by claiming that the ruling hegemonic majority is a victim of the disruptive invasion of the Other, and the support given those invaders by the "race relations industry." This victimization is often proclaimed and popularized by using cartoons showing ordinary citizens being battered by "the loony leftists," "fanatic liberals," or "radical teachers." The media is flooded with new vocabulary recasting racism in populist "commonsense" terms that play to those who experience themselves disenfranchised by the governing "elites" who control the society.[33]

Especially in the 1980s and 1990s, and on both sides of the Atlantic, the xenophobic national populists were able to gain ground in electoral and parliamentary systems by focusing on this strategy (above). They gave an "acceptable face" to their biases and strategies as the "reasonable right thing to do" to protect national identity and culture. They offered strong, simply stated solutions to two basic fears held by the hegemonic majority: (1) the loss of power and control due to the influx of vast numbers of immigrants and refugees of various colors, religions, and cultures from all over the globe into Europe and North America and (2) anxiety about the threat these movements posed for keeping the "old wealth" secure. These solutions were to be accomplished via mainstream political involvement.

Ambiguities among the mainstream political parties in Europe and North America made it easier for xenophobic ideas and actions to take hold. The complexities of the new issues brought about by globalization, immigrants, and refugees caught the mainline politicians without a vocabulary and a plan to address these issues in a popular commonsensical manner. Thus, conventional politicians found themselves in a defensive posture that required compromises and self-preserving strategies to "get tough on immigration." Numerous harsh draconian measures were passed on both sides of the Atlantic to limit immigration and fortify national identities. Many formal declarations about combating racism were brilliantly paraded, but they were weak, rarely enforced, and effectively utterly symbolic.

## THE COMPLICITY OF THE CHURCH AND THE IDEA OF RACE

The record of Christian churches concerning the ethics of power and racism, tribalism, and xenophobia is at best mixed. Across history, the actions of church leaders ranged from the biblical prophetic to the near demonic when they and lay Christians yielded to the pressures of their contexts and lost sight of the deepest convictions of respect, equality in Christ, justice, and charity.[34] Just as today, exemplified by the degree of compliance by Roman Catholics with magisterial teaching, authentic Christian praxis varied widely. Indeed, the stories that believers tell, rather than their knowledge of papal teaching or doctrines, express their appropriation of the Christian faith in their personal lives and are most influential for their moral actions.[35]

Thus, it is imperative that the church and its ministers not merely impart doctrinal and dogmatic condemnations of racial injustices of the past, but also proactively engage the faithful in experiential learning toward preventing racism's sinful violence, now and in the future. The challenge for present-day Christians and all people of good will is to learn from the past and honor the victims by not repeating the oppression. While never denying the horrific complicity of the Christian churches—the Roman Catholic church in particular—in oppression, slavery, or genocide, significantly and ultimately the official church held a line in favor of its ideals on at least two counts.

First, the church constantly returned to its fundamental position that each human person is created in the image and likeness of God and that each person bears an inviolable dignity that must be respected at all cost. How this foundational principle was interpreted in relation to those understood to be Other frequently had more to do with the current cultural and scientific understanding of the human person than theological tenets. Also, the influences of Greek dualism on Christianity allowed tolerating slavery, providing (cf. Philemon) there was a harmonious spirit of charity between masters and slaves.[36]

Second, the church held that in Christ, all persons are redeemed and redeemable. Doctrinally, the incarnation and the cross placed no one beyond the bounds of salvation. Thus, early Christians, influenced by their contexts and cultures, drew distinctions of difference, but they did not practice racism as we know it.[37] For example, Greeks allowed that barbarians could be civilized, Romans believed that all slaves could be emancipated, and Africans could be converted as was the Ethiopian (Acts 8:26–39). Space here is insufficient for an adequate examination of divergences from these liberating interpretations of human difference. But certainly, especially today, the church cannot rest on its ancient laurels.

## FACING THE DIAGNOSTIC DILEMMA

In 1988 the Pontifical Justice and Peace Commission promulgated the statement on the issue, The Church and Racism: Toward a More Fraternal Society.[38] It defines racism as "rooted in the reality of sin [as] . . . awareness of biologically determined superiority of one's own race or ethnic group with respect to others, developed above all from the practice of colonization and slavery at the dawn of the modern era" (§2). The commission then distinguished nine forms of racism:

- Exclusion and aggression (§8)
- Institutional racism (§9)
- Victimization and genocide of aboriginal peoples (§10)
- Religious and ethnic discrimination (§11)
- Ethnocentrism or tribalism (§12)
- Social racism against the third world (§13)
- Spontaneous racism [xenophobia] (§14)
- Anti-Semitism (§15)
- Artificial procreation and genetic manipulation (§16)

This document signaled a tremendous advancement in the church's willingness and capacities not only to denounce sinful practices, but also to utilize social analysis and act concretely to affect social, political, and economic change (§§24–32). Still, the emphasis is clearly on the conversion of heart: "Racial prejudice, which denies the equal dignity of all members of the human family and blasphemes the Creator, can only be eradicated by going to its roots, where it is formed; in the human heart" (§24).

Thirteen years later (2001) the Pontifical Council for Justice and Peace issued its Contribution to the World Conference against Racism, Racial Discrimination, Xenophobia, and Related Intolerance.[39] This document affirms the 1988 statement but goes further to tackle the need for reconciliation for past injustices (§§7–12). Additionally, it focuses on the need for teaching the values of human dignity, solidarity, and the common good in a variety of ways (§§13–17). Significantly, it supports concrete affirmative action (just opportunity) to mitigate past injustices and the denial of opportunity to peoples across the globe (§§18–19). The church also recognized the changing shape of racial injustice due to globalization and the unprecedented numbers of migrants and refugees in the world at the start of the new millennium (§§20–22).

With these ideas in mind, we turn once again to Memmi's work. It is critical that the church takes heed of what he calls "the discriminatory didactic" of the spiraling dynamics of racism: fear, followed by aggression, followed by more fear and aggression. Racists are fearful people. Underneath all racism, according to Memmi, racial affirmation is an instrument for negative self-definition that compensates for the feelings of personal vulnerability that accompanies fear. Indeed, racism in the narrow sense is easily defeated on its own weak logic. But racism in the broad sense requires the ability to generalize, and in order to generalize according to the skewed logic (illogic) required by racism, one needs support from a society and its structures. Memmi forewarns: "The relative structural coherence of racism in the narrow sense, even in its obsessive aggressiveness and self-interest, is confirmed precisely by the existence of racism in the broad sense."[40]

Thus, it cannot be stressed strongly enough, if the church is to be effective in combating racism and establishing racial justice, it must remain vigilant and deal with structural sin, not only personal sin. It must challenge oppressive social, economic, political, and sexual structures that frame the very world in which we would have "conversion of heart" take place. The church must not only proclaim doctrines and theological or moral principles, but also engage in training and forming moral agents who can critically analyze concrete realities in light of the gospel and view differences as gifts and as positive opportunities. On this count, the church has a long way to go. As Marquette University moral theologian Bryan Massingale showed in his classic analysis of U.S. (Catholic) Episcopal teaching on racism between 1990 and 2000, how racism is defined, analyzed, and diagnosed will also determine the judgment concerning what action is required to overcome it.[41] Shamefully, Massingale found that out of some twenty Catholic documents on racism promulgated between 1990 and 2000, only four adequately define racism as both structural sin and personal sin and address concrete corrective actions. Certainly we can and must do better!

Minimally, the very existence of official church teaching robs racism of any ethical legitimacy. But more fundamentally, while requiring a spiritual base, such teaching must stipulate that much can and must be done to create just social, political, and economic structures within which integral conversion can happen. Beyond that, actual commitment of real and substantive resources—time, talent, and treasure—must be given to such efforts.

Fortunately, there is hope on the horizon. The three most recent pastorals on race reflect adequate definition of racisms, accounting for structural and personal sin. The Bishops' Conference of England and Wales published and implemented exemplary in-house policy changes designed to model remedies for structural racism. Pastorals by Chicago's Cardinal George and Archbishop Hughes of New Orleans each gave substantive attention to "White Privilege" and implemented pastoral plans, engaging resources sufficient for the task.[42]

The obvious understatement is that all of this is not enough. Ultimately, it must be integral to the mission of all Christians, indeed for all people of goodwill, to define racisms adequately, develop the moral sensitivity to recognize this evil where it lurks, and then proactively dismantle it. If we do not do this, then like those convened in Edinburgh in 1910, racisms can easily define us and our work.

So let our commitment and our prayer be that, animated by the gospel, inspired by the Holy Spirit, and empowered by God's grace, we may proactively join our efforts to the deep yearning at the heart of Jesus' mission "that they all may be one . . ." (cf. John 17:22–23).

# 10

# A Beloved Earth Community

## *Christian Mission in an Ecological Age*

### David M. Rhoads and Barbara R. Rossing

Earth is in crisis. The planet is facing major ecological problems: global warming, loss of species diversity, loss of forests and arable land, disposal of garbage and toxic waste, pollution of air and land and water, overpopulation, depletion of nonreplaceable natural resources, diminution of food sources, ocean acidification and collapse of fisheries, among other degradations. Issues of human justice—discrimination, poverty, oppression, and displacement—are related to every ecological change. The issues are many and complex. And the survival of creation as we humans have known it is at stake.

When the Protestant missionary societies met in Edinburgh in 1910 to deliberate on evangelizing the earth before Christ returns, all of its eight study commissions paid scant attention to the impact of industrialization on nature. The Global North was still intoxicated with the fruits of scientific inventions and technological progress, and they perceived mission principally as sharing the gospel to the Global South, civilizing them through Christianity. At Edinburgh and for the better part of the century since then, the concept of mission has been anthropocentric, focusing almost exclusively on human beings and neglecting human responsibility to care for creation—as though nature were something neutral or a benevolent stage upon which humans play out their lives. Much to the contrary, human beings are absolutely embedded in nature.

We offer special thanks to Ogbu Kalu for his support and helpful suggestions in the preparation of this essay.

We *are* nature; and we humans cannot eat, breathe, sleep, act, work, or live without the rest of nature. Knowing this, we cannot now think of mission to people apart from God's mission to all creation.

A century later, the world is alarmed at the threats to the sustainability of the planet Earth due to human activities, to human ideologies that privilege the domination over nature, and to the human-centered conception of mission. Since the 1920s the church has realized that it does not exist for any other reason but mission—that the church should be the sign, presence, foretaste, and witness that the reign of God is here. So if the church exists for the sake of the world, it must pay attention to what is happening to the world and cease to concentrate on an individualistic spiritual mission of personal salvation without also addressing the need to restore creation as a whole. A holistic Christian mission connects the interrelationship between human beings and the rest of creation.

Recent developments have brought the issue of environmental degradation to the forefront worldwide. Al Gore's much-acclaimed 2006 film, *An Inconvenient Truth*, raised public awareness about global warming. In 2007, the Intergovernmental Panel on Climate Change (IPCC), representing the work of over three thousand scientists and other climate experts worldwide, released a series of four reports, *Climate Change 2007*, attesting that there is 90 percent certainty that human activity since the industrial revolution has been the major cause of global warming.[1]

In this twenty-first century, an adequate human response to the ecological state of the world—especially among industrialized countries—will require a transformation as great as the transformation that occurred in the United States and other Allied societies when they rose to the challenge of war in the 1940s. In the United States, for example, the whole economy was redirected to address the challenge of war. New industries arose overnight. Goods were rationed. People grew their own food. Cars were limited. Everyone made sacrifices. The resources of the society were marshaled to rise and meet the challenge. That is what industrial nations now need to do at national and global levels to address the challenge of the ecological crisis: embark on a transformation of industries to renewable energy, transition to eating local foods, transfer of resources to develop and share new technologies, limits on the use of pesticides, prohibitions against clearing forests, rationing of energy and water, protection of wetlands and wilderness, among many other things.[2]

Father Thomas Berry has said that from an evolutionary point of view, humanity is entering a new era, the Ecozoic Age—an age in which ecological issues will dominate our global life together. He argues that creating a sustainable environmental lifestyle on the planet is the "great work" of our time. It is a work in which all people can participate, a work that all must embrace if life on this planet is to be sustained.[3] This work is not easy: it will require intention and sacrifice.

The church is called to participate in this great work and, indeed, to offer leadership. There are many reasons why Christianity in general has failed to show much significant change of attitude toward Earth. Indeed, Christian traditions and practices have contributed significantly to the problems.[4] Nevertheless, since 1983, worldwide ecumenical organizations of churches—the World Council of Churches, the World Alliance of Reformed Churches, the Lutheran World Federation, and others—have held many meetings to covenant member churches to design new ways of developing a relationship with all of God's creation, to understand afresh how God works in the world of the nature around us, and to build and nurture beloved Earth communities. In the United States, for example, the National Partnership for the Environment was formed to foster care for creation among four representative groups: the National Council of Churches, the National Catholic Conference, the Evangelical Environmental Network, and the Coalition on the Environment and Jewish Life.[5] Clearly, the care for the creation is an emergent theme in contemporary mission.

In order for the church to rise to the occasion, however, it will need to go through a thoroughgoing reformation. Worldwide, churches must transform proclamation, preaching, worship, teaching, witnessing, communal formation, action, and advocacy so as to make care for all creation foundational to missional vocation. This is a reformation that will involve deep repentance, a *metanoia*—a mind change and a practice change. This is a reformation for the whole church. It will take diverse shapes in different cultures and countries and economies. Church bodies and congregations will need to be in solidarity with and to be inspired by each other.[6] Christians in the Global North will need to advocate for structural change that acknowledges the ecological debt that the North owes to the South, as well as to simplify life and lifestyle in order to minimize exploitation of Earth and people. Christians in the Global South will need to advocate for sustainable development practices and indigenous Earth practices such as tree planting and water conservation.

And this is a reformation that will unite rather than divide. As such, this reformation will not only be ecumenical but also interfaith, because all religions bear salient traditions and resources that can be garnered for crafting new ecoethics for Earth. Christians, Jews, Muslims, Buddhists, Hindus, Taoists, adherents of indigenous religions, among others—all will find together common ground (Earth!) in the collective calling to Earth care. We have much to learn from each other.[7] Perhaps the Rainbow Covenant contracted in Assisi in 1986 is an example of how the shift can be made to a creation mystique and an orthopraxis based on reciprocity.[8] It was achieved through rituals of confession, repentance, covenant renewal, and *conscientization*. Media facilities were employed, and an ecumenical mobilization of religious leaders and scientists ensured that the message reached the core of global culture.

So, if the church is to go through a comprehensive reformation, what principles might guide us? The following reflections suggest five key mandates to guide such a transformation of Christian identity and mission.

## LEARN ABOUT THE DEGRADATION OF GOD'S CREATION

The first mandate for mission calls the church to respond to the ecological state of the world. To do this, the church must be conversant with the scientific perspectives on the natural world in its current degraded state:

• Loss of species diversity. Scientist E. O. Wilson has estimated that at the current rate of extinction by human activity, the Earth is losing about one hundred species a day and will lose one half of animal and plant species by the end of the century! Diversity is the condition that enables life to adapt for survival.[9]

• Loss of forests (the lungs of the planet) is happening annually at the rate of the size of the nation Paraguay. Each year, worldwide, arable land (the food source of the planet) is being lost to desert at the rate of the size of the country of Oman.

• Pollution of the air, the water, and the land: emissions in the air; industrial and agricultural runoff in aquifers, lakes, rivers, and oceans; and pesticides, herbicides, and toxic waste in the land. The United States alone produces ten million metric tons of waste each year. Fifteen years ago, a University of Michigan scientist who had studied life in Antarctica for many years shared that his team had never examined a specimen of sea life or land animal that did not show traces of Styrofoam.[10]

• Population. The world has gone from one billion to six billion people in the last several centuries and will reach seven billion in 2012. In terms of the effect on plants and animals in many regions of the world, especially in the Global North, humans can be considered an invasive species.

• Global warming is the most dramatic and the most urgent ecological crisis. The IPCC has detailed the causes of global warming since the industrial revolution of the 1800s, including emissions from industrial stacks, cars, trucks, ships, airplanes, and houses as well as methane gases from raising cattle and other animals for human consumption—which turns out to be greater than emissions from all cars and trucks in the world. Before the industrial revolution, there were 275 parts per million of carbon dioxide in the atmosphere. The number is now approaching 385. This situation is trapping heat within the atmosphere and causing the average temperature of Earth to rise progressively.

Projections about the consequences of global climate have a wide range. According to the IPCC, global warming is happening much faster than scientists had previously forecasted. The melting of the polar ice sheet is an example of potentially irreversible feedback loops. The more the ice melts, the less light reflects back into outer space, and the greater the warming of Earth. As the permafrost melts, huge amounts of carbon deposits underneath, in the form of methane, will be released into the atmosphere. Warming temperatures cause dry conditions that increase fires, which in turn decimate forested areas. Such feedback loops are increasing the rate of global warming.

The consequences of global warming outlined by the IPCC are already evident: extreme and unpredictable weather patterns; rising oceans that are covering low-level islands and coastal regions; loss of freshwater reserves due in part to loss of glaciers; increased incidents of fires resulting from heat and dryness; shifting climates that change ecosystems and areas of food production; the depletion of oceanic ecosystems; the loss of plant and animal species as their natural climate conditions are lost. Every human population group on Earth is already and will be profoundly affected by these changes.[11] All of these problems are interrelated. Individually, they are alarming enough. Together, they are even staggering. Unless we face the size of these problems, we will not realize the size of the solutions necessary to address the problems.

There are some promising signs, particularly in retarding ozone depletion. Ozone depletion is caused mainly by chlorofluorocarbons rising to the upper atmosphere and destabilizing ozone molecules that protect Earth's surface from deadly ultraviolet rays. Holes have appeared in the ozone layer at the poles, and there is thinning throughout. The Montreal Protocol, an international treaty forged in 1989, has led to significant worldwide reduction in the carbon molecules that cause ozone depletion and has provided the conditions for the ozone layer to begin a process of restoration. Such cooperative efforts can serve as a model for nations to agree on ecological commitments and the sharing of appropriate technologies. Similarly, the 1992 Earth Summit in Rio de Janeiro began international efforts to lower greenhouse gases. The subsequent protocol developed in the 1997 summit in Kyoto, Japan, has now been signed, as of 2009, by 183 countries. Unfortunately, the United States and some other industrialized countries have not agreed to the provisions.

Humanity needs technological advances and cooperative efforts to transform the systems that are destructive of humans and nature. Individuals, organizations, factories, and corporations need to create a grassroots movement to diminish destructive human behavior. Religions are the largest grassroots organizations already in existence in the world. We are called to mobilize our energies and resources. Christians must be knowledgeable about ecological conditions so that we will repent, stop negative behavior, initiate positive actions to care for creation, and serve as a model for others to follow.

## RELATE ECOLOGY WITH HUMAN JUSTICE

The second mandate for mission is to embrace a Christian ethic that acknowledges the interrelationship between ecological conditions and issues of human justice. We have separated human justice and Earth care to our detriment. The social justice movement and the environmental movement have been separate and sometimes at odds with each other. James Cone, the well-known U.S. proponent of black theology, has observed that there is a common view by environmentalists that "Blacks don't care about the environment," and at the same time there is a common view among social justice advocates that "White people care more about the endangered whale and the spotted owl than they do about the survival of young Blacks in our nation's cities." The truth is, Cone concludes, *we need each other* because we "are fighting the same enemy—human beings' domination of each other and nature."[12] Brazilian theologian Leonardo Boff has made the same argument:

> Liberation theology and ecological discourse have something in common. . . . Both discourses have as their starting point a cry: The cry of the poor for life, freedom, and beauty (cf. Exodus 3:7) and the cry of the earth (cf. Romans 8:22–23). Both seek liberation of the poor . . . and a liberation of the Earth.[13]

In an effort to see the problems as one, people in these movements often speak in terms of ecological justice or ecojustice: the interrelated and integrated quest for justice for the whole Earth community.[14]

Human injustice is inextricably interrelated to injustice against Earth. One example of this is "environmental racism," especially evident in the United States, where it is well documented that a greater percentage of people of color live near polluting factories, waste incinerators, chemical brownfields, and other ecological hazards.[15] Another example is Hurricane Katrina, which hit the New Orleans area of the United States in August 2005. It was a disaster caused as much by human activity degrading the environment as by natural forces. The temperature in the Gulf of Mexico was one degree higher than usual, arguably due to global warming, which increased the intensity and length of the hurricane. The natural buffer of wetlands, which would have protected the mainland, had been developed into human projects. And the people most affected by Katrina were the poor, the elderly, the sick, people of color—people whose area of the city was most affected and who had the fewest resources to cope.[16]

This same dynamic is true of other global ecological crises, including global warming. The most vulnerable communities, particularly those who live close to the land, are bearing and will bear the brunt of these changes to our planet. Developing countries will be the most affected and will have the least resources with which to respond. For example, the melting of glaciers in the Andes and Himalayas is resulting in the loss of freshwater reserves for huge populations of South America and Asia. In Africa, environmental changes tend to have severe impacts on families: deforestation vitiates the energy supply, drought and soil degradation ruin the food sources, and there are few alternatives, which the West may have.[17] The loss of ice in the Arctic region and the burning of rain forests are making indigenous peoples into environmental refugees. Pollution of air is causing a tremendous increase in respiratory ailments, especially in inner cities, where the poor reside. Pollution of water in remote regions is the source of an alarming rise in water-borne diseases.

Cone's comment about "human beings' exploitation of each other and nature" is right on target. In "developed" societies in the North, we place profits above both people and nature. Much of our contemporary global economy is based upon the most efficient ways to strip resources from the land and pay the lowest wages to workers, without regard for their health and well-being. When we do that, we reduce land and people to commodities that serve the financial markets.

Consider the differences between standard commercial coffee and fair-trade coffee. Most coffee is produced by a system in which the coffee plants have been grown on plantations in the Global South, where the land is stripped; crops are made to grow by toxic fertilizers, pesticides, and herbicides; the workers (often including children) are paid below-standard wages; they are subjected to long hours in the sun and exposure to toxins; and there are about five middle people (landowners, producers, exporters, distributors, retailers) who get most of the profits (or 90–95% of the retail price). By contrast, fair-trade, shade-grown coffee is produced under quite different conditions: trees and shrubs are preserved on the land, and their foliage serves as fertilizer; the workers are in a cooperative; they are paid a living wage and work under healthy conditions; and there are few middle people. The production of most coffee is a common example of exploitation both of the poor and of Earth. The fair-trade alternative is humane to people and sustainable for nature. There is a need for fair-trade everything.

This second mandate for mission is important because we Christians cannot allow environmental commitments to lead us to ignore the commitment to social justice. Nor can we allow our commitment to human justice to lead us to neglect the environmental crises. We need to expand our commitment to include countering the degradations of Earth, and we need to double our efforts for human justice. It is all of one piece. As Christians, we all stand together in solidarity with the oppressed, the exploited, the marginalized, the poor, the sick, the elderly, people of color, women—*and now also endangered nature.*

## SEE CARE FOR CREATION AS BASIC
## TO VOCATION AND MISSION

The third mandate for mission is to recognize that the Bible presents care for creation as fundamental to our human vocation and mission. For the last centuries in the field of biblical studies, the Global North has read Christian Scripture through human-centered eyes, as if the Bible were about *human* salvation-history alone. In this view, the ancient Hebrew people were superior because they forsook the nature gods for a God who called primarily for morality among humans. Christianity tended to interpret the command in the creation stories to exercise dominion as though it had to do with domination and exploitation of nature for human use. By contrast, through creation-care lenses, interpreters are able to see that the Bible is really about salvation history of *all creation* and about the foundational mission of human beings to serve Earth as a means to serve God.[18]

Biblical creation stories teach the nature of the human relationship with creation. For example, the name given to the first human was "Adam," the masculine form of *adamah* ('ădāmâ), the Hebrew word for tillable soil, out of which Adam was created. The message is that human creatures belong to the earth (Gen. 2:5–15).[19] If for all these centuries we had translated "Adam" literally with the name "Earth" or "Earth-one," it would have made a difference in how we humans think about ourselves and our human relationship to Earth. Nature does not belong to us. We belong to nature. The writers of the Bible were indigenous people who knew this because they themselves were dependent upon the land.[20]

In the creation stories, the command to "exercise dominion" does not mean domination or exploitation. Rather, it is the word used of rulers who are to care for and be responsible to the people in their realm (Gen. 1:1–2:4). And the commands given to humans that are typically translated "to till and to keep" (2:15) are words used of slaves for their service to those to whom they were beholden. So we humans are to serve and to preserve the Earth (Gen. 2:5–15). This turns our relationship to Earth upside down. It puts qualifications even on our position of "dominion" by defining our responsibility in terms of serving—just as Jesus teaches us to "be last of all and servant of all" (Mark 9:35).

In the Bible, all creatures are valued for their own sake, not just for what they can do for humans. God's creation provides not just for humans but for the animals as well, as Psalm 104 tells it, because the grass is created for the cattle, the trees for the birds, the crags for the mountain goats—and God gives to all their food in due season. God created all living things and called them "good." In the creation stories, *all creatures*, not only humans, are commanded to be fruitful and multiply and fill the earth (Gen. 1:1–2:4). So we humans are to relate to the rest of creation in such a way that all creatures thrive together. The covenant given to Moses was primarily about God's relationship with humans, but it also provided for animals to rest on the Sabbath day and for the land to lie fallow in the Sabbath year. Even more creation-encompassing was the covenant God made with Noah and with the birds of the air and the fish of the sea and the land animals, to preserve Earth for all to thrive together (Gen. 9:8–17; Hos. 2:18).[21]

In the biblical view, all creation is sacramental. Earth is filled with God's glory (cf. Num. 14:21). Furthermore, all creation is called to worship and praise God—just by being what it is and doing what it does: "Let the sea roar, and all that fills it; let the field exult, and everything in it. Then shall the trees of the forest sing for joy" (1 Chron. 16:29–34). All of creation together, human and nonhuman creatures and the rest of the created order, is to "praise the name of the LORD" (Ps. 148). What a difference it would make to Christian worship practices if worshipers saw Earth as our sanctuary and all creation as partners in adoration![22]

In the Bible the degradation of creation is interrelated with human injustice. When there is injustice against fellow humans, the land withers, the grapevines dry up, and the granaries fail (Joel 1:1–20). In turn, salvation involves the restoration of creation. When Jesus announces that "The kingdom of God has arrived" (cf. Mark 1:15), he is announcing the restoration of creation to liberation and wholeness. Jesus ministered to the most vulnerable of the earth, which must now for us include also endangered creation. According to Paul, through Jesus "God was pleased to reconcile all things, whether on earth or in heaven, by making peace through the blood of his cross" (Col. 1:20).

Like the Old Testament, the New Testament does not envision personal salvation apart from community. Nor does it envision human salvation apart from all creation. Paul hears all creation groaning in labor pains for the "revealing of the children of God," who will manifest peace and justice for all creation (Rom. 8:18–25). And the book of Revelation has this astounding vision in which the writer hears the entire creation—everything in heaven, on the earth, under the earth, and in the sea—praising God and singing, "Blessing and honor and glory and might be to our God who sits upon the throne and to the Lamb forever and ever" (cf. 5:13).

The final vision of the new Jerusalem is that of a "renewed heaven and a renewed earth" (cf. Rev. 21:1–27). And God comes to dwell among people. In that vision, the river of the water of life flows down the middle of the city streets; it is available free of charge, so that the poor will never go thirsty. And on either side of the river is the tree of life, yielding fruit twelve months of the year, so that no one will go hungry. This is one glorious vision of God and humans and the rest of nature—the Creator and all creation—living in harmony together.[23]

This third principle is important because Christians must learn to read Scripture in creation-centered ways. When we read it through the lens of creation, we discover that humans and the rest of nature are one. We discover that loving and tending creation is fundamental to what it means to be human. It is our mission as Christians to create a sustainable future in which the whole Earth community survives and thrives. The Bible is about God's love for creation and God's mandate for humans to be Earth-keepers with God. Scripture teaches us that creation care is *not* just one more social issue among others. Rather, care for creation is foundational to our vocation as human beings. It is as basic as the great commandment: Love God, love your neighbor, and love creation.

## RECOGNIZE THEOLOGY AS SHAPING HOW WE ACT

The fourth principle is to realize that our mission to all creation leads us to see theology in new ways, because *how we think* shapes *how we act*. Christian theological ideas are often not Earth friendly. For the most part, they are anthropocentric, dualistic, and individualistic. They do not respect the intrinsic value and integrity of nature, nor do they affirm that God is really immanent in creation as well as transcendent. A test of theology in this century might be whether theological ideas promote the sustaining of the whole Earth community.

There are many insights from theology that can lead to thinking in Earth-friendly ways.[24] First is to strengthen our grounding in the first article of the (Nicene) creed, affirming our belief in God as creator. God did not create the world and then separate from it. Nor was Earth formed as we know it never to change. Rather, God is involved in the process of continuous creation.[25] It has taken about four and a half billion years for life to emerge on this planet to where we are today in the evolutionary process. And the Earth continues to change. God is in and with creation, influencing and shaping but not controlling. God is not above Earth, manipulating events and outcomes. Rather, as Paul says, "in everything God works for good" (Rom. 8:28 RSV). Because of this, life is to be considered sacred. A theology of reverence for all of life will serve Christians well. If we humans do not have reverence for creation, we will not care for it.

Reverence in religions of indigenous people can be a model for a rebirth of Christian theology. As we have said, the Bible itself was written by indigenous people living close to the land. Also, Native Americans have much to teach about reverence for Mother Earth.[26] Among the communities in the Global South, where many cultures still operate with preindustrial perspectives, indigenous worldviews still sacralize space and the world of nature: land, forests, and bodies of water under the guardianship of the Earth deity. In Africa, the Earth deity is so sacred that she is regarded as the guardian of morality. Earth and the ancestors together unite in creating a theory of obligation in communities where there is no secular theory of obligation.[27] For example, indigenous communities often practice rotational farming systems that allow parts of the community's land to renew itself. Christian theology can learn from such reverence.

A renewed Christian theology will consider the whole of creation as the realm of God's saving activity. God creates Earth, and God loves creation. As developed mammals, as higher primates and more, humans are embedded in creation. Along with God, humans are also now engaged in the process of the ongoing evolution of Earth, including the changes happening due to global warming and other degradations of Earth's ecosystems. Consequently, sin includes our injustices toward the rest of nature as well as toward other human beings: exploitation of life, lack of limits on our behavior, pursuit of a consumer lifestyle without regard to consequences. The spectrum of sins now includes not only personal and social sins but also ecological sins against God's creation. The degraded creation cries out for liberation and restoration from such human exploitation. As humans, therefore, we are called as partners to work with God to redeem and restore Earth for the sustainability of all life.

Second is to rethink the second article of the creed, our understanding of the work of Jesus Christ, so as to see redemption as a renewal of creation. God's creation was an act of love. The "new creation" through Jesus is also an act of love. As such, redemption is not an escape from matter or physical creation but the restoration of it. Jesus belonged to this Earth; and the New Testament affirms this humanity of Jesus. As Paul affirms, the Son was "born of a woman, born under the law" (Gal. 4:4). And 1 John states it as a test of belief that "Jesus Christ has come in the flesh" (1 John 4:2). In modern terms, the theological confession of the humanity of Jesus affirms that Jesus was in the gene pool, that Jesus too was a mammal—in solidarity not only with all humanity but also in solidarity with all creation.

Jesus was God incarnate in life, embodied Word. But theologically, Christians do not need to portray Jesus as the great exception, as if God is not present anywhere else in creation. Rather, Jesus can be seen as the great exemplar; as the definitive expression of God's incarnation: God is in all of life, and Jesus is what God looks like wherever God may be found. The movement of God is not to draw humans away from Earth but for Jesus to return and for God to be present on Earth. And the risen Jesus needs no longer to be seen as a reality dealing only with spiritual matters of the fate of individuals. Rather, the risen Jesus is a cosmic Christ, redeeming all of life, a Christ large enough to address the size of whatever problems Earth community faces.[28]

Third, we Christians need to rethink the concept of the Holy Spirit.[29] Theologically, the Holy Spirit is the renewer and sustainer of life. How much more ecological can this be—the Holy Spirit bringing about a renewed and sustained Earth? In the New Testament, the Spirit is given to the whole community; individuals experience the Spirit by virtue of being part of the community; and all have gifts that contribute to the well-being of the whole (1 Cor. 12). This is similar to the way a sustainable ecosystem works. Just so, the Holy Spirit works creatively in creation to guide humans to see our place in the Earth community so that we cooperate together with the rest of creation to be sustainable *as* creation. In this way, it is the "communion of the Holy Spirit" that secures the relationship with all creation as a communion of life.

This fourth principle for mission is important because, both consciously and unconsciously, human attitudes and actions toward nature are formed by religious worldviews and ethics.[30] We Christians need to become aware of how we think so that we can see the consequences of our thoughts and assumptions. We need to change our thinking about God and ourselves and Earth so as to provide a solid foundation for Earth-care action.

## INTEGRATE EARTH CARE WITH MISSION AND SPIRITUAL DISCIPLINE

The fifth principle for mission is that Earth-care action is integral to the mission of our Christian communities and our spiritual discipline. Neither systemic nor technological nor behavioral advances will work in the long run without also addressing the issues at a deeper level. At heart, the environmental crisis is a spiritual problem about our human estrangement from nature and our failure to see all of nature as sacramental. Many people, especially people from developed nations, no longer have close relationships to Earth that lead us humans to protect it. We Christians have spent centuries in cultivating the human relationship with God and the human relationship with one another. Now it is time for us to cultivate our relationship also with nature.

Because we are not spiritually, humanly rooted in Earth, we in the Global North tend not to realize the consequences to the Earth community of daily decisions, personal choices, and public policies. Furthermore, we have done much in the name of progress and market expansion without seeing the devastation we have left in our wake. Now we are in a place where Christians in the Global North must address the destructive implications of our daily actions for people in other parts of the globe. People in the Global North must make radical changes to embrace Earth-friendly lifestyles and engage in life-restoring actions,[31] including advocating for mandatory limits on carbon and other governmental policies, just as those in the communities of the Global South must also embrace sustainable actions. The spiritual recovery of the sense of reverence, of awe, of a creation mystique in nature is the first step toward a pro-active program for conserving Earth.

How then can we develop a spiritual discipline of Earth care as part of our identity and mission?[32] Many Christian communities of various denominations worldwide have been engaged in bringing care for creation centrally into their life and mission.[33] This is not an add-on, not a fad, not something a few do on behalf of the rest of the faith community. Rather, creation care is integral to how a congregation goes about doing everything. It is central to the worship life, the educational program, the maintenance of buildings and land, the discipleship of members at home and work, and the commitment to transform the world around them. People are hungry to connect their concern for the natural world to their faith and their faith communities.

Congregations can learn from the attitudes and behaviors of early Christian communities with their expectation of the end of the world and of their experience of an emerging new world.[34] Here are some relevant traits of those New Testament communities.

• There was a deep and urgent sense of mission to call individuals and nations to repent and change behavior, illustrated by the life of the apostle Paul and the mission charges in the Gospels (Mark 13:10; Matt. 28:19–20; Luke 24:47).

• Like Jesus, the early Christians were truth tellers. They fearlessly confronted the destructive powers-that-be, challenging their idolatry and hypocrisy, risking loss, persecution, and death. They made penetrating analyses both of themselves and of their culture, not just in terms of obvious evil, but also in terms of the dark side of goodness and compromises—transforming and replacing these dynamics with life-giving actions and stories.

• Like Jesus, they did prophetic acts. In a sense, their lives were prophetic symbols—healing the sick, feeding the hungry, eating with outcasts, forgiving sinners—all prophetic symbols of a new age impinging on the present.

• Many early Christians withdrew and dissociated from the behavior and lifestyles of the culture. Mark urged people to break with cultural values and institutions that were destructive (Mark 8:27–10:45). The author of Revelation admonished people to withdraw from participation in the social and economic life of idolatrous Rome (18:4).

• They not only broke from the cultures around them; they also formed alternative communities of the emerging new kingdom of God, apocalyptic pockets of countercultural reality[35] such as those reflected in the Gospel of John, the Acts of the Apostles (2:43–47), and the First Letter of Peter (2:9–10). They had a vision of the future and sought to live it now, in the present, so as to be a light for the world (Matt. 5:14–16). Perhaps the greatest mission of the church in our own time is to offer the world a vision for alternative communities that are signs of the kingdom of God.

• In all of this, the early Christians were willing to act *unilaterally* to create a new world without waiting for the leaders of the nation or the rest of the populace to lead the way or even to agree with them.

We can learn from this behavior of the early Christian communities facing what they believed to be the end of the world. Their example can be a means for us to discover alternative behaviors for our faith communities as we face ultimate choices for avoiding ecological disaster and for creating a new, sustainable life on earth.

We can also bear the spiritual witness as individuals in our daily lives. People in the Global South will often be negotiating a sustainable lifestyle with issues of immediate survival. People in the Global North can act in solidarity. We can recognize that our living spaces are directly connected to virtually every ecological issue we face. Consider the emissions from furnaces; the food that has been transported from a distance; beef, the production of which contributes more to global warming than do automobiles; the gas and oil in the car in the driveway; the water that comes in and goes out of the house; paper for office and household use; the cleaning products that enter the waste stream; the pesticides and herbicides used on lawns and gardens, which leech into the watershed; the electricity from power plants; the wood in the products purchased; the garbage that goes into landfills; and on and on. People can make choices every day that have an impact for good or ill on the well-being of God's Earth.

Accumulative decisions by individuals and faith communities to change lifestyle have the potential to make an enormous impact. In the face of our discouragement at what seem to be such puny efforts of our own, Stan Hallett, a Chicago environmentalist, gave this encouraging analogy about the aftermath of the eruption of Mount St. Helens, an active volcano in northwest United States. When the volcano blew in 1980, it completely destroyed all plant and animal life for miles around. The whole area was decimated. The incredible aspen stands were burned flat to the ground. For a long time, nothing grew. Then the moss came back, and the moss created the conditions for the lichen to grow. The lichen returned, and that created the conditions for the shrubbery to grow. The shrubbery returned, and that has created the conditions for the aspen to begin to grow again. And the animal life returned. All these small efforts we make at the grassroots are like the moss, creating the conditions for greater measures to be taken, which in turn create the conditions for more extensive changes to take place at the level of corporations and governments. Thus, even with small efforts, there is an important process of regeneration, indeed a process of resurrection, which is taking place among us.

And what if we Christians brought these commitments to labor—workplaces, factories, farms, businesses, organizations, corporations—with which we are affiliated? What if we collectively advocated for Earth-friendly laws and policies in the public realm? What if we participated in hands-on efforts to restore degraded habitats? What if it became part of our collective consciousness to avoid certain behaviors and embrace others—simply as part of our life together? Mission engagement with the world must include the deliberate engineering of salient ecoethics and radical changes of lifestyle as we make the commitments and the sacrifices, the new ways of living needed, for a just and sustainable world.

When we embrace the fact that the church exists for the sake of the world, our faith communities can become alternative communities. We can bear our mission by being a light to the world. We can show what it means to care for the wretched of the Earth as well as for the wretched Earth. We can manifest a lifestyle in contrast to the economic exploitation of nature and people that impacts so many cultures. We can be in the forefront of advocating for local practices, national laws and policies, and global treaties that bring us together on behalf of all.

What will motivate us for this labor of love? What will sustain us for the duration? Will we be motivated by fear? We have reason to be afraid, but fear would not sustain us for long, and it certainly would not motivate others. Will we be motivated by guilt or shame? These emotions might lead us to realize our culpability and make some changes but, again, these would not sustain us for the long haul. We certainly may be motivated by outrage at how much wanton destruction is happening and how little is being done, especially at the corporate and governmental levels. But anger would exhaust us before long. What about grief at the loss of life as we have known it? Again, this is an appropriate response but certainly not life sustaining. We may see all these emotions as alarm systems—fear, guilt, shame, anger, grief—all as appropriate signals in a warning system, but not good grounds for making wise decisions or for providing the nurture needed to sustain us.

In the end, we may discover the answer with the very God who impels our mission. What can sustain the whole of creation is the presence of God in all of life, as witnessed by Jesus. Gerard Manley Hopkins referred to this presence as the "dearest freshness deep down things."[36] Wendell Berry names it "the fund of grace out of which we all live."[37] This reservoir of God's presence in all of life and God's love for all creation does not quit. And it does nothing but generate more love and grace—in us. This is what empowers and sustains us for the mission ahead.

## CONCLUSION

These then are five principles of mission for the great work that lies before the churches, principles for a new reformation, for a transformation of the church into the twenty-first century, a movement that can serve to renew the church itself. These efforts are absolutely crucial for the future of the Christian church everywhere—and for the Earth. When we learn about the ecological crisis, we will be better prepared to contribute to humanity's efforts to restore Earth and make our life sustainable. When we understand the integrity of creation and justice, we will bear a witness to public ministry that is indeed holistic. When we worship God with creation and act on behalf of creation, we will recover our vital love of and reverence for Earth.

The early church announced an apocalyptic sea change that occurred as a result of the life, death, and resurrection of Jesus. This apocalyptic transformation continues today. It includes a call to withdraw "from the present evil age" (Gal. 1:4; Rev. 18:4–5) and to enter into a "new creation," which is coming into being (Gal. 6:15). Contemporary churches, in response to the enormity of the ecological crises we face, are challenged to be "transformed by the renewing of your minds to what is the good and perfect and acceptable will of God" (cf. Rom. 8:22–23) for our time—the mission to restore God's creation and to form a sustainable life for God's beloved Earth community.

# 11

# Mission as Dialogue

## An Asian Roman Catholic Perspective

EDMUND KEE-FOOK CHIA

## EVANGELIZATION 2000

Toward the end of the last millennium, Pope John Paul II (1920–2005) issued an apostolic letter titled *Tertio millennio adveniente*,[1] in which he exhorted Roman Catholic Christians everywhere to conscientiously prepare for the Jubilee Year 2000. A main thrust of this preparation was the review of efforts in evangelization as well as reevangelization. While those in the Human Rights and Nongovernmental agencies were busily campaigning for debt relief in the Jubilee Year, certain quarters of the church saw the Jubilee Year as occasion for proclaiming the coming of not only the reign of God but also the coming of the Lord Jesus Christ.

It was even reported that the greatest gift they were planning to present to Jesus on his 2,000th birthday was the conversion of the entire world to Christianity. In the words of an organization that called itself Evangelization 2000: "The Holy Father, Pope John Paul II, called for a 're-evangelisation, a renewal of the Christian Faith, a New Pentecost for the Catholic church and the Whole World within the Third Millennium,' so that all people will recognise and accept the Lord Jesus Christ as their only redeemer and saviour."[2] To accomplish this, they had offered the following prayer: "Open our hearts to Jesus. Give us the courage to speak His name to those who are close to us and the generosity to share His love with those who are far away. We pray that every person throughout the world be invited to know and love Jesus, as Saviour and Redeemer."[3]

## SYNOD FOR ASIA

As part of the Jubilee Year preparation Pope John Paul II also convoked a number of Synod of Bishops specifically to discuss the affairs of the different continents. Thus, between 1994 and the year 2000, bishops from all over the world met in Rome for synods for Europe, the Americas, Africa, Asia, and Oceania. Of interest to this essay is the Asian Synod, or what was officially named the "Special Assembly of the Synod of Bishops for Asia." It was not really a synod *of* Asia but one *for* Asia. In other words, this was an event not conceived by Asians but by Rome for the benefit of the peoples in Asia. It was, one might even add, a top-down synod. In any case, the synod was held in 1998 with about two hundred participants, the majority of them bishops and their consultors from Asia, but there was also a significant minority represented by the bishops and their consultors from Rome, specifically members of the Vatican's dicasteries (departments of the Roman Curia). In fact, the entire synod was prepared principally by officials of some of these dicasteries, with Pope John Paul II choosing the theme: "Jesus Christ the Savior and His Mission of Love and Service in Asia: '. . . That They May Have Life, and Have It Abundantly' (Jn. 10:10)."

Elsewhere I have reported at length about the dynamics of the synod, especially the creative tensions that came to light before and during the Special Assembly.[4] For the purposes of the present essay, it suffices to observe that the product of the synod, which took the form of an encyclical letter issued about eighteen months later, reiterated some of the main concerns of *Tertio millennio adveniente*. This document, officially called the Post-Synodal Apostolic Exhortation *Ecclesia in Asia* (*EA*), actually begins with Pope John Paul II expressing his hope that "just as in the first millennium the Cross was planted on the soil of Europe, and in the second on that of the Americas and Africa, we can pray that in the Third Christian Millennium a *great harvest of faith* will be reaped in this vast and vital continent" (§1). The document then explains that the Synod of Bishops for Asia was actually part of a "program centered on the challenges of the new evangelization" (§2). Quoting *Tertio millennio adveniente*, the pope points out that "the issue of the encounter of Christianity with ancient local cultures and religions is a pressing one," and that "this is a great challenge for evangelization, since religious systems such as Buddhism or Hinduism have a clearly soteriological character" (§2). He ends the section by informing readers that the Synod theme was carefully discerned so as to "illustrate and explain more fully the truth that Christ is the one Mediator between God and man and the sole Redeemer of the world, to be clearly distinguished from the founders of other great religions" (§2).

## CHRISTIANITY AND OTHER RELIGIONS

It has been a decade since Jubilee 2000; the whole of Asia has not converted to Christianity, much less the entire world, and Jesus did not receive his big birthday gift. If anything, the percentage of Christians might even be on the decline, as compared to the growth of religions such as Islam. Moreover, globally, the relations of Christianity with Islam have seen increased challenges, especially in the aftermath of September 11, 2001 (terrorist attacks via commercial jetliners in the U.S.A.), and October 7, 2001 (the day America dropped its first bombs on Afghanistan, prompting Muslims everywhere to regard "Christian" America's "War on Terror" as a "War on Islam"), and as evidenced in the flare-ups resulting from the Danish cartoons (September 30, 2005), Pope Benedict XVI's Regensburg address (September 12, 2006),[5] and a variety of other religiopolitical snafus.

That aside, the Roman Catholic Church's program of evangelization also met with stiff resistance from peoples of other religions. This was especially pronounced as the document *Ecclesia in Asia* was released by Pope John Paul II (on November 6, 1999) during his visit to India, the heartland of the Hindu religion. For the head of a religious community hitherto identified with European culture to visit another continent and boldly proclaim his hope that a "great harvest" would come from Asia is like visiting a neighbor's home and coveting not only their furniture but also their children. It came as no surprise that shortly after the pope's visit, a prominent Indian journalist-politician, Arun Shourie, pointed out that the pope's statement was proof that the Roman Catholic Church's ultimate goal was the conversion of all Asians to Christianity. This was certainly an affront to Asian religions such as Hinduism, and therefore Christianity had to be stopped, if not annihilated altogether. Hence, violence against Christian missionaries and churches was subtly justified, even if they were aggressions for other less-than-noble reasons. Shourie discussed all this in his book titled *Harvesting Our Souls*, in which he laid bare some of the imprudent missionary strategies employed by the church.[6]

## TOWARD A THEOLOGY OF DIALOGUE

The preceding is but an account of one approach to mission and evangelization. As was pointed out earlier, it was a program developed out of Rome *for* the Roman Catholic Church in Asia. It was not conceived on Asian soil but in Europe, then transplanted to Asia with the hope that it would take root and bear plentiful fruits. The church in Asia, however, has a totally different approach. It is as much concerned with evangelization, but its understanding of this Christian imperative differs substantially from how Rome understands it. I refer here to the works of the Federation of Asian Bishops' Conferences (FABC). Having served this institution for a number of years, I am more than familiar with how it operates, as well as its thrust and theology.[7] Let me now discuss where and how its theology differs from that of Rome's.

To begin, if one were to examine the documents that have been coming out of the FABC, one would find that the concept of "dialogue" features prominently in its theology. In its very first meeting in 1970, the Asian bishops who make up the FABC had this to say: "In the spirit of collegiality and dialogue so earnestly urged on us by the decrees of the Second Vatican Council, . . . we have sought to discover new ways through which we may be of greater and more effective service—not to our Catholic communities only—but [also] to our own peoples and to the future, pregnant with both fear and promise, which opens up before us" (Asian Bishops' Meeting [ABM], art. 2). At the end of the meeting, through the resolutions, the Asian bishops pledged themselves "to an open, sincere, and continuing dialogue with our brothers of other great religions of Asia, that we may learn from one another how to enrich ourselves spiritually and how to work more effectively together on our common task of total human development" (ABM, art. 12, Resolutions).[8]

Since then the FABC has insisted that this theme of dialogue must be kept at center stage, prompting Indian theologian Felix Wilfred, who served as FABC's theological consultant for a number of years, to assert that the word "dialogue" can more or less summarize the entire orientation of the FABC.[9] Dialogue is the way of being church in Asia, dialogue is also the method for doing theology in Asia, and dialogue is the mode of the church's mission. In this context we can sum up the FABC's theology as an Asian Theology of Dialogue.

## EVANGELIZING MISSION THROUGH THE TRIPLE DIALOGUE

What are the elements of this dialogue? Who does the church dialogue with, and why should the church do so? How does dialogue relate to the making of an Asian theology, and what are the constituents of this theology? What are the peculiar characteristics that make for a distinctive theology in Asia, and what does a theology of dialogue look like? These questions guide the search for an Asian Theology of Dialogue. To begin, we refer to the wisdom of Sri Lankan Aloysius Pieris, one of Asia's foremost theologians. In his seminal article "Toward an Asian Theology of Liberation," Pieris writes:

Any discussion about Asian theology has to move between two poles: the *Third Worldness* of our continent and its peculiarly *Asian* character. More realistically and precisely, the common denominator linking Asia with the rest of the Third World is its overwhelming poverty. The specific character defining Asia within the other poor countries is its multifaceted religiousness. These two inseparable realities constitute in their interpenetration what might be designated as the *Asian context*, the matrix of any theology truly Asian.[10]

The contextual reality referred to in the preceding quote has influenced the Asian bishops so much that they have come to speak of the evangelizing mission of the church as addressing the issues of poverty and attending to the religions of Asia. Such a mission is the task of every local church. Hence, the priority is the creation of authentic local churches, a task that can be accomplished only through an integral process of what has come to be known in FABC documents as the "triple dialogue" (FABC VII, part I, A:8).[11] Construing this as the threefold dialogue of the church—with the cultures, the religions, and the poor of Asia—the Asian bishops state categorically that this dialogue represents the primary means by which the church evangelizes in Asia. Through the process of dialogue, the church inculturates itself and contextualizes its mode of being and operating so as to give birth to a truly local church in Asia. This is a radical departure from the church of yesteryears, which espoused a colonial approach and continued to remain primarily a foreign church in Asia.

Advocating the triple dialogue, Aloysius Pieris points out that we can never effect the process of inculturation by merely translating or adapting Christian symbol systems. Inculturation, Pieris contends, "happens naturally." "It can never be induced artificially. The Christian tends to appropriate the symbols and mores of the human grouping around it only to the degree that it immerses itself in their lives and struggles. Thus, inculturation is the byproduct of an *involvement* with a people rather than the conscious target of a program of action."[12] In the context of Asia, inculturation is brought about, first of all, through the dialogue with Asia's poor, in view of facilitating their integral liberation. Second, because the other religions have their own views of what liberation and salvation mean and because the majority of Asia's poor owe their allegiance to these other religions, the process of inculturation, which entails the church's dialogue with the poor, must also include dialogue with the religions. In short, inculturation, interreligious dialogue, and the process of integral liberation are mutually involving ministries, all of which are integral to the evangelizing mission of the church in Asia.[13]

That Asia is poor is beyond dispute. The FABC has repeatedly recognized that Asia, with its teeming masses and underdevelopment, coupled with mismanagement and corruption as well as the ravages of conflict and war, is truly a suffering continent. It is therefore in need of the liberation that Jesus Christ offers and that the church can bring, provided it is in tune with the spirit of the gospel of Christ. Precisely in this situation of massive poverty, the church's mission of love and service is sorely needed.[14] In other words, Jesus and the church are necessary in Asia, not so much because the majority of Asians are not Christians but because they are suffering and poor.

## MISSION AND COLONIZATION

It does not take too much of a sociohistorical analysis to realize that the socio-economic poverty of Asia as well as its political chaos, such as the territorial wars and dictatorial regimes, are to a considerable extent the result of Asia's colonial history.[15] To appreciate that Asia's suffering has a direct correlation to its being colonized, we need only to think of the plunder of Asia's natural resources, the mass transplantation of people from one country to another in order to service the colonial exploitation of Asia's lands, and the divide-and-rule policies practiced by the imperial powers, which have left much of Asia segregated either by religion or ethnicity.[16] Commenting on the impact of European colonization of the third world, Belgian scholar Francis Houtart had this to say: "The conditions necessary for their development were completely overthrown, and . . . in any case their actual underdevelopment is the direct result of the growth of the West."[17]

That is not all. The exploitation and subjugation continues, even to this day. Reflecting on this, the late George Soares-Prabhu stated:

> This induced underdevelopment in Asia continues to be maintained by the more subtle but equally effective mechanisms of neocolonialism through which the metropolitan powers and their "global corporations" maintain a stranglehold on the economies of the Third World countries, and so perpetuate a system through which the rich grow richer at the expense of the poor, so that the gap between rich and poor grows steadily wider.[18]

In light of this, any Asian contextual theology will have to take this fact of poverty, oppression, and exploitation seriously. This is even truer if it is to be a Christian theology, since it was the Christian European West that committed the injustice of conquest, plunder, and domination upon the non-Christian Asian people of the East. By association, the church has as much a responsibility as former colonial powers to alleviate the suffering of the poor in Asia and to address the root causes of injustice and oppression. Such a responsibility calls for a theology that has a liberative thrust to it: a theology that includes the element of praxis, leading to the reality of liberation. For this purpose, an Asian perspective of interpreting the Bible is a necessary starting point.

## ASIAN BIBLICAL HERMENEUTICS

To begin this exploration into an Asian perspective of interpreting the Bible, we first need to clarify who exactly is meant by the poor, since the dialogue with the poor features prominently in Asian theology. Here we refer to the reflections of George Soares-Prabhu, who is renowned for his biblical theology. After searching through the Old and the New Testaments, Soares-Prabhu came to the conclusion that the poor refers to three principal concepts: (1) In the Bible, the poor (*'ănāwîm*) as a sociological group are deprived of the means or dignity to lead a full human existence—the economically afflicted, the dispossessed, the marginalized, the exploited, the oppressed. (2) Also in the Bible, the poor as a dialectical group are poor because another group has determined or caused them to be poor. The poor, therefore, stand in opposition to this other group. Poverty is an evil and has to be eliminated. The poor are blessed, but poverty itself is not blessed. (3) The Bible depicts the poor as a dynamic group, not as a pitiable group that is of no historical significance. Instead, because of their poverty and victimization, they are the beneficiaries of salvation as well as the mediators of this salvation to others.[19]

The above describes one group of people who are poor; they are not to be confused with another group who are also poor because they choose to be poor. The former are poor by circumstances: their poverty is forced upon them. The latter, on the other hand, are poor by choice: they embrace poverty voluntarily. Aloysius Pieris calls those who embrace the evangelical voluntary poverty the followers of Jesus (Matt. 4:19–22; Luke 5:28; etc.). They are the disciples of Christ. The other group who are forced into an antievangelical poverty and are poor not by choice are the vicars of Christ (Matt. 25:31–46; Mark 9:36–37, 41; etc.). They represent Christ, who said, "As you did it to one of the least of these my brethren, you did it to me" (Matt. 25:40 RSV). The two groups are necessarily related in that as "Yahweh's proxies on earth," the forced poor, the vicars of Christ, "share Yahweh's divine prerogative of making demands" on the followers of Christ, the disciples of Jesus. The poor by circumstances need the intervention of the poor by choice. The voluntary poverty of the disciples of Jesus must be oriented toward the alleviation of the forced poverty of the vicars of Christ as "the evangelical poor receive their mission through their solidarity with the socially poor." The disciples of Jesus are the proclaimers of God's reign; the vicars are its inheritors. In other words,

Pieris asserts, there is "no salvation outside God's covenant with the poor." For it is through this solidarity with the poor in discipleship praxis that the "Kingdom Community" is given birth.[20] In the words of the Asian bishops,

> Necessarily, the Kingdom of God confronts the forces of injustice, violence, and oppression. These forces combined form structures of sin, from which we need to be liberated. We uphold the preferential option for the poor, since they are victims of these structures. Hence, solidarity with the poor is a response to the Good News of God's Kingdom. Where this solidarity exists, there the power of Christ's Spirit is working. The work of the Spirit appears in the struggle for a better world in all its forms. We see people of all faiths participating in that struggle. (BIRA IV/10, art. 8)[21]

This brings us to the question of how the dialogue with other religions is related to the dialogue with the poor. How do we integrate interreligious dialogue with the ministry on behalf of integral liberation? How do we get the people of other faiths to participate with us in the struggle against mammon? How is the church accepted by the people of other faiths in the first place? In addressing these questions, Pieris draws our attention to the works of Flemish theologian Edward Schillebeeckx, especially the part where he points to the idea that Jesus' baptism under John the Baptist was Jesus' first prophetic gesture.[22] Through this prophetic act, Pieris discerns four missiological principles relevant for the church in Asia:

First, John the Baptist was from the Deuteronomic tradition of prophetic asceticism—one of liberative religiousness. Jesus opts for this brand of spirituality from among the many available during his time—the Zealots, the Essenes, the Pharisees, and so forth. Second, at the Jordan, Jesus comes before John the Baptizer as well as those to be baptized. The latter are the *anawim* (*'ănāwîm*), the poor, the outcast, the lepers, and others like them. By opting to be baptized instead of to baptize, Jesus joins the ranks of the latter group, identifying himself with the poor. Third, by submitting himself to baptism, Jesus receives his missionary credentials. It is in his baptism, an event carried out in the presence of the poor, that he receives his authority: "*Hear ye him*" (cf. Mark 1:11; 9:7). Fourth, the Jordan baptism is a self-effacing act on Jesus' part. By submitting himself humbly to be baptized, he is losing his identity. But it is precisely in this loss of identity that Jesus discovers his authentic selfhood: the Lamb of God, God's beloved Son, the Messiah.[23]

With his identity clarified and authority bestowed, Jesus sets off on his prophetic mission, a journey that sees him in defense of the poor and in confrontation with mammon. Pieris speaks of Jesus as God's defense pact with the poor and in a collision course with mammon.[24] It is this, especially his challenge of the ruling religious elites and colonial powers, that leads to Jesus'

death. The journey that has begun at Jordan in humility is to end on Calvary, not only in humility but also in shame; both the events, incidentally,
are described in the New Testament by the same word: "baptism" (Matt.
3:13–15; Mark 10:35–40; Luke 12:50). "The baptism of the cross, therefore,
is not only the price he paid for preaching the good news, but the basis of *all
Christian discipleship* (Mk. 8:34)."[25]

## FROM CHURCH IN ASIA TO CHURCH OF ASIA

The foregoing reflections clearly show that the task of developing a local
church has to be through the process of dialogue, where the term "dialogue"
is used loosely to refer to the interactions, relationships, and involvement
between one group and another. The dialogue with the contextual realities of
Asia, therefore, demands that the church take seriously the people who make
up the cultures and religions of Asia. In particular, the church, as disciples of
Jesus, must also walk in the footsteps of him who humbled himself in order to
serve the poor of his time. The events that took place at Jordan and Calvary
are significant markers from which the church in Asia can learn.

Significantly, it was at the river Jordan that Jesus received his first baptism.
This was a baptism into the religiousness of the culture of his time. Through
this act of baptism, Jesus received the necessary credentials to exercise his prophetic mission. Following in the footsteps of Jesus, the church in Asia also
has to take this first step, which is to submit itself to a baptism by the river of
Asia's religiousness. In effect, this means that the church must be extensively
immersed in and involved with Asia's other religions. Essentially, this first step
requires the church to fulfill "the prophetic imperative to immerse [it]self in the
baptismal waters of Asian religions" so that it becomes a local church, "'initiated' into the pre-Christian traditions under the tutelage of [Asia's] ancient
gurus." Because this is something the church has hitherto not done in many
parts of Asia, it continues to lack the authority to minister to the people in Asia.
In the words of Pieris, it would mean that the church "will continue to be an
ecclesiastical complex full of 'power' but lacking in 'authority.'" In this baptism,
the church, like its Master Jesus, will have to simply "sit at the feet of Asian
gurus not as an *ecclesia docens* (a teaching church) but as an *ecclesia discens* (a learning church), lost among the 'religious poor' of Asia, among the *anawim* who go
to their gurus in search of the kingdom of holiness, justice, and peace."[26]

The second baptism, the one of Calvary, which Jesus received is even more
significant. In current ecclesial language, one could refer to it as the sacra-
ment of confirmation. It was a confirmation of all of Jesus' signs, preaching,
teachings, and actions that began with the baptism of water at Jordan and

ended with his execution in what Pieris calls "the baptism of the cross." This was "a cross that the money-polluted religiosity of his day planted on Calvary with the aid of a colonial power (Lk. 23: 1–23)." It is not without connection that before arriving on Calvary, Jesus' journey had taken him through terrains where he had openly challenged the status quo and ruling elites. His was a "calculated strategy against *mammon* whom he declared to be God's rival (Mt. 6:24). The kingdom he announced was certainly not for the rich (Lk. 6:20–26). It takes a miracle for a rich person to give up wealth and enter the kingdom (Mk. 10:26–27). His curses on the 'haves' (Lk. 6:24–25) and his blessings on the 'have-nots' (Lk. 6:20–23) are sharpened by his dictum that it is in and through the poor (the hungry, the naked, etc.) that he would pass his messianic judgment on entire nations (Mt. 25:31–46)."[27]

As the Asian bishops also realize, "opting to be with the poor involves risk of conflict with vested interests or 'establishments,' religious, economic, social, political. It also involves for leaders of the church especially, *loss of security*, and that not only material but spiritual [as well]" (BISA I, art. 6).[28] But such is the way to Calvary and, more significantly, such is also the way by which the church would acquire its authority. It is in the losing of its security that the church will discover its identity: it is a "church of the poor," the same group with whom the church's Master had identified. This is the calling that the Asian bishops have been making ever since the 1970 Asian Bishops' Meeting, have reiterated forcefully at the First FABC Plenary Assembly in 1974, and have repeated ever since: The church must become a church of the poor if it is to be relevant to the people of Asia.

It is therefore quite clear that the only way by which the church in Asia can discover its identity and acquire its authority is if the church consciously submits to the challenge of the other religions and the challenge of the poor. Unless the Asian church is baptized in the "Jordan" of Asian religions and confirmed by the "Calvary" of Asian poverty, it will remain foreign and unacceptable by the majority of the people of Asia. Such is the process of inculturation and such is the challenge that the church knows it has to accept if it wants to become an authentically local church in Asia. Realizing this, the Asian bishops are of the mind that "the primary focus of our task of evangelization then, at this time in our history, is the building up of a truly local Church. . . . The local Church is a Church incarnate in a people, a Church indigenous and inculturated. And this means concretely a Church in continuous, humble and loving dialogue with the living traditions, the cultures, the religions" (FABC I, art. 9, 12).[29]

Implicit in this inculturation process is the transformation of the church's image and ways of functioning so as to embrace what the Asian bishops call the *New Way of Being Church*. This "new way" of "being" entails a relinquishing of the church's image of power and wealth in favor of a church that is meek and humble and involved in the lives and struggles of the people of Asia. When that happens, the church would have integrated itself into the Asian cultural fabric and be recognized and accepted as one of Asia's own. When that day comes, the church would have moved from being merely a church *in* Asia to becoming a church *of* Asia. It would no longer be a European church *in* Asia, but truly an *Asian* church serving the people of Asia.

## CONCLUSION

As is evident from the discussion above, the church in Asia has little choice but to be in dialogue with Asia's poor, as well as its cultures and religions. This is not only a matter of survival but also of being faithful to the gospel imperative of discipleship. Until and unless the church takes seriously this calling and vocation, its mission will forever be compromised. This is the mission toward which the church in Asia continues to strive. It is a mission that encounters challenges not only from forces outside of the church but also from those within it. Whatever it is, there certainly is no turning away from the church's mission of dialogue: its mission *is* dialogue, and its dialogue *is* mission.

# Notes

## Chapter 1: From Edinburgh to Edinburgh

1. Brian Stanley, *The World Missionary Conference, Edinburgh 1910* (Grand Rapids: Wm. B. Eerdmans Publishing Co., 2009), 16.

2. John R. Mott, "General Account of the Conference," in *Addresses and Papers of John R. Mott*, vol. 5, *The International Missionary Council* (New York: Association Press, 1947), 13; as quoted in Kosuke Koyama, "Carrying the Gospel to All the Non-Christian World," Lecture at the University of Edinburgh, April 2002, http://www.towards2010.org.uk/downloads/t2010paper01koyama.pdf, 1.

3. Stanley, *The World Missionary Conference*, 7.

4. James A. Scherer, "Edinburgh II—A New Springtime for Ecumenical Mission?" *International Bulletin of Missionary Research* 31, no. 4 (October 2007): 195.

5. Stanley, *The World Missionary Conference*, 87.

6. These reports were published as *World Missionary Conference, 1910*, 9 vols. (Edinburgh: Oliphant, Anderson, & Ferrier, 1910). Helpful summaries of each report can be found on the Web site of the Towards 2010 Committee, which is helping to coordinate the various centenary activities: http://www.towards2010.org.uk/papers.htm.

7. William H. Temple Gairdner, *Echoes from Edinburgh, 1910: An Account and Interpretation of the World Missionary Conference* (New York: Fleming H. Revell Co., [1910]), 53.

8. For a more complete survey of the delegates, see ibid., 47–58.

9. Charles Clayton Morrison, "The World Missionary Conference," *Christian Century* (July 7, 1910), http://religion-online.org/showarticle.asp?title=471, 1.

10. J. R. Mott, *The Evangelization of the World in This Generation* (1900; repr., New York: Student Volunteer Movement for Foreign Missions, 1905).

11. See Stanley, *The World Missionary Conference*, 7–12; Andrew F. Walls, "The Great Commission 1910–2010," lecture delivered at the University of Edinburgh, 2002, http://www.towards2010.org.uk/downloads/t2010paper01walls.pdf, 5.

12. See Stephen Neill, *A History of Christian Missions*, rev. Owen Chadwick, 2nd ed. (London: Penguin Books, 1986), 410–13.

13. Scherer, "Edinburgh II," 195, 198.

14. Stanley, *The World Missionary Conference*, 12. In a footnote Stanley writes that figures vary slightly for the white representatives, "depending on how one counts a few missionaries from one region or continent who served under a mission whose home base was in another region or continent." I have also found varying numbers for the total number of delegates.

15. Stanley, *The World Missionary Conference*, 13.

16. Ibid., 99. Gairdner, however—perhaps mistakenly—does speak of delegates from Africa: "And finally, men of African race, one, a negro of immense size glorying in his African race, from Liberia, the only independent negro organised state in Africa." See Gairdner, *Echoes from Edinburgh*, 58.

17. Ibid.

18. Ibid.

19. Brian Stanley, "Defining the Boundaries of Christendom: The Two Worlds of the World Missionary Conference, 1910," *International Bulletin of Missionary Research*, 30, no. 4 (October 1, 2006): 174.

20. See Stanley, *The World Missionary Conference*, 11–12; also Joan Delaney, "From Cremona to Edinburgh: Bishop Bonomelli and the World Missionary Conference of 1910," *Ecumenical Review* (July 2000), http://findarticles.com/p/articles/mi_m2065/is_3_52/ai_66279082.

21. Gairdner, *Echoes from Edinburgh*, 50.

22. Stanley, *The World Missionary Conference*, 11.

23. Walls, "The Great Commission 1910–2010," 4.

24. See Andrew F. Walls, "Culture and Coherence in Christian History," in *The Missionary Movement in Christian History: Studies in the Transmission of Faith* (Maryknoll, NY: Orbis Books, 1996), 16–25; Lamin Sanneh, *Whose Religion Is Christianity? The Gospel beyond the West* (Grand Rapids: Wm. B. Eerdmans Publishing Co., 2003); Philip Jenkins, *The Next Christendom: The Coming of Global Christianity* (New York: Oxford University Press, 2002).

25. See Ronald K. Orchard, ed., *Witness on Six Continents: Records of the Meeting of the Commission on World Mission and Evangelism of the World Council of Churches Held in Mexico City, December 8–19, 1963* (London: Edinburgh House, 1964, 175.

26. The literature on "missional church" is vast. See, e.g., Darrell L. Guder, ed., *Missional Church: A Vision for the Sending of the Church in North America* (Grand Rapids: Wm. B. Eerdmans Publishing Co., 1998); and Patrick J. Brennan, *The Mission Driven Parish* (Maryknoll, NY: Orbis Books, 2007).

27. See, e.g., the following important collections of two-thirds world theology and missiology: Max L. Stackhouse and Lalsangkima Pachuau, eds., *News of Boundless Riches: Interrogating, Comparing, and Reconstructing Mission in a Global Era*, 2 vols. (Delhi, India: ISPCK, 2007); Ogbu U. Kalu, ed., *African Christianity: An African Story* (Trenton, NJ, and Asmara, Eritrea: Africa World Press, 2007); Michael Amaladoss and Rosino Gibellini, eds., *Teologia in Asia* (Brescia, Italy: Queriniana, 2006); Wonsuk and Julie C. Ma, eds., *Asian Church and God's Mission* (Manila: OFM [Franciscan Order of Friars Minor] Literature; West Caldwell, NJ: MWM [Mountain World Mission], 2003).

28. Kenneth Scott Latourette, *A History of the Expansion of Christianity*, vol. 4, *The Great Century: Europe and the United States of America, A.D. 1800–A.D. 1914* (New York and London: Harper & Brothers, 1941); vol. 5, *The Great Century in the Americas, Australasia, Africa, A.D. 1800–A.D. 1914* (1943); vol. 6, *The Great Century in Northern Africa and Asia, A.D. 1800–A.D. 1914* (1944).
29. Stanley, *The World Missionary Conference*, 3.
30. Barbara Tuchman, *The Guns of August* (New York: Macmillan, 1972).
31. M. A. C. Warren, "Preface," in John V. Taylor's *The Primal Vision* (London: SCM Press, 1963), 10.
32. David J. Bosch, *Transforming Mission: Paradigm Shifts in Theology of Mission* (Maryknoll, NY: Orbis Books, 1991), 489. I have shifted Bosch's emphasis but have not, I believe, changed its meaning.
33. Ibid., for Bosch's phrase. For "prophetic dialogue," see *In Dialogue with the Word: Documents of the XV General Chapter SVD, 2000* (Rome: SVD Publications, 2000).
34. Bosch, *Transforming Mission*, 338.
35. Stanley, *The World Missionary Conference*, 4.
36. Ibid.
37. Quoted in ibid., 17.
38. Theresa Okure, "The Church in the Mission Field: Edinburgh, 1910: A Nigerian/African Response," lecture at New College, Edinburgh, April 26, 2003, http://www.towards2010.org.uk/downloads/t2010paper02okure.pdf, 18.
39. Kosuke Koyama, "What Makes a Missionary? Toward Crucified Mind Not Crusading Mind," in *Mission Trends No. 1: Crucial Issues in Mission Today*, ed. Gerald H. Anderson and Thomas F. Stransky (Grand Rapids: Wm. B. Eerdmans Publishing Co., 1974), 73–86.
40. David J. Bosch, "The Vulnerability of Mission," in *New Directions in Mission and Evangelization 2: Theological Foundations*, ed. James A. Scherer and Stephen B. Bevans (Maryknoll, NY: Orbis Books, 1994), 73–86.
41. Latin American Bishops' Conference at Santo Domingo, Dominican Republic, "Conclusions: New Evangelization, Human Development, Christian Culture," in *Santo Domingo and Beyond*, ed. Alfred T. Hennelly (Maryknoll, NY: Orbis Books, 1993), 125 (par. 108).
42. Stanley, *The World Missionary Conference*, 125.
43. "Towards 2010: Mission for the 21st Century; The Vision and the Process" (July 7, 2006), http://www.towards2010.org.uk/int_vision.htm. What follows is a summary of this document.

## Chapter 2: Mission from the Ground Up

1. On this, see esp. Shmuel Noah Eisenstadt, "Multiple Modernities," *Daedalus* 129, no. 1 (2000): 1–29.
2. Grace Davie, *Europe—The Special Case: Parameters of Faith in the Modern World* (London: Darton, Longman & Todd, 2002).
3. Joseph Ratzinger and Jürgen Habermas, *Dialektik der Säkularisierung: Über Vernunft und Religion* (Freiburg: Herder, 2005); ET, *The Dialectics of Secularization: On Reason and Religion*, ed. Florian Schuller, trans. Brian McNeil (San Francisco: Ignatius Press, 2006).
4. A number of these addresses have been collected in Jürgen Habermas, *Zwischen Naturalismus und Religion: Philosophische Aufsätze* (Frankfurt: Suhrkamp, 2005).
5. Charles Taylor, *A Secular Age* (Cambridge, MA: Harvard University Press, 2007).

6. Paul Collier, *The Bottom Billion: Why the Poorest Countries Are Failing and What Can Be Done about It* (New York: Oxford University Press, 2007). In August 2008 the United Nations increased the estimate of those who are living below the extreme poverty line (usually given as living on less than one U.S. dollar per day) to 1.4 billion, observing that $1.25 is a more accurate measure of the purchasing power of the extreme poor than $1.00.

7. On this, see Ulrich Beck, *Weltrisikogesellschaft* (Frankfurt: Suhrkamp, 2007).

8. On this point, see esp. Gunnar Heinsohn, *Söhne und Weltmacht* (Munich: Piper Verlag, 2008).

### Chapter 3: Globalization and Mission in the Twenty-first Century

1. A. G. Hopkins, *Globalization in World History* (New York: Norton, 2002); Hugh McLeod, *Secularisation in Western Europe, 1848–1914* (New York: St. Martin's Press, 2008).

2. Marshall McLuhan and Bruce R. Powers, *The Global Village: Transformations in World Life and Media in the 21st Century* (Oxford: Oxford University Press, 1989).

3. Thomas L. Friedman, *The World Is Flat: A Brief History of the Twenty-first Century* (New York: Picador, 2007).

4. See Francis Fukuyama's review of Benjamin R. Barber's *Jihad vs. McWorld: How the Planet Is Both Falling Apart and Coming Together and What This Means for Democracy* [New York: Times Books, 1995], in *Foreign Affairs* (November/December 1995), http://www.foreignaffairs.com/articles/51425/francis-fukuyama/jihad-vs-mcworld-how-the-planet-is-both-falling-apart-and-coming.

5. Charles Taylor, "On Religion and Violence," *Arts and Science Review* (University of Toronto) 2, no. 1 (Spring 2005): 31–35.

6. Rebecca T. Peters, *In Search of the Good of Life: The Ethics of Globalization* (New York: Continuum, 2000).

7. Pietra Rivoli, *The Travels of a T-Shirt in the Global Economy* (London and Hoboken, NJ: Wiley, 2006).

8. Arjun Appadurai, *Modernity at Large: Cultural Dimensions of Globalization* (Minneapolis: University of Minnesota Press, 1996); P. Beyer, *Religion and Globalization* (London: Sage, 1993); Mike Featherstone, Scott Lash, and Roland Robertson, eds., *Global Modernities* (London: Sage, 1995); R. Hackett, "Pentecostal Appropriation of Media Technologies in Nigeria," *Journal of Religion in Africa*, 28, no. 3 (1998): 258–77; R. Marshall-Fratani, "Mediating the Global and Local in Nigerian Pentecostalism," *Journal of Religion in Africa*, 28, no. 3 (1998): 278–315; Brigit Meyer, "Make a Complete Break with the Past," *Journal of Religion in Africa*, 28, no. 3 (1998): 350–73; David Lyon, "Wheels within Wheels: Globalisation and Contemporary Religion," in *A Global Faith: Essays on Evangelicalism and Globalization*, ed. M. Hutchinson and O. U. Kalu (Sydney: Center for the Study of Australian Christianity, 1998), 47–68; Jeff Haynes, *Religion and Politics in Africa* (London: Zed Press, 1996); Karla Poewe, ed., *Charismatic Christianity as a Global Culture* (Columbia: University of South Carolina Press, 1994); R. Robertson, *Globalization* (London: Sage, 1972); R. Robertson, "Globalization and Social Modernization: A Note on Japan and Japanese Religion," *Sociological Analysis* 47, no. 8 (1987): esp. 38–39.

9. Ogbu U. Kalu, *African Pentecostalism: An Introduction* (New York: Oxford University Press, 2008).

10. David Uru Iyam, *Broken Hoe: Cultural Reconfiguration in Biase Southeast Nigeria* (Chicago: University of Chicago Press, 1995), 205; Ogbu U. Kalu, *Power, Pov-*

*erty, and Prayer: The Challenges of Poverty and Pluralism in African Christianity,*
*1960–1996* (Frankfurt: Peter Lang, 2000), chap. 2.

11. Frieder Ludwig, "Tambaram: The West African Experience," *Journal of Religion in Africa,* 31, no. 1 (2001): 49–91.

12. Lamin Sanneh, "Theology of Mission," *The Modern Theologians,* vol. 1, *An Introduction to Christian Theology in the Twentieth Century,* ed. David F. Ford, 2 vols. (New York: Blackwell, 1989), 2:562; Susan B. Harper, *In the Shadow of the Mahatma: Bishop V. Azariah and the Travails of Christianity in British India* (Grand Rapids: Wm. B. Eerdmans Publishing Co., 2000).

13. Lamin Sanneh, *Whose Religion Is Christianity? The Gospel beyond the West* (Grand Rapids: Wm. B. Eerdmans Publishing Co., 2003), 12.

14. Presentation by Stephen B. Bevans, "The God of Jesus Christ: A Case Study for a Mission Theology," at Midwest Mission Fellowship, Chicago, October 27, 2007.

15. Darrell L. Guder, ed., *Missional Church* (Grand Rapids: Wm. B. Eerdmans Publishing Co., 1998): 77–182; D. L. Guder, *The Continuing Conversion of the Church* (Grand Rapids: Wm. B. Eerdmans Publishing Co., 2000).

16. Ogbu U. Kalu, "The Big Man of the Big God: Popular Culture, Media and Marketability of Religion," *New Theology Review,* 20, no. 2 (May 2007): 15–26. I have pursued this matter in greater detail in my *African Pentecostalism,* 103–22.

17. Stewart Hoover, *Mass Media and Religion: The Social Sources of the Electronic Church* (London: Sage, 1988), 21.

18. *Charisma* magazine, January 2006, 27–29.

19. Bruce D. Forbes and Jeffrey Mahan, *Religion and Popular Culture in America* (Berkeley: University of California Press, 2000); Imani Perry, *Prophets of the Hood: Politics and Poetics in Hip Hop* (Durham, NC: Duke University Press, 2004).

20. Michael Warren, *Seeing through the Media: A Religious View of Communication and Cultural Analysis* (Harrisburg, PA: Trinity International, 1997), 63.

21. Carmen M. Nanko-Fernandez, "Religion and Popular Culture: Reading between the Lines," *New Theology Review,* 20, no. 2 (May 2007): 78–81.

22. Quentin J. Schultze, *Televangelism and American Culture* (Grand Rapids: Baker Book House, 1991); Jeremy Carette and Richard King, eds., *Selling Spirituality* (London: Routledge, 2005); Marla F. Frederick, *Between Sundays: Black Women and Everyday Struggles of Faith* (Berkeley: University of California Press, 2003); Martyn Percy, "The Church in the Market Place: Advertising and Religion in a Secular Age," *Journal of Contemporary Religion,* 15, no. 1 (2000): 97–119, showing that much of what televangelists do in the U.S.A. and Africa (such as healing, miracles, and appeals for money) are banned by the watchdog, code of Advertising Standards and Practice, in Britain. These are regarded as exploitation of human inadequacy and degradation of the people to whom it appeals.

23. Berit Brethauer, "Televangelism: Local and Global Dimensions," in *Religions/ Globalizations: Theories and Cases,* ed. Dwight Hopkins et al. (Durham, NC: Duke University Press, 2001): 203–26, esp. 206; Brethauer's case study of Robert H. Schuller's ministry does not prove the assertion.

24. E. J. K. Asamoah-Gyadu, "Pentecostal Media Images and Religious Globalization in Sub-Saharan Africa," in *Belief in Media: Cultural Perspectives on Media and Christianity,* ed. Peter Horsfield, Mary Hess, and Adan Medrano (Aldershot, UK: Ashgate Publishers, 2004), 65–79, esp. 66.

## Chapter 4: Many Tongues, Many Practices

1. See James R. Goff Jr., *Fields White unto Harvest: Charles F. Parham and the Missionary Origins of Pentecostalism* (Fayetteville: University of Arkansas Press, 1988).
2. As recorded in the Matthean "apocalypse," Jesus said, "This gospel of the kingdom shall be preached in all the world for a witness unto all nations; and then shall the end come" (Matt. 24:14 KJV). Early Pentecostals widely believed that the gift of tongues they experienced was designed in part to enable them to preach the gospel to others in their own languages so as to fulfill the Great Commission in a more efficient manner; see D. William Faupel, "Glossolalia as Foreign Language: An Investigation of the Early Twentieth Century Pentecostal Claim," *Wesleyan Theological Journal* 31 (1996): 95–109. For more on the role of eschatology in early Pentecostalism, see also D. William Faupel, *The Everlasting Gospel: The Significance of Eschatology in the Development of Pentecostal Thought* (Sheffield: Sheffield Academic Press, 1996).
3. See Allan Anderson, *Spreading Fires: The Missionary Nature of Early Pentecostalism* (London: SCM, 2007), esp. chaps. 8 and 10.
4. The following summarizes ibid., chap. 9.
5. For one case study that fills in the details of how early Pentecostal missions were almost completely co-opted by the colonial paradigm, see Eric Newburg, "The Pentecostal Mission in Palestine, 1906–1948: A Postcolonial Assessment of Pentecostal Zionism" (PhD diss., Regent University School of Divinity, 2008).
6. The following derives from Gary B. McGee, *This Gospel Shall Be Preached: A History and Theology of Assemblies of God Foreign Missions*, 2 vols. (Springfield, MO: Gospel Publishing House, 1986–89).
7. Ibid., 1:97.
8. McGee discusses this campaign in ibid., vol. 2, part 2, "Global Conquest (1959–1967)."
9. See, e.g., Steve Brouwer, Paul Gifford, and Susan D. Rose, *Exporting the American Gospel: Global Christian Fundamentalism* (New York and London: Routledge, 1996).
10. L. Grant McClung, *Globalbeliever.com: Connecting to God's Work in Your World*, rev. ed. (Cleveland, TN: Pathway Press, 2004), 257.
11. McGee, *This Gospel Shall Be Preached*, 1:97, noting this development.
12. E.g., Melvin L. Hodges, *The Indigenous Church and the Missionary* (South Pasadena, CA: William Carey Library, 1978).
13. Melvin Hodges, *A Theology of the Church and Its Mission: A Pentecostal Perspective* (Springfield, MO: Gospel Publishing House, 1977), 95.
14. Roland Allen published *The Ministry of the Spirit* (Grand Rapids: Wm. B. Eerdmans Publishing Co., 1960); see also idem, *The Compulsion of the Spirit: A Roland Allen Reader*, ed. David Paton and Charles H. Long (Grand Rapids: Wm. B. Eerdmans Publishing Co.; Cincinnati: Forward Movement Publications, 1983).
15. See Paul A. Pomerville, *The Third Force in Missions: A Pentecostal Contribution to Contemporary Mission Theology* (Peabody, MA: Hendrickson Publishers, 1985).
16. See ibid., 137–43; cf. John V. York, *Missions in the Age of the Spirit* (Springfield, MO: Logion Press, 2000), esp. chaps. 1–5.
17. See also Veli-Matti Kärkkäinen, *Toward a Pneumatological Theology: Pentecostal and Ecumenical Perspectives on Ecclesiology, Soteriology, and Theology of Mission,*

ed. Amos Yong (Lanham, MD: University Press of America, 2002), chaps. 15–16; and John Michael Penney, *The Missionary Emphasis of Lukan Pneumatology* (Sheffield: Sheffield Academic Press, 1997), esp. chap. 5.

18. McGee, *This Gospel Shall Be Preached*, 2:106–7; and York, *Missions in the Age of the Spirit*, 129–30.

19. See Philip Jenkins, *The Next Christendom: The Coming of Global Christianity* (New York: Oxford University Press, 2002).

20. See Larry D. Pate, "Pentecostal Missions from the Two-Thirds World," in *Called and Empowered: Global Missions in Pentecostal Perspective*, ed. Murray Dempster, Byron D. Klaus, and Douglas Petersen (Peabody, MA: Hendrickson Publishers, 1991), 242–58.

21. On the migration of Afro-Caribbeans to the United Kingdom, among other sources see Malcolm J. C. Calley, *God's People: West Indian Pentecostal Sects in England* (London and New York: Oxford University Press, 1965); Nicole Rodriguez Toulis, *Believing Identity: Pentecostalism and the Mediation of Jamaican Ethnicity and Gender in England* (Oxford and New York: Berg, 1997); and Joel Edwards, "Afro-Caribbean Pentecostalism in Britain," *Journal of the European Pentecostal Theological Association* 17 (1997): 37–48.

22. For a rich ethnography of the fortunes of a West African Afro-Pentecostal congregation in Britain, see Hermoine Harris, *Yoruba in Diaspora: An African Church in London* (New York: Palgrave Macmillan, 2006). A more diverse set of discussions is in André Droogers, Cornelis van der Laan, and Wout van Laar, eds., *Fruitful in This Land: Pluralism, Dialogue and Healing in Migrant Pentecostalism* (Zoetermeer, the Netherlands: Uitgeverij Boekencentrum; Geneva: WCC Publications, 2006). See also a briefer discussion by Edith A. Miguda, "Encountering History: Christianity and Identity in Nigerian Diaspora Churches," in *Religion, History, and Politics in Nigeria: Essays in Honor of Ogbu U. Kalu*, ed. Chima J. Korieh and Q. Ugo Nwokeji (Lanham, MD: University Press of America, 2005), 216–29.

23. One church that has been more intentional about an international missions program that both serves the needs of African migrants as well as seeks to fulfill the Great Commission is the Ghanaian Church of Pentecost; see Opoku Onyinah, "Pentecostalism and the African Diaspora: An Examination of the Missions Activities of the Church of Pentecost," *PNEUMA* 26, no. 2 (2004): 216–41.

24. See Roswith Gerloff, "Pentecostals in the African Diaspora," in *Pentecostals after a Century: Global Perspectives on a Movement in Transition*, ed. Allan H. Anderson and Walter J. Hollenweger (Sheffield: Sheffield Academic Press, 1999), 67–88; and "'Africa as Laboratory of the World': The African Christian Diaspora in Europe as Challenge to Mission and Ecumenical Relations," in *Mission Is Crossing Frontiers: Essays in Honour of the Late Bongani A. Mazibuko, 1932–1997*, ed. Roswith Gerloff (Pietermaritzburg, South Africa: Cluster, 2003), 343–81; cf. Amos Yong, "Justice Deprived, Justice Demanded: Afropentecostalisms and the Task of World Pentecostal Theology Today," *Journal of Pentecostal Theology* 15, no. 1 (2006): 127–47.

25. For overviews, see Manuel Silva, "A Brazilian Church Comes to New York," *PNEUMA* 13, no. 2 (1991): 161–65; and Jill DeTemple, "Chains of Liberation: Poverty and Social Action in the Universal Church of the Kingdom of God," in *Latino Religions and Civic Activism in the United States*, ed. Gastón Espinosa, Virgilio P. Elizondo, and Jesse Miranda (Oxford and New York: Oxford University Press, 2005), 219–31.

26. Thus it is said that "neo-Pentecostalism promotes an anti-hierarchical rupture in Brazilian society, precisely because it both valorizes and wages warfare on the spirits of the past"; see Patricia Birman, "Conversion from Afro-Brazilian Religions to Neo-Pentecostalism," in *Conversion of a Continent: Contemporary Religious Change in Latin America*, ed. Timothy J. Steigenga and Edward L. Cleary (New Brunswick, NJ, and London: Rutgers University Press, 2007), 115–32, esp. 117.

27. Berge Furre, "Crossing Boundaries: The 'Universal Church' and the Spirit of Globalization," in *Spirits of Globalization: The Growth of Pentecostalism and Experiential Spiritualities in a Global Age*, ed. Sturla J. Stålsett (London: SCM, 2006), 39–51, esp. 41.

28. Virginia Garrard-Burnett, "Stop Suffering? The Iglesia Universal del Reino de Dios in the United States," in Steigenga and Cleary, *Conversion of a Continent*, 218–38, esp. 30. At the same time, observers have also pointed out that more often than not, IURD missionaries seem to think it possible to transport many other aspects of the Brazilian version of the church's beliefs and practices without much sensitivity to the cultural distinctives of their "mission" fields; cf. Paul Freston, "The Transnationalisation of Brazilian Pentecostalism: The Universal Church of the Kingdom of God," in *Between Babel and Pentecost: Transnational Pentecostalism in Africa and Latin America*, ed. André Corten and Ruth Marshall-Fratani (Bloomington and Indianapolis: Indiana University Press, 2001), 196–215; and "The Universal Church of the Kingdom of God: A Brazilian Church Finds Success in Southern Africa," *Journal of Religion in Africa* 35, no. 1 (2005): 33–65.

29. Ari Pedro Oro and Pablo Séman, "Brazilian Pentecostalism Crosses National Borders," in Corten and Marshall-Fratani, *Between Babel and Pentecost*, 181–95.

30. See Mark R. Mullins, "The Empire Strikes Back: Korean Pentecostal Mission to Japan," in *Charismatic Christianity as a Global Culture*, ed. Karla Poewe (Columbia: University of South Carolina Press, 1994), 87–102.

31. Hyeong Sung Bae, "Full Gospel Theology and a Korean Pentecostal Identity," in *Asian and Pentecostal: The Charismatic Face of Christianity in Asia*, ed. Allan Anderson and Edmond Tang (Oxford: Regnum; Baguio City, Philippines: APTS Press, 2005), 527–49.

32. Hong Young-Gi, "The Influence of His [David Yonggi Cho's] Church Growth on Korean Society," in *Charis and Charisma: David Yonggi Cho and the Growth of Yoido Full Gospel Church*, ed. Hong Young-Gi and Myung Sung-Hoon (Oxford: Regnum, 2003), 197–217; and Ig-Jin Kim, *History and Theology of Korean Pentecostalism: Sunbogeum (Pure Gospel) Pentecostalism*, Mission Series 35 (Zoetermeer, the Netherlands: Uitgeverij Boekencentrum, 2003), chap. 15.

33. For a discussion of South Korean Pentecostal missions, see Kim, *History and Theology of Korean Pentecostalism*, chap. 14.

34. As posed by Chris Sugden, "Mission Leadership and Church Growth," in *David Yonggi Cho: A Close Look at His Theology and Ministry*, ed. Wonsuk Ma, William W. Menzies, and Hyeon Sung Bae (Goonpo, Korea: Hansei University Press; Baguio City, Philippines: APTS Press, 2004), 209–20, esp. 218.

35. Leo Oosterom, "Contemporary Missionary Thought in the Republic of Korea: Three Case-Studies on the Missionary Thought of Presbyterian Churches in Korea" (Utrecht-Leiden: Interuniversitair Instituut voor Missiologie en Oecumenica, 1990), 82; cited in Kim, *History and Theology of Korean Pentecostalism*, 283.

36. This is worked out more fully in my *In the Days of Caesar: Pentecostalism and Political Theology* (Grand Rapids: Eerdmans, 2010).

37. See Amos Yong, *The Spirit Poured Out on All Flesh: Pentecostalism and the Possibility of Global Theology* (Grand Rapids: Baker Academic, 2005), 27, 83–86.
38. For much further expansion of these motifs, see Amos Yong, *What in the World Is the Holy Spirit Doing Today? Explorations in Luke-Acts* [working title] (Brewster, MA: Paraclete Press, forthcoming).
39. See, e.g., Stanley Hauerwas and William H. Willimon, *Resident Aliens: Life in the Christian Colony* (Nashville: Abingdon Press, 1989); and idem, *Where Resident Aliens Live: Exercises for Christian Practice* (Nashville: Abingdon Press, 1996).
40. Hauerwas would represent the latter and more oppositional stance, while John Howard Yoder has adopted the former and more dialogical approach. For more on Yoder's use of the Jeremiah 29:7 motif—"But seek the welfare of the city where I have sent you into exile, and pray to the LORD on its behalf, for in its welfare you will find your welfare"—see his *The Jewish-Christian Schism Revisited*, ed. Michael G. Cartwright and Peter Ochs (Grand Rapids and Cambridge, UK: Eerdmans, 2003), 202–60.
41. Representative of the former is Vernon K. Robbins, "Luke-Acts: A Mixed Population Seeks a Home in the Roman Empire," in *Images of Empire*, ed. Loveday Alexander, Journal for the Study of the Old Testament Supplement Series 122 (Sheffield: Sheffield Academic Press, 1991), 202–21; arguing the latter is Kazuhiko Yamazaki-Ransom, "God, People, and Empire: Anti-Imperial Theology of Luke-Acts in Light of Jewish Portrayals of Gentile Rulers" (PhD diss., Trinity Evangelical Divinity School, 2006), esp. 195–211.
42. This diversity of early Christian responses to empire is overviewed in Warren Carter, *The Roman Empire and the New Testament: An Essential Guide* (Nashville: Abingdon Press, 2006), esp. chaps. 2 and 8.
43. I expand on this theme of hospitality vis-à-vis Christian mission in Amos Yong, *Hospitality and the Other: Pentecost, Christian Practices, and the Neighbor* (Maryknoll, NY: Orbis Books, 2008), esp. chaps. 4–5.
44. Among other scholarship see Judith Herrin, *The Formation of Christendom* (Princeton, NJ: Princeton University Press, 1987); and Alan Kreider, *The Change of Conversion and the Origin of Christendom* (Harrisburg, PA: Trinity Press International, 1999).
45. Peter Brown, *The Rise of Western Christendom*, 2nd ed. (Malden, MA: Blackwell, 2003); here I draw esp. from Brown's chap. 16, "Micro-Christendoms."
46. This is actually what allowed for the rise of powerful bishops like Athanasius, or imposing religious figures (or "holy saints") like Antony; see the thorough discussion in Timothy D. Barnes, *Athanasius and Constantius: Theology and Politics in the Constantinian Empire* (Cambridge, MA, and London: Harvard University Press, 1993), esp. chap. 17; reissued as an ACLS Humanities E-Book (Ann Arbor, MI: University of Michigan, Scholarly Publishing Office, 2002).
47. Brown, *Rise of Western Christendom*, 16.
48. See Stanley M. Burgess, *The Holy Spirit*, 3 vols. (Peabody, MA: Hendrickson Publishers, 1984, 1989, 1997).
49. See Lamin Sanneh, *Disciples of All Nations: Pillars of World Christianity*, Oxford Studies in World Christianity (Oxford and New York: Oxford University Press, 2008).
50. Here I have in mind also images of how the symbol of Christ, and even the christological systems we have formulated, can be used either for or against empire; see Joerg Rieger, *Christ and Empire: From Paul to Postcolonial Times* (Minneapolis: Fortress Press, 2007).

## Chapter 5: Mission from the Rest to the West

1. David B. Barrett, George T. Kurian, and Todd M. Johnson, eds., *World Christian Encyclopedia*, 2nd ed. (New York: Oxford University Press), 2002.
2. The original migration mentioned here began with Columbus's discovery of the Americas in 1492 and lasted for four and a half centuries; it has shaped the modern world. In this migration, millions of people left Europe and found homes in other parts of the world. These migrants and their descendents established hegemony over much of the world.
3. Samuel Escobar, "Mission from Everywhere to Everyone: The Home Base in a New Century," http://www.towards2010.org/downloads/t2010paper06escobar .pdf.
4. Ibid., 15.
5. This phrase is used in this chapter as a historical construct rather than a geographical construct. Stuart Hall, who was the first one to use this expression, argues that during the age of exploration and conquest, Europe began to define itself in relation to the existence of many new "worlds," profoundly different from itself. "West" came to include North America. For further discussion, refer to Stuart Hall, "The West and the Rest: Discourse and Power," in *Formations of Modernity*, ed. Stuart Hall and Bram Gieben (Cambridge, UK: Polity Press, 1992), 279–80.
6. Kenneth R. Ross, "Non-Western Christians in Scotland: Mission in Reverse," *Theology in Scotland* 12, no. 2 (Autumn 2005): 71, http://www.ctbi.org.uk/pdf_ view.php?id=210.
7. Dana Robert, "Shifting Southward: Global Christianity since 1945," *International Bulletin of Missionary Research* 24 (April 2000): 53.
8. Ibid.
9. Philip Jenkins, *The Next Christendom: The Coming of Global Christianity* (Oxford: Oxford University Press, 2002), 2.
10. For instance, the number of those who embraced Christianity from the work of the Scottish missionaries far exceeds the total population of Scotland itself. For further detail, refer to Ross, "Non-Western Christians in Scotland," 71–89.
11. Callum G. Brown, *The Death of Christian Britain* (London: Routledge, 2001), 1; quoted in Kenneth R. Ross, "'Blessed Reflex': Mission as God's Spiral of Renewal," *International Bulletin of Missionary Research* 27, no. 4 (October 2003): 162.
12. See http://al.feria.free.fr/StuartMurrayEmergentChurch.htm.
13. Ross, "'Blessed Reflex,'" 163.
14. Ibid.
15. Ibid.
16. Jenkins, *The Next Christendom*, 8.
17. Michael Jaffarian, "What the *WCE*[2] Numbers Show?" *International Bulletin of Missionary Research* 26 (July 2002): 130. See note 1 (above) for *WCE*[2].
18. Robert Eric Frykenberg, *Oxford History of the Christian Church: From Beginnings to the Present* (Oxford: Oxford University Press, 2008), vi.
19. This total makes Korea the second largest missionary-sending country in the world, ranking only after the United States in its number of overseas missionaries. This number is conservative, for it includes only missionaries belonging to mission agencies, not independent missionaries sent directly by a local church.

Nor does it include workers who committed themselves to missionary service for less than two years, or those who have given up Korean citizenship for the sake of their work. At present there are approximately 1,000 new missionaries being sent out each year from Korea to 162 countries. In 2000 only the United States sent missionaries to more (197) countries. The largest number of Korean missionaries serve in Asia (47.3 percent). The rest are active in the Eurasian countries of the former USSR (14.6 percent), followed by North America (9.3), Africa (7.7), Latin America (5.8), the Middle East (4.5), Western Europe (3.9), the South Pacific (2.9), and Eastern Europe (2.0), with the remainder in itineration and headquarters (2.0 percent). For further details, refer to Steve Sang-Cheol Moon, "The Protestant Missionary Movement in Korea: Current Growth and Development," *International Bulletin of Missionary Research* 32, no. 2 (April 2008): 59–62, http://krim.org/files/moon_on_korean_mission.pdf.

20. G. Rosales and C. G. Arevalo, eds., *For All the People of Asia*, vol. 1 (Manila: Claretian Publications, 1997), 130; quoted in Michael Amaladoss, "Mission Institutes in the Millennium," in *The West and the Rest of the World in Theology, Mission and Co-funding: Lectures on the Occasion of the 10th Anniversary of the Nijmegen Institute of Missiology*, ed. Frans Dokman (Nijmegen: Nijmegen Institute for Missiology, 2005): 66.
21. In 1963, the first Commission on World Mission and Evangelism (CWME) met in Mexico City under the theme of "Mission in Six Continents." The perspective of mission was enlarged to encompass every continent and not only those of the South.
22. Michael Amaladoss, "Foreign Missions Today," *East Asian Pastoral Review* 25 (1988): 104–18; quoted in Amaladoss, "Mission Institutes in the Millennium," 67.
23. Ibid., 69.
24. Claudia Währisch-Oblau, "Mission in Reverse: Whose Image in the Mirror?" *Anvil* 18, no. 4 (2001): 261.
25. Escobar, "Mission from Everywhere to Everyone," 16.
26. Roswith Gerloff, "Editorial," *International Review of Missions* 89, no. 354 (July 2000): 275–80, esp. 276; Gerloff is guest editor of this issue on the Millennial Conference at Westminster College, Cambridge, UK, on September 16–20, 1999: "Open Space—the African Christian Diaspora in Europe and the Quest for Human Community."
27. Ross, "Non-Western Christians in Scotland," 77.
28. Cited in Andrew F. Walls, "Migration and Evangelization: The Gospel and Movement of Peoples in Modern Times," *Covenant Quarterly* 63, no. 1 (February 2005): 24.
29. Gerloff, "Editorial," 275.
30. Walter J. Hollenweger, in the foreword to Roswith Gerloff, *A Plea for British Black Theologies: The Black Church Movement in Britain in Its Transatlantic Cultural and Theological Interaction* (Frankfurt am Main: Peter Lang,1992), ix.
31. Ross, "Non-Western Christians in Scotland," 81.
32. Andrew F. Walls, "Mission and Migration: The Diaspora Factor in Christian History," *Journal of African Christian Thought* 5, no. 2 (December 2002): 10–11.
33. John Olorunfemi Onaiyekan, "African Bishops Come to the Aid of Europe," *The Tablet*, November 20, 2004, 33; cited in Ross, "Non-Western Christians in Scotland," 82.

34. Rufus Ositelu, "Missio Africana: The Role of an African Instituted Church in the Mission Debate," *International Review of Mission* 89, No. 354 (July 2000): 385–86.
35. A document of the Evangelischen Kirche in Deutschland, "Zur ökumenischen Zusammenarbeit mit Gemeinden fremder Sprache oder Herkunft," EKD-Texte 59 (1996); quoted in Gerloff, "Editorial," 276.
36. Gerrie ter Haar, *Halfway to Paradise: African Christians in Europe* (Cardiff, UK: Cardiff Academic Press, 1998), 58; quoted in Ross, "Non-Western Christians in Scotland," 82.
37. Währisch-Oblau, "Mission in Reverse," 262.
38. Ibid.; cf. idem, http://www.warc.ch/miu/rw004/obl.html.
39. Währisch-Oblau, "Mission in Reverse," 262.
40. David F. D'Amico, "Evangelization across Cultures in the United States: What to Do with the World Come to Us?" http://www.ethnicharvest.com/links/articles/damico5.htm.
41. George R. Hunsberger, "The Newbigin Gauntlet: Developing a Domestic Missiology for North America," *Missiology: An International Review* 19 (October 1991): 391.
42. Ross, "'Blessed Reflex,'" 163.
43. Ibid., 166.
44. Kenneth R. Ross, "The Centenary of Edinburgh 1910: Its Possibilities," *International Bulletin of Missionary Research* 3, no. 4 (October 2006): 177.
45. David Bosch, *Transforming Mission: Paradigm Shifts in Theology of Mission* (Maryknoll, NY: Orbis Books, 1991), 338.

**Chapter 6: Expanding the Boundaries, Turning Borders into Spaces**

1. Eleanor Wilner, "Emigration," in *Vital Signs: Contemporary American Poetry from the University Presses*, ed. Ronald Wallace (Madison: University of Wisconsin Press, 1989), 91.
2. See "Global Migrants Reach 191 Million," BBC News, June 7, 2006, http://news.bbc.co.uk/2/hi/americas/5054214.stm.
3. *Anderson Cooper 360°*, CNN, August 2007.
4. Mike Parnwell, *Population Movements and the Third World* (London: Routledge, 1993), 29–30.
5. Nikos Papastergiadis, *The Turbulence of Migration* (Cambridge, UK: Polity Press, 2000), 40, 44.
6. For example, Frenchman Jean-Marie Le Pen, who asserted that immigration will lead to "the submersion of our country, our people, our civilization," got enough votes in the 2002 presidential elections to challenge President Chirac in the second and final round. In other cases this nationalism provokes a violent backlash. Pim Fortuyn, a popular and outspoken anti-immigration politician in the Netherlands, also advocated for the cessation of immigrants, particularly those from the Muslim world. Fortuyn argued that Muslim immigrants were eroding Dutch national identity and threatening the traditional liberal Dutch tolerance for homosexuality and commitment to equality for women. Fortuyn was assassinated by a Dutch Muslim jihadist in 2002.
7. On the positive side, Agence France-Presse (AFP) in "Migrant Workers to Remit Home 225 Billion Dollars in 2005: World Bank," October 25, 2005, http://www.mywire.com/a/AFP/Migrants-workers-to-remit-home/1061157?&pbl=27, cites a study by World Bank that showed remittances playing a key role in slashing

poverty rates in developing economies. Still, most scholars maintain that such an effect is not across the board nor critical enough to lift third-world countries out of their impoverishment.

8. Filipino overseas workers, for instance, even have their own political party (aptly named Migrante International, http://migrante.tripod.com/), with its own representative and staff in the Philippines and branch offices worldwide.

9. Elizabeth Apuya, "Money or a Day Off," *TNT Hong Kong* 2, no. 2 (March 1996): 5.

10. English spoken with a Cantonese accent, as could be the case with Singlish (Singaporean English) or Spanglish (Spanish English), could be hard to decipher for someone who is not used to speaking or hearing it. For example, many Chinese in Hong Kong have a problem pronouncing the letter "r," which often becomes "l," as in "fry" becomes "fly." Moreover, some employers have problems with correct grammar or sentence construction.

11. Vicky, "Cook Yourself," *Tinig Filipino*, July 1992, 48; as quoted in Nicole Constable, *Maid to Order in Hong Kong* (Ithaca, NY: Cornell University Press, 1997), 177–78.

12. Gregg Easterbrook, "Religion in America: The New Ecumenicalism," January 1, 2002, http://www.brookings.edu/articles/2002/winter_religion_easterbrook.aspx.

13. Kathleen Sullivan, "St. Mary's Catholic Church: Celebrating Domestic Religion," in *Religion and the New Immigrants: Continuities and Adaptations in Immigrant Congregations*, ed. Helen Rose Ebaugh and Janet Saltzman Chafetz (Walnut Creek, CA: Alta Mira Press, 2000), 197.

14. Simon Jacob and Pallavi Thakur, "Jyothi Hindu Temple: One Religion, Many Practices," in Ebaugh and Chafetz, *Religion and the New Immigrants*, 153.

15. See Justice in the World, *Justicia in mundo*, §6 http://www.osjspm.org/major doc_justicia_in_mundo_offical_test.aspx.

16. Nelle Morton, *The Journey Is Home* (Boston: Beacon Press, 1985), xix; quoted by Letty Russell in her *Household of Freedom: Authority in Feminist Theology* (Philadelphia: Westminster Press, 1987), 67.

17. See "Filipino Migrant Workers in Hong Kong," *Asian Migrant* 7, no. 1 (January–March 1994): 7.

18. In the Dutch city where I used to live, for instance, Filipinas married to Dutchmen are instrumental in bringing religion not only into the lives of their Dutch husbands but also to their children as they become active members in the Filipino Dutch community, which gathers monthly for the Eucharist (also regularly for social events), followed by a festive meal.

19. For more on this immigrant church, see Fenggang Yang, "Chinese Gospel Church: The Sinization of Christianity," in Ebaugh and Chafetz, *Religion and the New Immigrants*, 180–95.

20. "Filipino Migrant Workers in Hong Kong," 6–7.

21. Gerrie ter Haar, *Halfway to Paradise: African Christians in Europe* (Cardiff, UK: Cardiff Academic Press, 1998), 92.

### Chapter 7: Short-Term Missions as a New Paradigm

1. Arthur G. McPhee, *The Road to Delhi: J. Waskom Pickett Remembered* (Bangalore, India: SAIACS Press, 2005), 194–96.

2. Robert Wuthnow and Stephen Offutt, "Transnational Religious Connections," *Sociology of Religion* 69 (2008): 218.

3. Robert J. Priest and Joseph Paul Priest, "They See Everything, and Understand Nothing: Short-Term Mission and Service Learning," *Missiology: An International Review* 36 (2008): 53–73.
4. Wuthnow and Offutt. "Transnational Religious Connections," 218.
5. Jenny Trinitapoli and Stephen Vaisey, "The Transformative Role of Religious Experience: The Case of Short-Term Missions," essay (2008) in *Social Forces: International Journal of Social Research* 88, no. 1 (September 2009).
6. Kyeong-Sook Park reports even higher rates of involvement in STM abroad (75%) in her account of 869 Bible college students. She surveyed both students in core required courses and students in some mission courses that were not required of all students—which may well account for this higher report. Nonetheless, her work provides additional evidence that Bible college students participate in short-term missions at very high rates. See her report, "Researching Short-Term Missions and Paternalism," in *Effective Engagement in Short-Term Missions: Doing It Right!* ed. Robert J. Priest (Pasadena, CA: William Carey Library, 2008), 499–522.
7. Cited in McPhee, *The Road to Delhi*, 342.
8. Robert J. Priest and Joseph Paul Priest, "They See Everything, and Understand Nothing," 57.
9. Scott Moreau, "Short-Term Missions in the Context of Missions Inc.," in Robert J. Priest, *Effective Engagement in Short-Term Missions*, 1–33.
10. Kurt Ver Beek, "Lessons from the Sapling: Review of Quantitative Research on Short-Term Missions," in Robert J. Priest, *Effective Engagement in Short-Term Missions*, 475–97; and Robert J. Priest, Terry Dischinger, Steve Rasmussen, and C. M. Brown, "Researching the Short-Term Mission Movement," *Missiology* 34, no. 4 (2006): 431–50.
11. Scott Meier, "Missionary, Minister to Thyself: The Real Reason behind Mission Work," *Youthworker* 17, no. 5 (2001): 24-28.
12. Paul Borthwick, "Short-Term Missions, Tape of GMC Triennial Chinese Mission Conference Sponsored by Ambassadors for Christ, Philadelphia, 12-29-2004."
13. Charles A. Cook and Joel Van Hoogen, "Towards a Missiologically and Morally Responsible Short-Term Ministry," *Journal of Latin American Theology* 2 (2007): 49.
14. See, e.g., Harri Englund, "The Quest for Missionaries: Transnationalism and Township Pentecostalism in Malawi," in *Between Babel and Pentecost: Transnational Pentecostalism in Africa and Latin America*, ed. André Corten and Ruth Marshall-Fratani (Bloomington: Indiana University Press, 2001), 235–55; and Harri Englund, "Christian Independency and Global Membership: Pentecostal Extraversions in Malawi," *Journal of Religion in Africa* 33, no. 1 (2003): 83–111.
15. Englund, "The Quest for Missionaries," 244.
16. Miguel Angel Palomino, *Misión en la ciudad* (Lima, Peru: SERCY, 1990).
17. Robert Putnam, *Bowling Alone: The Collapse and Revival of American Community* (New York: Simon & Schuster, 2001), 66.
18. Ibid., 22.
19. Ibid., 23.
20. Ibid., 22.
21. Michael Woolcock, "Managing Risk, Shocks, and Opportunity in Developing Economies: The Role of Social Capital," in *Dimensions of Development*, ed. Gustav Ranis (New Haven, CT: Yale Center for International and Area Studies, 1999), 197–212.

22. Robert Wuthnow, "Religious Involvement and Status-Bridging Social Capital," *Journal for the Social Scientific Study of Religion* 41 (2002): 669–84.

23. C. M. Brown, "Friendship Is Forever: Congregation-to-Congregation Relationships," in Robert J. Priest, *Effective Engagement in Short-Term Missions*, 209–37.

24. Kersten Bayt Priest, "Women as Resource Brokers: STM Trips, Social and Organizational Ties, and Mutual Resource Benefits," in Robert J. Priest, *Effective Engagement in Short-Term Missions*, 257–75.

25. Hunter Farrell, "Cleaning Up La Oroya," *Christianity Today*, April 20, 2007, http://www.christianitytoday.com/ct/2007/april/37.70.html.

26. Kersten Bayt Priest, "Caring for the Least of These: Christian Women's Short-Term Mission Travel" (PhD diss., Loyola University, Chicago, 2009).

### Chapter 8: "Do Not Fear: Go"

1. Osvaldo D. Vena, *Evangelio de Marcos* (Miami, FL: Sociedades Bíblicas Unidas, 2008), 363–364.

2. Julia Esquivel, "Cuando llegue la hora," http://mypage.direct.ca/j/julio/julia.html."

3. Amy-Jill Levine, "Matthew," in *The Women's Bible Commentary*, ed. Carol A. Newsom and Sharon H. Ringe (Louisville, KY: Westminster/John Knox Press, 1992), 262.

4. Ester A. de Boer, "The Lukan Mary Magdalene and the Other Women Following Jesus," in *A Feminist Companion to Luke*, ed. Amy-Jill Levine (New York: Sheffield Academic Press, 2002), 155.

5. *Evangelio de María Magdalena* (Fragmento P.Ryl. III 463), in *Los Evangelios Apócrifos: Colección de textos griegos y latinos, Versión crítica, estudios introductorias y comentarios*, ed. Aurelio de Santos Otero, 8th ed. (Madrid: Biblioteca de Autores Cristianos, 1993), 96–97.

6. Cf. Susan Thorne, "Missionary-Imperial Feminism," in *Gendered Missions: Women and Men in Missionary Discourse and Practice*, ed. Mary Taylor Huber and Nancy C. Lutkehaus (Ann Arbor: University of Michigan Press, 1999), 39–65. By using the concept, I am referring broadly to the phenomenon of relatively privileged women who (sometimes with the best of intentions) replicate patterns of injustice in their mission work in the Global South.

7. Mirta Bazán, Margarita Canteros, Amanda Farías, Blanca Geymonat, and Hilda Gómez, "La palabra de mujeres a partir bíblico-teológico en la interculturalidad," in *El mundo palpita, economía, género y teología*, ed. Nancy Bedford and Marisa Strizzi (Buenos Aires: ISEDET, 2006), 90–92.

8. On the question of the land, see Ana María Jose Hrycaniñk, "La cuestión de tierras entre los indígenas Toba Q'om argentinos," http://www.indigenas.bioetica.org/inves11.htm#_Toc39412472.

9. Patricia Hill Collins, *Black Sexual Politics: African Americans, Gender, and the New Racism* (New York: Routledge, 2004), 11.

10. On this, see Mrinalini Sebastian, "Mission without History? Some Ideas for Decolonizing Mission," *International Review of Mission* 93 (January 2004): 77.

11. Mercy Amba Oduyoye, "Calling the Church to Account: African Women and Liberation," *Ecumenical Review* (October 1995), http://findarticles.com/p/articles/mi_m2065/is_n4_v47/ai_18069979.

12. Letty Russell, *Church in the Round: Feminist Interpretation of the Church* (Louisville, KY: Westminster John Knox Press, 1993), 90; as she points out on this same page, her doctoral dissertation was about "Tradition as Mission" (Union Theological Seminary, New York, 1969).

13. Russell, *Church in the Round*, 94,

14. Ibid., 110.

15. Gnana Robinson, "Solidarity as Missionary Principle," in *Many Voices in Christian Mission: Essays in Honour of J. E. Lesslie Newbigin*, ed. T. Dayanandan Francis and Israel Selvanayagam (Madras, India: Christian Literature Society, 1994), 98.

16. Ibid., 104.

17. See Mary Schaller Blaufuss, "Relationships rather than Frontiers: Contributions of Women-in-Mission and of Women's Issues to the Field of Missiology," in *Ecumenical Missiology: Contemporary Trends, Issues, and Themes*, ed. Lalsangkima Pachuau (Bangalore, India: United Theological College, 2002), 185–86.

18. Musimbi Kanyoro, "Thinking Mission in Africa," in *A Feminist Companion to the Acts of the Apostles*, ed. Amy-Jill Levine (New York: T&T Clark International, 2004), 66.

19. Ibid., 67.

20. Ibid., 70.

21. Lalrindiki Ralte, "The Struggle of the Mizo Women Vegetable Vendors: A Challenge to the Mission of the Church," in *Re-routing Mission: Towards a People's Concept of Mission (Indian Perspective)*, ed. George Mathew Nalunnakkal (Tiruvalla, India: CSS [Christava Sahitya Samithi] Books, 2004), 6–67.

22. Kirsteen Kim, *The Holy Spirit in the World: A Global Conversation* (Maryknoll, NY: Orbis Books, 2007), 181.

23. Katja Heidemanns, "Missiology of Risk? Explorations in Mission Theology from a German Feminist Perspective," *International Review of Mission* 93 (January 2004): 105–18.

24. Susan Smith, "The Holy Spirit and Mission in Some Contemporary Theologies of Mission," *Mission Studies* 18 (2001): 104.

25. Ibid., 105.

26. The bodily, material dimension of the *imago Dei* is central; as Irenaeus puts it, "The soul and the spirit are certainly a *part* of the human, but certainly not *the* human; for the perfect human consists in the commingling and the union of the soul receiving the spirit of the Father, and the admixture of that fleshly nature which was molded after the image of God" (*Adversus haereses* 5.6.1).

27. Linda Thomas, "Anthropology, Mission and the African Woman: A Womanist Approach," *Black Theology* 5 (2007): 11–19, esp. 13–14.

28. See Judy Root Aulette, Judith Wittner, and Kristin Blakely, *Gendered Worlds* (Oxford: Oxford University Press, 2009), 223–29. They quote Peggy Reeves Sanday's work in looking for comparatively rape-free societies (such as that of a group in Central Thailand) and rape-prone societies, such as that of the Yanomami people in Brazil. Cf. Peggy Reeves Sanday, *Fraternity Gang Rape: Sex, Brotherhood, and Privilege on Campus*, 2nd ed. (New York: New York University Press, 2007).

29. See Dana Roberts, "World Christianity as a Women's Movement," in *International Bulletin of Missionary Research* 30, no. 4 (October 2006): 180–88.

30. Women's voices are even underrepresented in the publications. For example, of the 20 testimonies on "My Pilgrimage in Mission" published in the *International Bulletin of Missionary Research* (during January 2003 through April 2008), only one was written by a woman, and one by a couple.

31. Nam-Soon Kang, "The Centrality of Gender Justice in Prophetic Christianity and the Mission of the Church Reconsidered," *International Review of Mission* 94 (April 2005): 289.

## Chapter 9: Defining "Racisms"

1. Stephen Bevans, "From Edinburgh to Edinburgh: Toward a Missiology for a World Church" (2008 Scherer Lecture, Lutheran School of Theology at Chicago, February 19, 2008), heretofore unpublished but now appearing as chap. 1 (above), see the section "From Power to Vulnerability."
2. On the Web site *Remembering the Past: Redefining the Future*, in the "Archive for the 'V. S. Azariah' Category," see the section "The Courage to Speak Your Mind," http://missionstudygroup.wordpress.com/category/visionaries/vs-azariah/.
3. Ibid.
4. Bevans, in chap. 1 (above), "From Edinburgh to Edinburgh," in the section "From Power to Vulnerability."
5. Margo Monteith and Jeffery Winters, "Why We Hate," *Psychology Today*, May/June 2002, 45.
6. Jeremy Manier, "Recesses of the Mind," *Chicago Tribune*, October 13, 1996, Perspective Section, 1.
7. Sandra Harding, ed., *The "Racial" Economy of Science: Toward a Democratic Future* (Bloomington: University of Indiana Press, 1993); see also UNESCO (1950, 1951, 1964, 1967).
8. Dwight N. Hopkins, *Being Human: Race, Culture, and Religion* (Minneapolis: Fortress Press, 2005), 131.
9. George M. Fredrickson, *Race: A Short History* (Princeton, NJ: Princeton University Press, 2002), 53.
10. David Brion Davis, "Constructing Race: A Reflection," in *In the Image of God: Religion, Moral Values, and Our Heritage of Slavery*, ed. David Brion Davis (New Haven, CT: Yale University Press, 2001), 307–42.
11. Fredrickson, *Race: A Short History*, 1–6.
12. Albert Memmi, *Racism*, trans. Steve Martinot (Minneapolis: University of Minnesota Press, 2000), 100.
13. Ibid., xvii.
14. Ibid., xviii.
15. Ibid., xix.
16. Ibid., 92.
17. Ibid., 93.
18. Ibid., 94.
19. See Michael Omi and Howard Winant, *Racial Formation in the United States: From the 1960s to the 1990s*, 2nd ed. (New York: Routledge, 1994), 117–18; Gargi Bhattacharyya, John Gabriel, and Stephen Small, *Race and Power: Global Racism in the Twenty-first Century* (London: Routledge, 2002), 28–59, 125–26.
20. Memmi, *Racism*, 43.
21. Ibid., 45.
22. See Omi and Winant, *Racial Formation in the United States*, 117; and Neil Mac-Master, *Racism in Europe, 1870–2000* (New York: Palgrave, 2001), 193–208.
23. MacMaster, *Racism in Europe*, 2.
24. See Kelly Brown Douglas, *What's Faith Got to Do with It? Black Bodies and Christian Souls* (Maryknoll, NY: Orbis Books, 2005).

25. D. W. Waruta, "Tribalism as a Moral Problem in Contemporary Africa," in *Moral and Ethical Issues in African Christianity*, ed. J. N. K. Mugambi and A. Nasimiyu-Wasike (Nairobi, Kenya: Initiatives Publishers, 1992), 2.
26. E. Cashmore, "Xenophobia," in *Dictionary of Race and Ethnic Relations*, ed. E. Cashmore et al. (London: Routledge, 1994), 346.
27. MacMaster, *Racism in Europe*, 190–91.
28. J. M. Voster, "Racism, Xenophobia and Human Rights," *Ecumenical Review* 54, no. 3 (July 2002): 7.
29. See http://www.davidduke.com/index.php?p=350.
30. MacMaster, *Racism in Europe*, 192.
31. Ibid., 194.
32. Ibid.
33. Ibid., 195–98.
34. See Joel S. Panzer, *The Popes and Slavery* (New York: Alba House, 1996).
35. Timothy E. O'Connell, *Making Disciples: A Handbook of Christian Moral Formation* (New York: Crossroad, 1998), 116–27.
36. See Christopher A. Frillingos, "'For My Child, Onesimus': Paul and Domestic Power in Philemon," *Journal of Biblical Literature* 119, no. 1 (Spring 2000): 91–104.
37. See Ivan Hannaford, *Race: The History of an Idea in the West* (Baltimore: Johns Hopkins University Press, 1996); also see Lloyd A. Thompson, *Romans and Blacks* (Norman: University of Oklahoma Press, 1989); and see also Frank M. Snowdon Jr., *Before Color and Prejudice: The Ancient View of Blacks* (Cambridge, MA: Harvard University Press, 1983).
38. Pontifical Justice and Peace (Justitia et Pax) Commission's statement, "The Church and Racism: Towards a More Fraternal Society" (November 3, 1988), http://www.inaword.com/svd/church%20and%20racism.pdf.
39. Pontifical Council for Justice and Peace, "Contribution to World Conference against Racism, Racial Discrimination, Xenophobia and Related Intolerance," http://www.vatican.va/roman_curia/pontifical_councils/justpeace/documents/rc_pc_justpeace_doc_20010829_comunicato-razzismo_en.html.
40. Memmi, *Racism*, 96.
41. Bryan N. Massingale, "James Cone and Recent Catholic Episcopal Teaching on Racism," *Theological Studies* 61, no. 4 (December 2000): 700–730.
42. See Francis Cardinal George, OMI, "Dwell in My Love: A Pastoral Letter on Racism" (April 4, 2001), http://www.archchicago.org/cardinal/dwellinmylove/dwellinmylove.shtm. See also Archbishop Alfred Hughes, STD, "'Made in the Image and Likeness of God': A Pastoral Letter on Racial Harmony" (published by the *Clarion Herald*, December 16, 2006), http://www.louisianacatholicconference.org/bins/site/content/louisiana/docs/Archbishop%27s%20Racial%20Harmony%20statement.pdf?_resolutionfile=ftppath%7Clouisiana/docs/Archbishop's%20Racial%20Harmony%20statement.pdf.

### Chapter 10: A Beloved Earth Community

1. For reports of the Intergovernmental Panel on Climate Change, go to www.ipcc.ch.
2. On social transformation, see David Korten, *The Great Turning: From Empire to Earth Community* (San Francisco: Berrett-Koehler, 2006); Lester Brown, *Plan B 3.0: Mobilizing to Save Civilization* (New York: W. W. Norton, 2008); Bill McKibben, *Deep Economy: The Wealth of Communities and the Durable Future* (New York: Henry Holt, 2007); and Van Jones, *The Green Collar Econ-*

*omy: How One Solution Can Fix Our Two Biggest Problems* (New York: Harper-One, 2008).

3. Thomas Berry, *The Great Work: Our Way into the Future* (New York: Bell Tower, 1999). On the environmental movement, see Paul Hawken, *Blessed Unrest: How the Largest Social Movement in History Is Restoring Grace, Justice, and Beauty to the World* (New York: Penguin Books, 2008).

4. See David Kingsley, "Christianity as Ecologically Harmful and Christianity as Ecologically Responsible," in *This Sacred Earth*, ed. Roger Gottlieb (New York: Routledge, 1996); and various chapters in Dieter T. Hessel and Rose-mary Radford Ruether, eds., *Christianity and Ecology* (Cambridge, MA: Harvard University Press, 2000).

5. See http://www.nrpe.org.

6. David Hallman, *Ecotheology: Voices from South and North* (Maryknoll, NY: Orbis Books, 1994).

7. Michael Barnes, ed., *An Ecology of the Spirit: Religious Reflections and Ecological Consciousness* (Lanham, MD: University Press of America, 1994); David Kinsey, *Ecology and Religion: Ecospirituality in Cross-Cultural Perspective* (Englewood Cliffs, NJ: Prentice-Hall, 1995); and Laurel Kearns and Catherine Keller, eds., *Ecospirit: Religions and Philosophies for the Earth* (New York: Fordham University Press, 2007). For in-depth analysis of different religions, see the Religions of the World and Ecology series, edited by Evelyn Tucker and John Grim for Harvard University Press (1997–).

8. See Richard John Huggett, *Fundamentals of Biogeography* (New York: Routledge, 1998), 218.

9. E. O. Wilson, *The Creation: An Appeal to Save Life on Earth* (New York: W. W. Norton, 2006).

10. In private conversation with David Rhoads in the mid-1980s.

11. Elizabeth Kolbert, *Field Notes from a Catastrophe: Man, Nature, and Climate Change* (New York: Bloomsbury, 2006); and Stephan Faris, *Forecast: The Consequences of Climate Change, from the Amazon to the Arctic, from Darfur to Napa Valley* (New York: Henry Holt, 2008).

12. James Cone, "Whose Earth Is It Anyway?" in *Earth and Word: Classic Sermons on Saving the Planet*, ed. David Rhoads (New York: Continuum), 142.

13. Leonardo Boff, *Cry of the Earth, Cry of the Poor* (Maryknoll, NY: Orbis Books, 1997), 104.

14. On ecological ethics, see Dieter Hessel and Larry Rasmussen, eds., *Earth Habitat: Eco-injustice and the Church's Response* (Minneapolis: Fortress Press, 2001); Michael Northcott, *Environment and Christian Ethics* (Cambridge, UK: Cambridge University Press, 1996); Larry Rasmussen, *Earth Community, Earth Ethics* (Maryknoll, NY: Orbis Books, 1996); and Willis Jenkins, *Ecologies of Grace: Environmental Ethics and Christian Theology* (Oxford: Oxford University Press, 2008).

15. See, e.g., the essays in Robert Bullard, ed., *The Quest for Environmental Justice: Human Rights and the Politics of Pollution* (San Francisco: Sierra Club, 2005).

16. See Jones, *Green Collar Economy*.

17. See Rosemary Ruether, *Women Healing Earth: Third World Women on Ecology, Feminism, and Religion* (Maryknoll, NY: Orbis Books, 1996), 143–60.

18. On biblical interpretation, see Ronald Simkins, *Creator and Creation: Nature in the Worldview of Ancient Israel* (Peabody, MA: Hendrickson Publishers, 1994); Dianne Bergant, *Israel's Wisdom Literature: A Liberation-Critical Reading* (Minneapolis: Fortress Press, 1997); Terence Fretheim, *God and World in the Old*

*Testament: A Relational Theology of Creation* (Nashville: Abingdon Press, 2005); and Norman Habel and Peter Trudinger, eds., *Exploring Ecological Hermeneutics* (Atlanta: Society of Biblical Literature, 2008). See esp. the five volumes in the Earth Bible series edited by Norman Habel et al. for Sheffield Academic Press (2000–). For a copy of the New Revised Standard Version with passages related to nature highlighted, see *The Green Bible* (New York: HarperCollins, 2008).

19. Theodore Hiebert, *The Yahwist's Landscape: Nature and Religion in Early Israel* (Oxford: Oxford University Press, 1996).

20. Ellen Davis, *Scripture, Culture, and Agriculture: An Agrarian Reading of the Bible* (Cambridge, UK: Cambridge University Press, 2009).

21. Bernard Anderson, "Creation and Noachic Covenant," in *Cry of the Environment*, ed. Philip Joranson and Ken Butigan (Santa Fe, NM: Bear & Co., 1984), 510–51.

22. See worship resources at www.seasonofcreation.com. See also Gordon Lathrop, *Holy Ground: A Liturgical Cosmology* (Minneapolis: Fortress Press, 2003); and Paul Santmire, *Ritualizing Nature: Renewing Christian Liturgy in a Time of Crisis* (Minneapolis: Fortress Press, 2008).

23. Barbara Rossing, "River of Life in God's New Jerusalem: An Ecological Vision for Earth's Future," in *Christianity and Ecology*, ed. Rosemary Radford Ruether and Dieter T. Hessel (Cambridge, MA: distributed by Harvard University Press for the Harvard University Center for the Study of World Religions, 2000), 205–24.

24. H. Paul Santmire, *The Travail of Nature: The Ambiguous Theological Promise of Christian Theology* (Philadelphia: Fortress Press, 1985); and idem, *Nature Reborn: The Ecological and Cosmic Promise of Christian Theology* (Minneapolis: Fortress Press, 2000); Steven Bouma-Prediger, *The Greening of Theology: The Ecological Models of Rosemary Radford Ruether, Joseph Sittler, and Jürgen Moltmann* (Atlanta: Scholars Press, 1995); Sallie McFague, *The Body of God: An Ecological Theology* (Minneapolis: Fortress Press, 1993); idem, *A New Climate for Theology: God, the World, and Global Warming* (Minneapolis: Fortress Press, 2008); and Viggo Mortensen, ed., *Concern for Creation: Voices on the Theology of Creation* (Uppsala: Tro & Tanke, 1995).

25. See Thomas Berry and Brian Schwimme, *The Universe Story: From the Primordial Flaring Forth to the Ecozoic Era—A Celebration of the Unfolding of the Cosmos* (New York: HarperCollins, 1992); and Christopher Southgate, *The Groaning of Creation: God, Evolution, and the Problem of Evil* (Louisville, KY: Westminster John Knox Press, 2008).

26. Jace Weaver, ed., *Defending Mother Earth: Native American Perspectives on Environmental Justice* (Maryknoll, NY: Orbis Books, 1996).

27. Ogbu U. Kalu, "Gods as Policemen: Religion and Social Control in Igboland," in *Religious Pluralism in Africa*, ed. K. Olupona and S. Nyang (Berlin: Mouton de Gruyter, 1993).

28. Joseph Sittler, "Called to Unity," in *Evocations of Grace: The Writings of Joseph Sittler on Ecology, Theology, and Ethics*, ed. Steve Bouma-Prediger and Peter Bakken (Grand Rapids: Wm. B. Eerdmans Publishing Co., 2000), 38–50.

29. Mark Wallace, *Fragments of the Spirit: Nature, Violence, and the Renewal of Creation* (Harrisburg, PA: Trinity Press International, 2002); Joseph Sittler, *Evocations of Grace*, 59–75; Dennis Edwards, *Breath of Life: A Theology of the Creator Spirit* (Maryknoll, NY: Orbis Books, 2004).

30. Mary Evelyn Tucker and John Allen Grim, "The Emerging Alliance of Religion and Ecology," *Worldviews: Environment, Culture, Religion* 1, no. 1 (April 1997):

3–24; excerpt, http://environment.yale.edu/pubs/The-Emerging-Alliance-of-Religion-and-Ecology/.

31. Michael Schut, ed. and compiler, *Simpler Life, Compassionate Life: A Christian Perspective* (Denver, CO: Living the Good News, 1999); and Barbara Kingsolver, *Animal, Vegetable, Miracle: A Year of Food Life* (New York: Harper-Collins, 2007).

32. On ecospirituality, see Sarah McFarland Taylor, *Green Sisters: A Spiritual Ecology* (Cambridge, MA: Harvard University Press, 2007); and Howard Clinebell, *Ecotherapy: Healing Ourselves, Healing the Earth* (Minneapolis: Fortress Press, 1996).

33. Care-for-creation resources for faith communities are offered at www.web ofcreation.org. On stewardship as a Christian environmental model, see R. J. Berry, ed., *Environmental Stewardship: Critical Perspectives—Past and Present* (New York: T&T Clark, 2006).

34. See David Rhoads, "Who Will Speak for the Sparrow: Eco-Justice Criticism of the New Testament," in *Literary Encounters with the Kingdom of God: Essays in Honor of Robert Tannehill*, ed. Sharon Ringe and Hyun Chul Paul Kim (New York: T&T Clark, 2004), 64–65.

35. Brian Blount, *Go Preach! Mark's Kingdom Message and the Black Church Today* (Maryknoll, NY: Orbis Books, 1998), 15–16.

36. Gerard Manley Hopkins, "God's Grandeur," in *Poems of Gerard Manley Hopkins*, 4th ed., ed. W. H. Gardner and N. H. Mackensie (Oxford: Oxford University Press, 1967).

37. Wendell Berry, "Original Sin," in *Given: New Poems* (Emeryville, CA: Shoemaker Hoard, 2005), 35.

## Chapter 11: Mission as Dialogue

1. Pope John Paul II, Apostolic Letter, *Tertio millennio adveniente* (November 10, 1994), http://www.vatican.va/holy_father/john_paul_ii/apost_letters/documents/hf_jp-ii_apl_10111994_tertio-millennio-adveniente_en.html.

2. See http://www.evangelisation2000.com/Welcome-e.htm.

3. Evangelization 2000 Prayer, http://www.evangelization2000.org/let_us_pray .htm.

4. See Edmund Chia, "Of Fork and Spoon or Fingers and Chopsticks: Interreligious Dialogue," *Horizons* 28 (Fall 2001): 294–306; repr., in *The Asian Synod: Texts and Commentaries*, ed. Peter Phan (Maryknoll, NY: Orbis Books, 2002), 273–83.

5. See Edmund Chia, "Regensburg and Dialogue," *Studies in Interreligious Dialogue* 17 (2007): 70–82.

6. Arun Shourie, *Harvesting Our Souls: Missionaries, Their Design, Their Claims* (New Delhi, India: ASA [African Studies Association of India] Publications, 2000).

7. See Edmund Chia, "Thirty Years of FABC: History, Foundation, Context and Theology," in *FABC Papers 106* (Hong Kong: FABC, 2003), 1–56, http://www.ucanews.com/html/fabc-papers/fabc-106.htm.

8. Federation of Asian Bishops' Conferences, "Message and Resolutions of the Asian Bishops' Meeting [Manila, Philippines, November 29, 1970]," in *For All the Peoples of Asia*, vol. 1, *Documents from 1970 to 1991*, ed. Gaudencio Rosales and C. G. Arévalo (Quezon City, Philippines: Claretian Publications, 1997), 3, 9.

9. Felix Wilfred, "The Federation of Asian Bishops' Conferences [FABC]: Orientations, Challenges and Impact," in ibid., xxiii, http://www.ucanews.com/html/fabc-papers/fabc-69.htm.

10. Aloysius Pieris, "Toward an Asian Theology of Liberation," in *An Asian Theology of Liberation* (Quezon City, Philippines: Claretian Publications, 1989), 69.
11. Federation of Asian Bishops' Conferences, *For All the Peoples of Asia*, vol. 3, *Documents from 1997 to 2001*, ed. Franz-Josef Eilers (Quezon City, Philippines: Claretian Publications, 2002), 4.
12. Aloysius Pieris, "Asia's Non-Semitic Religions and the Mission of the Local Churches," in *An Asian Theology of Liberation* (Quezon City, Philippines: Claretian Publications, 1989), 38.
13. See Edmund Chia, "Wanted: Interreligious Dialogue," *Studies in Interreligious Dialogue* 12, no. 1 (2002): 101–10.
14. The theme of the Seventh Plenary Assembly of the FABC was "A Renewed Church in Asia: A Mission of Love and Service"; see "FABC VII" in FABC, *For All the Peoples of Asia*, 3:1.
15. The case of East Timor exemplifies this political chaos. A colony of the Portuguese for nearly 400 years, civil war broke out when the local resistance fighters declared independence for the nation. This was then followed by the neighboring Indonesian invading force, whose occupation of the nation lasted from 1975 to 1999, at a cost of hundreds of thousands of human lives. See Georg Evers, *Human Rights in East Timor: The Difficult Road to Statehood* (Aachen, Germany: Missio [Pontifical Mission Society, Human Rights Office], 2001), 5–8, http://www.missio-aachen.de/images/mr%20osttimor%20englisch_tcm14-12079.pdf.
16. In a paper presented at a conference in Berlin, I discussed Christian-Muslim relations in Malaysia by looking at its roots in the colonial policies of the British, which divided the people in order to rule better. This partly accounts for the continued racial and religious polarization that so pervades the country. See Edmund Chia, "The Multifaceted Mission in Malaysia," in *Church in the Service of Asia's Peoples*, ed. Jacob Kavunkal, Errol D'Lima, and Mathew Jayanth (Pune, India: Jnana-Deepa Vidyapeeth, 2003), 99–112.
17. Francis Houtart, "Underdevelopment: An Induced Phenomenon," *Vidyajyoti Journal of Theological Reflection* 39 (1975): 62. Elucidating on this with a specific example, Matthew Kurien comments: "The total wealth transferred from India by British imperialism has been variously estimated at between 500 million and 1,000 million pounds." Little imagination is needed to make the connection that Britain's wealth and developed status might have something to do with India's poverty and underdevelopment. See Matthew Kurien, "Socio-Economic and Political Reality in Asia," in *Asia's Struggle for Full Humanity*, ed. Virginia Fabella (Maryknoll, NY: Orbis Books, 1980), 64.
18. George Soares-Prabhu, "Inculturation—Liberation—Dialogue: Challenges to Christian Theology in Asia Today," in *Biblical Themes for a Contextual Theology Today*, ed. Isaac Padinjarekuttu (Pune, India: Jnana-Deepa Vidyapeeth, 1999), 55.
19. George Soares-Prabhu, "Class in the Bible: The Biblical Poor as a Social Class," in *Theology of Liberation: An Indian Biblical Perspective*, ed. Francis D'Sa (Pune, India: Jnana-Deepa Vidyapeeth, 2001), 93–109.
20. Aloysius Pieris, *God's Reign for God's Poor: A Return to the Jesus Formula* (Kelaniya, Sri Lanka: Tulana Research Centre, 1999), 42, 60–61.
21. Tenth Bishops' Institute for Interreligious Affairs [BIRA] on the Theology of Dialogue, "BIRA IV/10 (Sukabumi, [Indonesia,] 1988)," in FABC, *For All the Peoples of Asia*, 1:314.

22. See Pieris, "Asia's Non-Semitic Religions and the Mission of the Local Churches," 45.
23. Ibid., 46–48.
24. Pieris, *God's Reign for God's Poor*, 57.
25. Ibid., 49.
26. Ibid., 47.
27. Ibid.
28. First Bishops' Institute for Social Action, "BISA I (Novaliches, [Philippines,] 1974)," in FABC, *For All the Peoples of Asia*, 1:200.
29. First Plenary Assembly of the Federation of Asian Bishops' Conferences, "FABC I (Taipei [City, Taiwan], 1974)," in FABC, *For All the Peoples of Asia*, 1:14.